Who We Meet Along the Way

Brandon Tosti

Parker,

Good luck with your career!
Let me know if you need help down
the road!

Brandon Tosti

11/30/22

Printed in the United States of America

ISBN 978-1-7365815-1-3 (hardcover)

ISBN 978-1-7365815-0-6 (paperback)

ISBN 978-1-7365815-2-0 (ebook)

Canoe Tree
Press

4697 Main Street

Manchester Center, VT 05255

Canoe Tree Press is a division of DartFrog Books.

Dedication

This book is dedicated to Silvio "Spadio" Tosti

To my grandfather I never met, I want to let you know your kids turned out okay, especially your youngest son, Raymond "Ray" Michael. He did not buy a fatherhood ops manual to guide him, nor did he attend a seminar. He led from the heart and pushed me always to do my best and to chase my dreams.

Our daughter Emily's middle name is Katherine, chosen to honor your loving wife, Katherine "Katie" Limone Tosti. When her parents emigrated to the United States, her father was concerned the other students would make fun of her because of the unique-sounding last name. He changed their name to Lemon to blend in better. She was my sweet Italian Mamaw, a gentle soul, and her homemade biscotti always hit the spot.

Grandpa Silvio, I have always been told you were friendly and you loved people. As I write this last line, I realize this is an unspoken gift you passed onto me. Your gift has guided me during my first forty-six years and will continue to serve me well as I meet more wonderful people along the way.

Author's Note

The book you have in your hand was not written in a traditional format. It is a collection of social media posts that were written over ten years with no intention of turning them into a book. There are plenty of colorful characters, twists, and turns, but the stories are true. Please note I wrote the columns as moments in time; you may encounter a few storylines that don't line up cohesively or notice a repetitive story reference. I worked with editors to smooth this out as much as possible while retaining the posts' original words and meaning.

It is often said that life's journey is a path. Each of us walks a different one, and it is filled with curves, speed bumps, and moments in the fast lane. We encounter a bit of everything, but one element that we share is the inspiring people we meet in life. They coach, love, support, and challenge us, one story and one mile at a time.

Foreword
By David Blankenship

The glass is half full. The power of positive thinking. Looking at the world through rose-colored glasses. These catchphrases could describe the author's outlook on life. Of course, having such a life view does not make him unique; being optimistic and proactive are characteristics many, many people aspire to achieve.

If you have met Brandon, the distinction between aspiration and being is evident. Brandon, or "Tosti," as friends and even business associates call him, simply just is optimistic. He is an overachiever. He looks for the good in everyone, and, while having seen and experienced troubles both in and around his life, he looks for the best outcomes for any situation. In that, Brandon is unique. What we all hope or try to be, he simply is.

In this world where first impressions define you forever, some may think him "fake." Undoubtedly, one might think in this day and age of cynicism and skepticism, this guy has to be a "salesman"; beneath the guy lies the same jadedness many of us, myself included, feel when viewing the world, such as it is, from time to time.

Nope. Sorry. I find it annoying on occasion, but he is who he is. What you see is what you get. While he has never told me exactly why, I was honored when Brandon asked me to write the foreword to this, his first book. When he asked, I knew exactly what to say about this guy and why this book is (a) a long time coming and (b) needed to be written . . . by him.

As of this writing, I have not read a page of the book you are holding. I do not need to, because, at the end of the day, no matter what he says in this book, I know why he wrote it. Brandon, being the person that he is, probably hopes this book makes you think back to the good times of your life or simply makes you smile. That would probably be the upper limit of what he would say his aspirations are for this book.

What he will not say, I will. This book should serve as encouragement for us all. It should encourage us to keep in touch with our friends and our family. In a day and age where access to high school or college friends is but a search and click away, think about all the people who have improved your life in some way. When is the last time you have simply reached out and said hi or thank you? In this book, Brandon has shown that when you honestly "keep in touch," those people who improved your life then can continue to do so today.

It should encourage us to increase our circle of friends. Meeting new people gives you a new outlook and experiences, which can only enrich the person you are today. Brandon is a guy from a tiny town in eastern Kentucky. He has increased his circle of friends to the point it spans the nation. How can that be a bad thing for you?

It should encourage us to set goals . . . to have dreams . . . and do something about it. You share experiences with The People You Meet Along the Way. Those experiences, good and bad, go a long way in defining who you are. Complacency is easy; it is comfortable. It also does not let you interview Olympic swimmers or play a scrimmage game against the Women's Olympic Basketball Team. Or, hell, coach your kid's basketball team. Here is a secret. Brandon did not play basketball past eighth grade. That did not stop him from learning enough about coaching and getting to have those memories of coaching his son.

Brandon is a good guy who hopes this book makes your day just a little bit better. We can all learn a little from that.

—David "Dave" Blankenship

Paintsville, Kentucky

Along For the Ride: Advance Praise

The book's Advance Praise section is formatted differently for a reason. I felt it was important to include a few friends, teachers, and other important leaders who impacted my life along my journey. I reached out to people from my hometown, my college, and my home city for the past twenty years.

PAINTSVILLE, KENTUCKY

"After a few pages of *Who We Meet Along the Way*, you will want to keep reading. Tosti's mastery of the art of storytelling will have you hooked. You will be amply rewarded as you are simply drawn into his world, a world of no pretense, just a love of his work and his life."

—Clyde Pack, retired educator, journalist, and Brandon's high school English and journalism teacher

"As you read through the stories in this book, you will discover how one person can influence so many lives. We all have a choice to leave a positive or negative mark. Maybe sometimes microscopic in nature, but a mark that leaves a moment with one feeling a little better or a little worse about their day or circumstance. This book's pages are uniquely woven together with memories of people affected by one person's courage, compassion, love, and laughter.

"There was a time when I would frequently say, "This boy is going to drive me crazy." Brandon and I grew up together. We argued together. We laughed and cried together. He was my best friend. Our friendship remains today because we have always loved and respected each other for who we are and who we have become. I am just one of the countless people along the way impacted by Brandon and his genuineness, but I am so glad I was one of the first. Enjoy this book. Be motivated by this book to live a little kinder and sweeter life with a whole lot of love, laughter, and tears along the way."

—Sabrina (Moore) Rader, Brandon's dear childhood friend

Brandon Tosti is and always has been one of the best people walking the earth. I could tell you story after story from our childhood and even a couple of years ago when, despite us only checking in with each other a few times a year, he traveled by himself from Colorado to Kentucky to honor my mother when she passed.

The good news is that a lot of the stories and many more are in the book. Read it and have your children read it. It will inspire you to be a better person and your children to grow into the adults you wish they would. Brandon is an inspiration.

—Marty Preston, one of Brandon's oldest friends

"Brandon and I have been friends since kindergarten. As you will see in this book, we shared many adventures. He has always been more than a friend to my family, and my parents considered him their third son. Brandon was and remains my closest friend. He knows all my secrets, including my good and bad decisions, not because I had to tell him but because he was always there by my side. Having a lifelong friend like Brandon is a blessing. His book will take you on a fascinating journey as you watch an amazing little boy become an even more amazing man. Enjoy!"

—Vincent "V" Grino, one of Brandon's best friends

"It has been an honor and a privilege to know Brandon Tosti for the last forty-plus years! From the early days of sleepovers in your basement to playing Little League together to neighborhood bike rides to now hanging out with our families and watching our children do the same things. I would not trade any of it for the world! I feel blessed that we ended up living thirty minutes from each other on the other side of the country many years later. We truly have come full circle! Thanks so much for letting me be a part of this book project, for being such an incredible friend over the years, and for always being YOU!"

—Brian Hardison, one of Brandon's neighborhood buddies

"Paintsville was unique with a diverse population: racial, cultural, religious, and economic. However, there was acceptance and respect despite these differences. As a teacher, I hoped I was making a positive impact on the lives of my students. But I have realized I was also the one who grew in this slower-paced lifestyle. Each relationship and experience shaped us in some small way. The results of life's lessons, good or bad, depend on how we apply them in our daily living. Those years were special because they reminded my family to appreciate the simple things in our lives."

—Mrs. Johnsie Tucker, Brandon's fifth- and sixth-grade teacher

LEXINGTON, KENTUCKY

"We all have at least one friend who could write a book because of his or her life journey, ability to tell a story, or means to entertain; Brandon has all three. Since our college days over two decades ago, Brandon has captivated individuals, groups, and businesses with his colorful, heartfelt experiences and coaching mentorship. This collection of thoughts will be hard to put down."

—Jon Andrews, close friend of Brandon and designer of the book cover

"These stories show time and time again that it is not the plans you make in life, or even the events themselves, but the people who are with you along the way that really matter. Throughout my twenty-five-year friendship with Brandon, I have always admired his constant positivity, his earnestness, and his genuine curiosity about other people. He has always greeted the world with an open mind and an open heart, and the stories in this book clearly illustrate that."

—Tom "Tommy Boy" Williams, close college friend of Brandon

"I have known Brandon for twenty-five years. Having been fortunate enough to meet many accomplished people in my lifetime, I have found no one to possess the combination of character, empathy, and drive that he does. From formally serving with him on student leadership boards to kicking around ideas as friends, Brandon's servant leadership and influence have made me a better person, father, and professional. There is no greater achievement than the impact of positive influence in the service of others. Brandon has successfully used his experiences to generate a good that has impacted and moved our world to a better state than it was prior to his efforts."

—Mike "Guelch" Guelcher, Brandon's close college buddy

"Brandon has captured in these stories how important it is to have a passion for helping others. His enthusiasm and energy to do the right thing has extended from Paintsville, Kentucky, to Lexington, Kentucky, New Orleans, and Denver. The stories truly bring out the goodness in a man I have known for over twenty years. Reading his stories made me think about the first day I met him in my office at the University of Kentucky. I could tell that he was a very compassionate and ambitious young man who needed some direction. We decided on an academic path, and the rest is history. Brandon has taken advantage of every opportunity and has elegantly shared his experiences in *Who We Meet Along the Way*. Thank goodness we have people in the world like Brandon who are willing to help those in need without expecting something in return."

—Dr. Steve R. Parker, Associate Professor for Sport Leadership and Teacher Education at University of Kentucky and Brandon's undergraduate advisor

"Brandon has been one of my closest friends for twenty-five years. We were roommates in a tiny dorm room at the University of Kentucky and somehow survived as roommates in various apartments and houses for another four years after that. The defining qualities that struck me about Brandon were his optimism, passion for life, and love for people. He was always ready to try something new or embark on a last-minute road trip to visit a friend he had not seen in a while. I never fully appreciated his written storytelling ability until 2016, when he started a Lent challenge called Focus on Friends. Each day he would write a Facebook post about a different friend and what they meant to him. I would eagerly wait for each post, and as I read each one, I felt like I knew that person. His heartfelt words and love for each person were captivating.

"Brandon will inspire you to enjoy life, call that old friend, volunteer for a cause you care about, and just be a better person. As you read these stories of his life, relationships, and experiences, you will understand why so many people call him a friend."

—Chad Randall, Brandon's best friend and college roommate who is responsible for the book's concept

New Orleans, Louisiana

"This is a story of people who make a difference in people's lives. Tosti and Sports For a Cause were a ray of hope to New Orleans–area schools, coaches, and athletes who were still struggling with the seemingly insurmountable issues created by the breaking of our levees after Hurricane Katrina. Brandon's strong character remains intact today, giving up a career in sports to spend more time with his family and coach his kids' teams—giving a whole new meaning to the words Sports for a Cause."

—Jay Cicero, President and CEO of the Greater New Orleans Sports Foundation, Brandon's friend and the ultimate resource and networker in New Orleans

"Every so often, God surprises and blesses us with experiences that open up our eyes, even more, to what's important in life. It enlarges our heart to give more of ourselves to life, to bring into the life of others help, wisdom, inspiration, whatever is needed and what our gifts can provide. Such was my experience when He sent Brandon to our church to help paint our gym floor. The group of volunteers did a fantastic job.

"What struck me about Brandon and his wife was their togetherness, this oneness, this unity of purpose to share the unique gifts that God had given each of them. They have committed themselves to each other wholly and to the vision they have been given, so the world can become a better place through selfless giving of time and resources in an outreaching of love from the heart. His example, her example together is an example of how we can be a blessing to our world. Keep your eyes on the prize my friend going forward; as He leads you all along the ways He would have you to go . . . again, from the heart, from Hope United Church . . . We thank you!"

—Pastor Donald Nicholas, a.k.a. "Pastor Nick," Hope United Baptist Church in the Gentilly neighborhood of New Orleans, Louisiana

"After New Orleans was devastated by Hurricane Katrina in 2005, I received a call from a man named Brandon Tosti. He said he lived in Denver, Colorado, and wanted to bring a group of volunteers to New Orleans to help renovate playgrounds, schools, and/or recreation facilities. He also offered to bring used athletic equipment for various sports! His team restored one particular playground that had been destroyed and brought school supplies and equipment. We were then able to hold a successful baseball clinic for kids in that area. Brandon made possible a special experience for children who had been so traumatized. Their world had become forever changed. So many lost their homes, their schools, entire neighborhoods, and in some cases, loved ones during the storm.

"Brandon is one of the most dedicated and unselfish people I have ever met. It was very obvious that he really wanted to make a difference in people's lives. Brandon is a very special person, and people like him were one of the main reasons that New Orleans was able to recover."

—Ron Maestri, Retired Baseball Coach and Director of Athletics, University of New Orleans

DENVER, COLORADO

"Brandon is one of those gifted storytellers who anchors himself in the sense of place. He invites you to enter that place with a kind smile and a warm welcome. He begs you to sit awhile and share a story, and you are always glad you did. His stories are modern folk art that weave together past and present, heartache and joy. He is part country music song and part inspirational quote. You will be better for the read, and, like your favorite song or quote, his stories will become part of your story.

"I know Brandon as Coach. He was my kid's first-grade basketball coach. I am not sporty; in fact, writing the word *sporty* made me uncomfortable, but I train my kids to be grateful. After every practice, I would make my son say, "Thank you, Coach," and I would wave or give the manly head nod. My son took to basketball, and he improved every week. I knew that was not my doing, and I questioned whether it was even genetically possible.

"Brandon coached him. He coached him in basketball and on what it meant to be part of a team, and he affirmed his style of playing. He is a great coach. He wove a story around basketball that my young son could understand and make his own. It is the same with this book. He coaches you into understanding more fully, into caring more deeply and sharing your story more generously.

"I have seen what happens when Brandon is your coach. The results instill in you a lifetime of learning and a belief that you can be the person you are meant to be. This book is no different. We all need a great coach in our life, and Brandon is one of the best."

—Carl Johnson, Brandon's unofficial Life Coach

"Brandon brings positive energy to every one of life's endeavors. Having met Brandon a decade and a half ago, I feel fortunate to have been 'Along for The Ride,' or at least for part of it. This book is your chance to follow Brandon's adventures from Kentucky to Colorado—and seemingly everywhere in between."

—Josh Gross, dear friend of Brandon and Vice President of Business Operations for the San Diego Seals

"'The road traveled' would be an excellent description of my longtime friendship with Brandon. What started as merely client–customer communication developed through the months and years into a meaningful relationship based on shared values, wild ideas, and a level of genuine compassion that you only find in the best of friends.

"Here is an example of what I mean . . . in 2008, when he was simply my vendor and I was only his client, a good friend of mine who was a young mother of three soccer-loving kids was diagnosed with terminal cancer. I shared this news during a casual conversation with Brandon while he was an employee of the Colorado Rapids soccer team. What followed that conversation was nothing short of incredible. First, the kids were treated to the most amazing Rapids VIP game-day treatment ever received . . . jerseys, on-field meet-and-greet, box seats, the works.

"In the weeks that followed, he would donate event space for a family fundraiser, secure auction items, provide food, and even volunteer his own time. Because this family was important to me, they became intensely important to him, and his influence inspired his colleagues to join. Brandon delivered a memorable experience for this family he had never met, just because he could.

"The day after my friend succumbed to her illness, a huge bouquet, along with a signed card, was quietly delivered to the home of her widowed husband, signed by the Colorado Rapids. Its simplicity is what made it special . . . a compassionate and unprompted gesture, facilitated by a true friend, never forgotten by the family or me.

"Brandon has the unique ability to make everyone he encounters *feel* like one of those friends, and this book is a genuine reflection of who he is and what he values. No topic is truly safe from exploration! Through the years, he and I have talked about sports, business, relationships, cancer, philanthropy, politics, real estate . . . you name it. So, what you are getting in the coming pages is *all* of him. Consider yourself lucky!"

—Nate Baldwin, close friend and co-owner of a future entrepreneur venture with Brandon

Chapter One
Home, Hills and Hollers

Home is a simple word, but it carries a deep meaning for me. It set the tone for my path in life. I was raised in the heart of Appalachia and am proud of the little town that built me. Home is warm, safe, and comfortable. I count myself lucky because I grew up in a house filled with love, positivity, and unconditional support.

Paintsville was small but mighty, supported by kind and proud citizens. I could spend pages trying to portray the town with praise and accolades, but the word that I keep coming back to is . . . safe. As kids we were free to roam the neighborhood, and it was not an issue if you left your bike out overnight. I respected the police chief for apparent reasons, but he was not someone I feared because he was also my best friend's dad. Teachers were your neighbors, a close buddy's Mom, or your Sunday school teacher.

I wrote a few reflective columns about my hometown and what it means to me. A trip home always soothes my soul. It is not just a minor part of my story; it's everything.

Home

April 2016 🌐

I have lived in four places in my forty-six years of life. I was born in Pikeville, Kentucky, and lived there for five years, then made two more stops in the Bluegrass State. I spent my childhood in what I consider one of the best small towns in America. It blessed me with a great childhood and wonderful neighbors who treated me like their own grandson. Beth and I have lived in Denver for twenty years, but Paintsville is what I think of when I hear the word *home*. As I get older, I realize not everyone has fond memories of home. I was lucky, and I never take it for granted. Little did I know that a kind stranger on a plane ride would remind me of this important lesson.

On a flight from Chicago to Denver, I sat beside a sophisticated woman dressed in stylish clothes, including an expensive watch. She noticed my writing journal. She asked me if I often wrote, because she could tell by the number of pages that I was not just scribbling to kill time or jotting down random brainstorms. We talked the entire flight home about our families, our upbringings, and our differing perspectives on home. She was born in India. Her father worked as an international banker, and during her childhood she had lived not only in India but also in Africa, London, and New York City. She mentioned that her family had always had a driver. Her childhood was unique and one that another might long for. Yet, because she moved often, she did not have friends from her neighborhood. In India and Africa, she routinely saw wild animals and was accustomed to seeing lions, tigers, and other big game animals from afar, but she did not have a pet dog or cat.

Once again, it reminded me that money could not buy happiness. Alpa, thank you for reminding me how lucky some of us are and how memories of home are not always warm and fuzzy for everyone.

The Big Move

April 2016 🌐

For twelve years, Beth and I called home a 900-square-foot ranch house built in 1951 and nestled in the Cory-Merrill neighborhood. Cory-Merrill is a tree-lined, warm, inviting community. It is located ten minutes south of downtown and a few blocks from the University of Denver campus. The location of our little house was perfect. We were close to downtown Denver and within walking distance of a light-rail station, the Tech Center, Washington Park, and I-25. We were also a short bike ride to great restaurants and upscale shopping in Cherry Creek. (We did not frequent the last part, but we may or may not have been on a first-name basis with the owners of Bonnie Brae Ice Cream and Bonnie Brae Tavern. God, I am going to miss their pizza.)

Nine hundred square feet is, by local standards, a small house. Our kitchen was small and cozy, to put it lightly. The closets were tiny, and we learned to maximize every nook and cranny. In the kitchen, you could not open the doors on two appliances because they would hit one another. I often joked with Beth, our next house could be 3,000 square feet, but the kitchen would be a 2,000-square-foot gourmet masterpiece. Thankfully, we had an additional 900 square feet in the finished basement for our TV and the kids' play area. We shared our living room and dining room in one space. One could say we outgrew this house several years ago, and we would agree, but we did not mind most days. Simply put, we are not big house people.

My dad worked for the power company, and he always told me: "You can have the largest house you want, son, but remember you must heat it, cool it, and furnish it." The advice stuck with me. Parents who understood the value of a buck raised Beth and me to remember that the size of a house should be measured not in square footage but by the amount of love on the inside.

We have a lot of splendid memories and stories from this little starter home. We thought we would stay in the house for five years, then upgrade. Over time, you get comfortable and adapt. Plus, moving is painful, and life gets busy. You do not think about it after a while. In this little house, we started a family. Two beautiful kids took their first steps in this house. We hosted some epic Kentucky Derby parties and somehow squeezed more than sixty people inside its tight walls one year. I am sure we violated the fire code a few times along the way.

In life, we do not get to choose our neighbors. Somehow, this young couple lucked into some of the best neighbors in the world and an eccentric one. Those relationships and friendships will stay in our minds and hearts forever. We hope to be those good neighbors in our new neighborhood, and we pray to the Good Lord that we will not have a neighbor who blows his leaves from dusk to dawn.

We researched and looked at popular neighborhoods and multiple suburban areas from Littleton to Arvada in the past three years. Beth and I always swore off the suburbs, even though we knew we could get a much bigger house and the kids would have access to better schools. Public schools can be challenging, regardless of the location. Every school has a few issues, but this played a significant role in our decision. We finally cast our vote with Arvada. There is a historic section of the city called Olde Town. It is filled with mom-and-pop restaurants, locally owned businesses, and quaint retail shops. It feels like it has a little soul to it. Plus, we have several friends who moved there over time and liked it. We hope we will too.

We will leave more than a house behind. We will miss a group of friends dearly, and those are the kids and families I coached for the past two years in baseball and basketball. I was blessed to coach youth basketball for close to a decade, and this group of kids means the world to me. I am bummed I will not coach them in basketball next year, because I think they will go undefeated.

It is a YMCA league, and the referee does not keep score, but our kids always knew the score and our win/loss total. They continuously let me know if we were up or down during our timeouts. Yes, the kids are seven years old, but I would bet the ranch a few of them will play at the high school level and excel in multiple sports. A few of them understood the game early on and possessed a healthy competitive spirit—plus, they never quit.

The parents of these Little League kids were not too shabby either. I never had to ask or look for an assistant coach, because multiple dads immediately volunteered to help. Some were my assistants from day one, and others jumped in for a practice or two to help lead a fast break or a simple rebounding drill. The moms were cut from the same cloth. They always wanted to help me, and they planned our season parties and assisted with the team communication process, which is never a minor task.

I love coaching, and sometimes I wonder what the parents who watched us practice thought of me. We only practiced for an hour each week. It was not as if we had two or three hours to rehearse offensive sets or intricate defenses. I get excited about little things in life, and when a hyper group of elementary school kids picked up a drill after a few times, I would yell positively, "Nice work, gentlemen. Awesome! Let's get better tonight; what do you say? Let's improve!" I preached the importance of setting goals and asked the kids to write one thing they wanted to improve on at the beginning of the season. After our last game, I handed out certificates with some terrible clip art commemorating each player's accomplished goal.

I cannot teach a kid passion, but I hope they always demonstrate good sportsmanship and play until the clock hits :00. Dream big, fellas, always dream big! Something tells me our son and a few of his old teammates will cross paths again on a baseball diamond or a basketball court several years from now. *[By the way, the basketball team went undefeated the following year. —B.T.]*

Life is full of decisions and changes. We are excited about this next chapter of our lives. It was a hard decision wrought full of anxiety, uncertainty, excitement, and faith. Here's hoping our new home and neighborhood provide us with wonderful memories, mom-and-pop restaurants, and a team of kids for me to coach.

Growing Up in a Small Town

October 2017 🌐

I have lived in Colorado for sixteen years, and people still ask me where I am from and where I call home. Sometimes it is the first question, and other times they wait a few minutes before they ask. They usually guess Texas for whatever reason, probably because of my Southern accent.

A few years ago, I worked at Denver International Airport (DEN), managing the Beer Flights event. I met people from all over the world, and, as one might imagine, I heard a lot of different accents. The Concessions Department at DEN created a temporary Colorado microbrewery concept where passengers could sample local beers. Passengers could taste ten beers (two ounces each), and it was a neat event. We had visitors from forty-nine states and at least ten foreign countries. Our event staff did a bit of everything for the event, but my favorite days were when I could pour samples and tend bar.

This part of the job was fun for me because I talked to hundreds of people daily and realized I should have been a college bartender. I saw multiple people coming and going, but my two favorite groups were two firefighters from Houston and a group of ex-Marines who had been out of the service for twenty years but still got together every year for a guy's trip. This year they were traveling to Colorado Springs. I am not sure why they talked with me for most of the time they were in the beer garden, but I thanked them for their service, and they asked me to follow them around the beer garden because they wanted to hang out for a post-shift drink. One wife told me all their nicknames and what type of jobs they currently hold. As they left for the weekend, we took a group photo. I prayed they did not break my back with their bear hugs.

I told the firefighters about our son, Kaden, and how much he loves fire trucks. Anytime we pass a fire department vehicle parked near our house, he wants us to turn around to see the house number since he knows where two or three are located. They were great guys. If I ever have time to visit, I might have to stop by in person and say thanks. They gave me an extra "Houston FD House 19 5th Ward" patch for Kaden, which I thought was cool.

I am from Kentucky—or "the Deep South," for a few of my Ohio friends—and I am okay with it. My roots in Southern hospitality is one reason I relish hosting people at our house for dinner, watching a game, or even celebrating the Kentucky Derby with as many friends as we can squeeze into our small house. I am not perfect, nor do I claim to be, but I try to be nice to everyone I meet and to greet them with a genuine smile and a firm handshake. I do not waste time on people who dislike me or do not respect me, because I cannot change opinions, but I usually appreciate everyone until they give me a reason not to.

I do not travel home nearly as often as I should, but I try to call my parents every weekend, if not more. I try to keep in touch with friends and family from back home. Here are some other thoughts and anecdotes about my tiny hometown:

Yes, we speak with an accent, and we sometimes root a little too much for the UK Wildcats. We feel the need to outwork big-city folks or people who attended a better school than we did. We stick together when adversity strikes. We have some grand stories; only people from similarly small towns would understand and appreciate them—such as tales of all the surfaces we played basketball on: dirt, grass, concrete, and rubber (Virgie High School's court).

Yes, we have a Dairy Queen located five feet from a busy main road, and often the line backs up to the road, and it has never been a safety issue. It is a must-do when everyone comes home, but I must admit I have never eaten the famous hot-dog sauce and probably never will.

It is true that some people drink too much pop. We have big hearts and sometimes cook delicious and unhealthy meals, kind of like New Orleans. I am a healthy eater, but I love country ham!

In a rural area, the word *community* means a little more to people. You take care of one another, and you look out for the well-being of family, friends, and friends of friends, regardless of what school color they wear for Friday night football games. After you leave for college, people still ask about you, and you do the same. Our parents always keep us filled in on each other's whereabouts, successes, mishaps, and other life stories.

In rural small towns, you create your activities. You generate things to do in your spare time, some good, some bad, but you do not repeat the bad ones because you know better. My generation's screen time was the Atari console for an hour after we played Wiffle Ball, rode our bikes, and swam for two or three hours. Today's society differs from the '80s, and I hate what kids have to deal with these days.

My good friend Courtney Daniels' grandmother had a house near the heart of downtown, and I remember the times we would sit on her front porch in the giant rocking chairs, talking about dreams and life. It was peaceful and comforting because we did not have a care in the world. When life gets rough, that porch is one place I wish I could return to and let my mind wander.

When I was in high school, I was eager to go away to college like every other kid, but now I am forty and a little wiser. I often reminisce about and miss parts of home, my friends, and experiences. A lot has changed, yet a lot has remained the same. The next time someone asks me where I am from, I might say, "Just a small town you've never heard of, but I can promise you it is a great one."

The Paintsville High School gymnasium.

A (Much-Needed) Visit Back Home

2019 🌐

Each time I visit home, I always leave with a full heart and a deep appreciation for my childhood. For the past twenty years, Denver has been where we call home. It is such a great city, and we count our blessings; we can call it our adopted home. However, sometimes you miss your childhood home and need to visit for no other reason than to enjoy time with family and regain a proper perspective on life.

Life is not always easy, and when I run a quart or two low on energy, I know that a trip to Kentucky usually provides a sense of calm and the rest that my body needs. We all need to recharge our minds, and this time I loved spending time with my family and a few dear friends. I can honestly say it was a special visit, and my heart is full for many reasons. On the plane, I thought about what home means to me, and I wrote down my thoughts to share here.

Home is:

Where I learned to say *sir* and *ma'am*, and the root of my Southern hospitality, and where you sit on the porch and talk about everything (my parents have three porches).

Tiger pride citywide, and Golden Eagle pride countywide.

Texting an old college buddy, Aaron Silletto, last-minute to ask if I can (at age forty-three) crash on a couch, laugh at old stories with his rock-star wife, Sara, and finally meet their adorable three-year-old son.

Where I want to run to when a tragic event occurs.

Family, lots of hills, outstanding teachers, and excellent country cooking.

Old money versus new money, with positive energy fighting for progress and innovation battling small-town politics.

Where you will find some of the nicest people in the world, and where I learned to work hard and always to dream big.

Battling stereotypes and national news stories focused on the wrong things.

Johnson County Buddy Basketball, the youth league where I fell in love with the game.

1980s Pizza Hut with Dig Dug, Hogan's Alley, and Ms. Pac-Man video games.

The Sipp Cinema, which had the world's best cherry Pepsi (I can still see the old-school Tupperware squeeze bottle with the red syrup slowly dripping down the side).

Growing up with a WWII veteran neighbor whose wheelchair did not stop him from driving and being heavily involved in the community, and understanding why you should *never* park in a handicapped space.

Running into a stranger who became more like an angel by helping me find closure after an old friend's funeral when I could not get home in time.

Driving three hours one way to spend two hours with my ninety-five-year-old Italian great-aunt Nancy and eat her homemade delicacy of rigatoni, marinara sauce, and meatballs.

A special place you can leave, but a piece of your heart never will.

Chapter Two

Family

Family is essential for a lot of reasons, but I love mine for their unconditional support. We all have a cousin who is more like a sibling or share a special bond with a grandparent who provides a lifetime of memories. Sometimes you might disagree or drive one another crazy, but family is what you miss the most when you leave home. Over time, I wrote a few columns to remind my parents what they mean to me and that I am grateful for the life lessons, the work ethic they instilled in me, and a few priceless memories.

My parents, Ray and Linda, raised my sister, Brittany, and me to work hard, have fun, and always put money aside for a rainy day. They instilled in us at an early age that helping others is not a unique activity that you do once or twice a year; it's something one must do often and without concern for receiving credit or attention for the act.

I was six years old when Brittany was born. I was a huge Star Wars fan, and my parents thought it was a good idea for my new sibling to bring me a gift. My little sister's gift to me was the full-sized Millennium Falcon. I was excited and told Mom and Dad that I wanted more siblings if it meant I would receive cool Star Wars toys.

Being six years apart was a challenge because we were at different stages in life, but Brittany and I got along mostly. Still, the sibling rivalry was always there in some form or fashion. She and I always joke about how I was a good big brother and rarely aggravated her (my side of the story). Britt's opinion is slightly different, and I always remind her I was never mean to her because as soon as I was within ten feet of her, she would scream at the top of her lungs. It is a running joke that we still laugh about all these years later.

The Many Hats of Motherhood

May 2014 🌐

I spent some time thinking about all the things a mom does for her children and family. Sometimes people refer to parenting as the best job in the world, but it is not a job; it is more like a privilege. It is utterly unique when you think about everything a mom can do and how well they can do it all.

Most moms have never spent a day reviewing cases for law school or donned a pair of scrubs for a residency in an emergency room. Nor did they major in international relations, yet somehow, they could quickly jump in as a foreign diplomat or stand in for a hostage negotiator during a time of crisis.

They can clean and dress significant flesh wounds, splint a broken arm, heal a broken heart, negotiate, argue with a crying four-year-old and solve a crisis between two teenagers and a clueless father. Let us not forget about coaching a sport, leading a Scout pack, and teaching the finer points of budgeting and finance or how to prepare a meal worthy of being served at the finest restaurants in the world.

Moms are superheroes who will never appear in a comic book or a movie, but they will capture your heart and teach you what it means to genuinely care for someone. The love a mom has for her child is possibly the strongest bond in the world and something we can all learn from as we stumble and fight through this thing called life.

My mom taught Brittany and me many things and has always been there for us. This remained true even if we disagreed on a situation. A mother's love is unconditional, and if we appreciate them, then we should tell them every chance we get, not just on their special day in May.

I love you, and I am glad you are still here.

Thank You, Mom!

May 2015 🌐

Happy Mother's Day to all the moms in the world! I want to thank my beautiful mom and share some of my favorite stories from some other moms who helped me and my friends survive the everyday ups and downs of life.

Mom, thanks for always being there for Brittany and me, regardless of how big or small the issue was at the time. I appreciate your teaching me the importance of volunteering in the community and giving back to those less fortunate. Another essential life lesson you taught me was the value of a credit card and why not to abuse it. I had one point in my life where I forgot the lesson, but once I paid it off, it never happened again.

Thank you for being there at our darkest hour when Beth and I needed you the most. Thank you for always lighting a candle for my friends when they were dealing with some adversity. Your example taught me how to support my friends.

Thank you for encouraging me to bring home as many of my college friends as we could fit in our small house for the Kentucky Apple Festival. You would prepare enough food and desserts to feed an army.

Thank you for teaching me how to iron my clothes. I think I was the only student at UK who ironed khakis and dress shirts.

Thank you for teaching me how to ride a bike, clean anything, parallel park, and work hard.

Thank you for teaching me to root for my favorite teams even when they were terrible: University of Kentucky football and the Atlanta Braves. Dad was not a baseball fan, but I would rush home after playing with my neighborhood friends to watch baseball with you. This was our summer tradition for five or six seasons. Dale Murphy was our favorite player.

Thank you for teaching me to welcome people into our home and treat party guests like family—Kentucky Derby party, anyone??? Thanks for sending us bourbon balls for our Derby party to make sure we had extras for Kieran Cain and B.K.

Thanks for always supporting my crazy career choices and dreams even though you wanted me to find a stable government job. No need to worry about me—twenty-five years later, I finally listened to you.

Thanks for teaching me what it means to respect one's mother. I smarted off to you only one time during my teenage years, and Dad told me I would not drive for many years if I ever did it again. It was the first and last time I smarted off to you.

Thank you for trusting me with your life every time you visit Colorado. We have snowshoed in Rocky Mountain National Park and survived snowmobiling in Grand Lake, where I got lost for a little while. You rode the alpine slide in Steamboat Springs even though you despise any kind of thrill ride.

Thank you for having such a wonderful sense of humor, plus an extra helping of sarcasm and wit as you get older.

Thank you for our family tradition of visiting a Hallmark store each Christmas to pick out an ornament. When Brittany and I moved away, we had enough ornaments to decorate our family Christmas trees. Beth and I happily passed on this tradition to our kids. No matter my age, I appreciate the sentimental value and memories associated with each ornament. Each year as I unpack the forty-plus ornaments, I share with Emily and Kaden the background of what was going on in my life during that time.

Thank you for loving this ADHD, night-owl, sports-nut, talkative, and overall crazy kid.

Thanks for being the best mom a kid could ever ask for and always reminding me to "make it a good day."

Beth, you are such a great mom; the kids adore you. I would be lost without you, but you already know that fact. Life is busy for families everywhere, and you are, without a doubt, General Manager and Head Coach of the Tosti household. I do not know how you do it, but I try to say thanks as much as possible. I love you for lots of reasons, and I appreciate everything you do for the kids. They are lucky to have you as a mom, and I am glad you are my best friend and wife! Thank you for everything!

Penny Grino, thank you for always bringing me and V pepperoni pizza on Fridays during Lent at midnight. I also appreciate your treating me like a third son for thirteen years.

Final thoughts: I tip my hat to all the single moms in this world. I am in awe of what you accomplish, because I struggle when it's me and the kids for a day or two. You are some of the strongest women on this Earth. I enjoy reading about your kids and all their accomplishments. Please take a moment, pat yourself on the back, and smile, because you are loved and appreciated more than you know.

I am thankful for all the supportive moms I have encountered through coaching basketball, T-ball, and soccer. I have been fortunate enough to coach in three cities. I know this is not always the case for coaches, regardless of the age or skill level, and I never take it for granted. I hope all the moms in the world had a great day!

Me and Mom in Pikeville, Kentucky, in 1978.

Mom, Kaden, and Emily in Arvada, Colorado, 2018.

A Day for Dad: Blessings and Reflections

June 2015 ⊗

Being a father is such an honor and one of the best things in life. I often tell friends getting married is one of the best things you can do, but having a child is *the* best thing. Without your children, you would not be a father. I feel as if Father's Day is a special day to thank and honor kids as well as fathers. I know someday Kaden and Emily will not want to be seen in public with Beth and me, but for now, they still call me Dad or Daddy, and I try to savor every smile. Like all parents, I try to forget the epic temper tantrums, crying spells, and other meltdowns, but then I realize we did the same thing when we were little. Plus, I know someday those temper-tantrum stories will become perfect tales to share when the high school years roll around.

Time is the best gift you can give your children. I like to play golf even though I rarely break 100. Like most recreational golfers, I can hit a decent tee shot and even a smooth approach shot once every nine holes, but then I mimic Happy Gilmore and sky the ball across the green from the front edge. The issue with golf is the time it takes to play a round of 18. I decided to walk away from golf, not out of frustration but because of my focus and priorities. I have played only four rounds in the past three years because I feel as if the weekends are sacred. We see the kids for only two to three hours a night during the week. Golf is an excellent game, but I do not feel as if it is worth missing half a weekend day with our kids. I look forward to introducing the game to both kids at the right time. At that point, the five hours can be quality time spent outside on a golf course.

Kaden and I enjoy playing putt-putt golf, and it is our favorite father-and-son activity—although we added a basketball hoop to our driveway yesterday, and Kaden played on it nonstop for the first two hours we had it. He loves it, and we have already practiced multiple times. It is adjustable, and we set it at seven feet. I can dunk for once in my life, and it reminded me of my high school days playing "dunk ball" at the Riddles' house, minus losing the ball down the long, steep hill.

The best part of being a dad is coming in the door after a crappy day of work and having one or both kids run up and give me a bear hug. When kids ask you to play outside, it makes you remember the important things in life. I also enjoy watching our kids overcome a fear or perfect a skill—those times they practice over and over and it takes them a while to achieve the result. The mile-wide smile is heartwarming and makes everything else fade away. I hope both of our kids always approach life's trials with a positive attitude and determination to fight through adversity.

My grandfathers worked in the coal mines—one in Pikeville, Kentucky, and one near Welch, West Virginia. John Emery Justice had only an eighth-grade education. He worked his way up to one of the top supervisor positions in the coal mines and was by far the hardest-working man I have ever met in my life. When I was little, I could not say Grandpa or Papaw; I called him Ping. He went by various nicknames, such as Papaw John, Papaw, and John Emery, but he was and will always be Ping to me. He is where Kaden's middle name, Emery, comes from.

I have fond memories of the time I spent with Ping. He was 160 pounds at 5' 8", but he was a healthy individual in both spirit and mind. Beth and I dated for six years before we got married, and once Ping asked me if I was making sure that she was the one. Yes, he said it in front of her.

The Italian side of my family has an interesting history. My grandfather had roots in southern Italy, and my grandmother Katherine was from the northern part of the country. Back then it was rare for those two areas to mingle. Silvio was killed in a coal-mining accident when my dad was six years old and my uncle Louie was eight. I have heard a few stories about him and what he was like, but not many. I have a few pictures of him, and my favorite one is at a swimming pool with my dad and my uncle Louie clutching onto each of his legs with big smiles on their faces.

I always wondered how Dad knew how to be a wonderful dad to my little sister and me despite having lost his own father so young. Did he learn from his friends' dads, or did he try different approaches and see what worked? Did he ask for advice or read a book? I have never asked him, and the truth is it does not matter, because he is one hell of a dad who also is one of my best friends. He is now retired. I often call to say hi because I can. I know not everyone has the luxury, and I do not take it for granted.

*John Emery "Ping" Justice deep in a coal mine in Pike
County, Kentucky, in the late '50s or early '60s.*

*Silvio Gilmore Tosti, my grandfather I never knew.
This photo was taken in the early '40s.*

On the lighter side, here are a few funny stories involving my dad

One summer in high school, we were driving back from Lexington with Mom and my girlfriend. It was a hot and muggy day. I yelled, "Dad, why don't you turn on some A/C?" He responded, "Brandon, we're not listening to that crap!" Mom, the girlfriend, and I both doubled over in laughter, because he thought I was referring to AC/DC.

When I turned sixteen, Dad told me my little brown Buick Skyhawk was like magic: If I came home with a speeding ticket, then the car would disappear.

One of my best childhood friends, V Grino, and I were habitually late for Mass. Once we turned sixteen and started driving ourselves, we would arrive a few minutes late to dodge the responsibility of being altar boys. Well, Ray Tosti was not okay with our plan, so he told the priest to wait two minutes because he knew V and I would be arriving shortly. After we graduated, he told us what he had done, and we still laugh about it to this day.

Speaking of dads, I cannot forget about Beth's dad, Joe Obergfell. He is a character and a funny guy. When I asked him for Beth's hand in marriage, he smiled and said, "You are asking the wrong person. You need to ask Beth, not me." Thanks for putting up with me, Joe, and for building us two makeshift golf holes in your backyard for all of us to utilize during our summer visits.

I will not reveal his age, but Joe is one of the few grandfathers I know who has ridden water slides with his grandkids. He is a great bowler and not a bad Boggle player either, but his specialty is euchre. Joe, I wish I had a tenth of your handyman skills, because you never cease to amaze me with your ability to fix almost anything.

As a child, I always wished I could have met my grandfather Silvio Tosti. I am forty-one now and a dad myself, but my longtime wish has changed. To my dad, I hope Silvio knows how great of a dad you are and continue to be for Brit and me. I tell you this often and every year in a card, but thank you for everything, most of all, your love and support.

My dad, or "Big Ray," as a few of my friends call him, has played a vital role in my life. Below are a few instances that come to mind. Thank you, Dad:

For being my best man at our wedding.

For passing on your passion for event management to me. I know the

Kentucky Apple Festival might not mean much to some people, but they do not know the hours you have volunteered annually for more than thirty years to make sure our little town had a great event.

For teaching me to be honest with people, not necessarily East Coast honest, but Southern honest.

For walking around the house breaking things so I could help you repair them and complete my Home Repairs merit badge for Boy Scouts. There was one project we could not fix, and we had to call in a professional.

For teaching me to respect my mom. I try to teach Kaden and Emily this lesson every day.

For pushing me never to be satisfied.

For passing on your gift of gab and your genuine love for people.

For teaching me to stand up for what I believe in even if I am in the minority, and for teaching me to fight for those who cannot fight for themselves.

For asking about our friends and how they are doing, especially during hard times.

I love you, Dad. Happy Father's Day!

Northfork, West Virginia, 1960s.

*Dad and I backstage at the Kentucky Apple
Festival Country Concert, 1994.*

Fran Diz and Father Dan Noll

Crossing Paths, a Priest, and a Heartfelt Thank-You From an Old Friend

February 2017—Part 1 of 3 ⊙

Two personality characteristics run deep on my dad's side of the family. Those are sarcasm and the gift of gab. Whether it is my dad, my uncle Louie, or their cousins Jeannine and Fran Diz, you always need to be prepared for either a witty response or a hilarious one depending on the situation. These four grew up together and were more like best friends than cousins.

Fran Diz enjoyed life to the fullest and loved the city of Lexington, particularly the horse industry. She left us when she suffered a massive heart attack. They rushed Fran to the ER, but unfortunately she did not survive. She was seventy-nine, but you would never know it by her fun attitude and sharp mind. Fran and Jeannine were sisters by blood but more like best friends; they were extremely close. Jeannine had to forge ahead on her own path without Fran. I asked for thoughts and prayers as she prepared for that challenging journey.

I kept in touch with my mom and little sister during those stressful and frantic days as I sat in Denver, feeling utterly helpless. Our family circle was getting smaller, and I wanted to fly home for the funeral, but unfortunately it did not happen. However, a photo and a text from my mom provided both tears and a sense of calm.

Father Dan Noll was at the hospital and walked into Fran's room. Since he is a priest at Fran and Jeannine's church, I assumed Jeannine had called him or he had heard the news from a fellow priest. When my mom asked who notified him, he said, "God called me." It was such a perfect Father Dan response. Soon after, he led our family in a beautiful prayer and administered the Last Rites, the final Catholic sacrament that prepares the dying person's soul for death. It provides absolution for sins by penance, sacramental grace, and prayers for the relief of suffering through the anointing and the Eucharist's final administration.

Father Dan, I cannot thank you enough for being there for our family when we needed it the most. It was something we will never forget, and I will appreciate it for years to come.

The Paths of Life

February 2017—Part 2 of 3 🌐

It is often said you cross paths with people for a reason. The statement rang true for my family. During the darkest hour and when our family needed it the most, a friend from my past showed up unannounced and blessed our family with serenity, kindness, and God's grace.

Father Dan, as our UK Catholic Newman Center friends know him, was the priest during our college years. He knew Beth and me very well, and he will always be one of our favorite people. He knew the people we dated, what our dreams were, and what we feared the most. Besides, he was my boss for one year when I lived at the Newman Center and served as the Student Ministry Intern. He would often challenge you to do more and see the good in others without caring about accolades or press coverage. He knew how to reach young people during his Homily and in everyday life.

He made such an impact on our lives during our college years. When we got married, Beth and I knew who we wanted standing at the altar with us. We paid for his flight to Denver, and he arrived a day early for the rehearsal dinner and met all our wonderful Denver friends. It was a joyful reunion for some of our Kentucky friends and a peculiar experience for our Denver ones. To this day, our friends still talk about how cool Father Dan was, and about the fact that he liked beer!

The other neat thing Father Dan did for me was to insist that I walk down the aisle to start the wedding ceremony. He put his hand on my shoulder, smiled, and said, "If Beth has to do it, then you do, too." At the time, I remember I was both frustrated and scared to death. Twelve years later, I look back in complete gratitude because it was honorable, and I do not recall another guy friend who can say he shared that experience with his better half.

My Favorite Memory of Fran

February 2017—Part 3 of 3 ❸

When I turned twenty-one, Fran invited me to Keeneland, which is the world-famous horse-racing track in Lexington. She told me about the most successful jockeys, what the various distances meant, and the crucial advice on how to pick a winning horse. She bought me my first legal Bourbon and Coke, and we quickly huddled to plan our bets for the upcoming race. I frantically tried to digest everything Fran had told me, and I rehearsed my bet. I thought that after placing our bets we could sit down, relax, and take in the beautiful scenery. Fran had other ideas, and she told me to hurry to the rail. I did not realize how close we would be able to get to the track. I took my place against the rail and could smell the dirt mere inches from my feet.

I had been to the track before but never experienced it like this madness. It is my favorite memory of Fran. When I take Kaden and Emily to Keeneland someday, you can bet your $2 betting slip that I will tell them this story and make sure they have their lungs primed and a rolled-up racing guide in hand, ready to scream and yell for their horse, just like Fran taught me.

Rest in peace, Fran.

What I Really Want to Give Our Kids for Christmas: A to Z

December 2015 🌐

Like most parents, Beth and are discussing what gifts to buy for our kids at Christmas. It is always a delicate balance. It requires a lengthy discussion of priorities: what is essential, and what they need versus what they want. Of course we will buy an Olaf or an Elsa plush doll and a Star Wars light saber, but I thought of other gifts that are far more valuable because, unlike toys, they cannot be bought.

A—Appreciation. Appreciate good food, good friends, and great memories.

B—Believe. Always believe in yourself and your ability to make a difference in someone's life.

C—Cancer-free world. There is a fifty percent chance the BRCA1 gene mutation will be passed onto our children. I hope and pray neither one of them has to deal with this stupid disease.

D—Determination. Life will provide plenty of challenges, but stay focused and push forward. Your dad has a proverb written on an envelope of job rejection letters: "Fall down seven times, stand up eight."

E—Engage. Get involved in your community and make something positive happen.

F—Fight. Take a stand for something you believe in.

G—Grateful. Count your blessings.

H—Hustle. Do not be afraid of hard work.

I—Imagine. Dream big, and then go after it with everything you have.

J—Joke. Everyone needs a good laugh. Repeat this one often.

K—Kin. Family is everything. When you get older, you will understand the reasons Pinky and Nan both sacrificed three months of their lives to help us when Mommy was fighting breast cancer.

L—Love. This one will hurt more than once. Do not give up, but do not chase it, either. It will appear when you least expect it. Trust me.

M—Manners. These never go out of style.

N—Network. This is the key to success in whatever career path you choose. A good networker will never be out of a job for long.

O—Optimism. It is free and one of the most powerful mental tools in the world. Plus, the world always needs more of it.

P—Passion. Life can be boring without it. We all need a reason to live. Find yours, and never let it go.

Q—Question. Ask a ton of questions because this is a great way to learn.

R—Respect. Remember to respect life, other people's beliefs, your parents and grandparents, the elderly, and the lowest person on the totem pole at work.

S—Sincerity. Be yourself, be real, and be genuine.

T—Teamwork. You cannot do everything by yourself. Early in your life, I hope you learn the importance of working with others and the simple power of everyone pushing toward the same goal.

U—Understand. Listen, learn, and help others. Take time to see what makes people tick. It will spare you a lot of frustration and make you a better person along the way.

V—Volunteer. Do this often. It not only helps others in need, it also keeps your spirit and priorities in place.

W—Win with class. This one is especially important. I preach this to Kaden and Emily every time we play, whether it is sports, Memory, Trouble, or Operation. Shake hands with your opponent and tell him or her, "Good game."

X—X chromosome. Do not let society define what you can or cannot do based on your gender.

Y—Young. Regardless of what your age is, always stay young at heart.

Z—Zest. I hope you never lose your zest for life. When people ask me why I love life so much or how I can be positive all the time, I tell them LIFE is the greatest gift from God.

Christmas Memories

December 24, 2018 🌐

Our little family always attends the 5:00 p.m. Christmas Mass on Christmas Eve in Denver. This particular year, we arrived ten minutes early, which is a Christmas miracle of epic proportions. If there is any doubt, ask either set of parents or any parishioner from St. Michael's Parish about my track record for arrival time the entire school year of 1992. It was a team effort between myself and my lifelong buddy, Vincent "V" Grino.

We sat down, and a young Marine in his Class A uniform sat down in front of us. He did not look a day over eighteen, but he carried himself like a forty-year-old. He was constantly helping his elderly grandparents throughout the service. I tapped Kaden on the shoulder and said, "Kaden, you know what to do when it is time to offer peace and shake hands?" Before I could say any more, he stopped me and said, "Dad, I know, I know."

When the time came to shake hands during the sign of peace offering, Kaden extended his hand to the Marine, gave him a firm handshake, and said with a stern and clear voice, "Thank you for your service." It blew me away, because sometimes Kaden is shy and gets embarrassed when prompted to do something. I have always told our kids to approach police officers, firefighters, and military members and thank them for what they do for us.

Our daycare person's husband was a Denver police officer. For four-plus years, Kaden and Emily saw a glimpse of what it was like for him to come home and take off his gun belt, uniform, and boots every day. He never talked about his day, but they were always excited to see Eric walk through the door. They were too young to grasp the danger of the job entirely, but someday they will.

As parents, we often critique ourselves and question everything as it relates to our parenting skills. Are we too soft? Are we too strict? Sometimes it is nice to know our children listen to us. That day Kaden thanked the Marine was not about me but more about the real meaning behind the word *respect*. I hope both kids never forget to thank these individuals every time an opportunity presents itself.

The second gift from tonight happened after dinner. The kids were riled up because yours truly let them devour some Bonnie Brae ice cream—but they both picked it over cookies, to be fair. Beth and I were clearing the dishes, and the kids sprinted downstairs in matching REI base layer outfits, laughing hysterically and dancing in unison. Another family tradition followed this with a little twist this year.

We usually read "'Twas the Night Before Christmas" to each child in their respective beds. However, this year, they jumped into the guest bed and insisted we read it to both of them. We convinced them to take turns reading one page each, and we filled in once or twice. It was adorable, and they giggled the entire time.

Tomorrow, Beth and I will open our usual gifts, including books, a box of Ghirardelli chocolates, and most likely a sweater. I am excited for Beth to open her two books, but after tonight, my heart is full because I already have the best gift of all: a Christmas memory to last a lifetime.

Chapter Three
The Lent Challenge—Focus on Friends

Friends are special people who enjoy the ride, and the good ones do not leave when the road gets rough. No, they buckle up, hang on tight, and ride along with you. Each one has a defining characteristic that is unique and memorable, which makes it easy to appreciate their unconditional support. It is never a bad time to remember and reflect on the special moments you've shared with friends.

Lent is a significant season for various religions throughout the world. Beginning on Ash Wednesday, Lent is a season of reflection and preparation before the celebration of Easter. By observing the forty days of Lent, Christians replicate Jesus Christ's sacrifice and time spent in the desert for forty days.

It is common during Lent for individuals to "give up" something they like, such as chocolate, fast food, or watching TV. Beth asked me what I was giving up for Lent, and I told her I did not know. I have given up chocolate before, and potato chips. Shortly after this conversation, I chose a unique approach. I wrote forty columns in which I highlighted forty or more random friends and relived some of our good times. Life is short, and I believe it is crucial to embrace our stories and reflect on the great moments we've shared with friends. I want them to know that even if we rarely talk or see each other, their friendship means a lot to me.

This was a creative writing challenge for me and a significant time commitment that I did not fully comprehend until a week into it, but this project received the most comments and feedback of all my columns. Originally, I numbered the posts 1 through 40 for the forty days of Lent. In this book, though, for the sake of clarity I have grouped the columns based on the cities I reference throughout the book. I have edited most of the columns for length.

Paintsville, Kentucky

Marty Preston

March 2016 ⊗

My friendship with Marty began in kindergarten. He and I went to Our Lady of the Mountains (O.L.M.) Catholic School. I blame Marty—or, I should say, give him credit—for instilling in me his passion for everything sports-related. He was an avid Pittsburgh Steelers fan, and I gravitated to the Dallas Cowboys. He was always the best athlete. It did not matter if it was basketball, golf, or tennis; this kid always knew how to play the game at a high level.

We played a Commodore 64 computer basketball game on a floppy disk for hours at a time. It featured Dr. J and Larry Bird. The graphics were awful, but it was our favorite game. If we were not dunking on the UK hoop that was loosely fastened to Marty's bedroom door, then we were launching the electronic version of three-point shots. Somewhere in between, we were escaping WWE wrestling holds and other forms of friendly torture from Marty's older brother, Rusty, and Rusty's crazy friend, Steve Belcher.

I cannot tell you the number of Friday nights I spent at Marty's house or vice versa. We would return home only to dodge and survive a gauntlet that would rival American Gladiators. The two older guys practiced wrestling moves on us, chased us around the house, and "gently" hazed us in between their multi-day legendary Monopoly games.

Our love for basketball extended to the real court, and we played for our school and ultimately won the league championship. One game, I remember hitting a half-court shot to end the third quarter, and Marty made the game-winning free throws. His mom, Stella, videotaped every game and provided some play-by-play commentary. Stella was, and still is, my second mom. I love her dearly, and her positive attitude and magnetic personality are still going strong.

Her basketball passion was clear, because she would yell at the referees and had some of the best one-liners. It was always cheerful and never rude, unlike things we routinely hear these days from parents at the gym or the baseball diamond. I would like to show Kaden one of those video-tapes, but we threw away our VCR about fifteen years ago.

One of my fondest memories was riding to McDonald's on Friday nights with Marty's dad, Russell. Russell had this long two-door silver Cadillac, and we both rode in the front seat to pick up Chicken McNuggets with sweet-and-sour sauce. We thought we were cool kids!

I went home for a few days and stopped by Marty's childhood home to visit with Stella, who was battling leukemia. We sat and talked for an hour or two, and all those childhood memories kept rushing back. The furniture and layout had changed, as you would imagine, but my mind was reliving 1984. It was good to see her, and I am glad we made it a priority to visit with her and not just for five minutes. She has not changed a bit.

Memories of My Second Mom

December 5, 2018 🌐

Stella Preston courageously fought cancer but ran out of time. I never say people "lose their fight with cancer," because cancer does not fight fair. I have never met someone fighting cancer who would not do everything in their power to beat the disease. I flew home for a few days to pay my respects to someone I dearly cared about who played a vital role in my life. I also wanted to make sure one of my best friends, Marty Preston, did not have to bury his mom by himself.

During our middle school years, the Paintsville Tigers earned a trip to the Kentucky High School Basketball Tournament (commonly referred to as the Sweet Sixteen) three years in a row. I still remember watching the police escort the buses out of town. The following year, Stella took Marty and me to Lexington to watch the tournament. The game began with the Tigers crossing half-court, and a player from Fairdale (Louisville) stole the ball and dunked ferociously. It was the first time we saw someone dunk in person, and our eyes were as big as saucers. I thought, *Oh man, this is going to be a long day for our Tigers.* The team shook it off, brought the ball down the court, and started the next possession. I vividly remember shooting hoops in our high school gym during summer with Marty and the Tigers point guard, telling us what it felt like to experience it. He was my favorite Tiger because he worked his tail off, was down to earth, and was nice to everyone. When you are a middle school basketball player in our town, the Paintsville High School basketball players are your heroes.

Stella was our loudest cheerleader by far, and she made sure the refs knew when she felt they were doing a lousy job. She was vocal and hilarious but never rude or disrespectful. The worst part was that she knew the names of every kid (on both teams) *and* every referee. It was not a typical "Hey ref, you stink." It was more like, "Now, William Fraley, you know these boys are playing their hearts out. You need to do better, and I know you can. Step it up!"

Stella videotaped every game with one of those circa-1980 camcorders the news stations used back then. I know it was not light. The end product must have resembled *The Blair Witch Project*, because there is no way the camera remained steady or straight more than 45 seconds at a time. I told Marty it would be fun someday to sit down with V, Brian Bailey, Charles Lusk, Paraag Maddiwar, and others to watch one of those game videos.

Marty's family owned one of the local funeral homes, and as kids, we practically lived there during the week because it was our after-school landing spot. We knew the drill when we came in the front door. We were always quiet and respectful and headed straight to the back office. Once there, Russell, Marty's Dad, would let us "buy" one Pepsi or Nehi each by letting us borrow his key to unlock the pop machine. They came in ten-ounce bottles with Styrofoam wrappers. We thought we were something special.

As a kid, you might have questions about death and the role the funeral home plays. Stella had a heart of gold, and she would explain everything to us, from the business operations to the family side. I always wondered why someone would choose a career in the funeral industry, but now it makes total sense. Stella did not have a mean bone in her body and was always a positive light to everyone she met. She had a dynamic personality and could make you laugh and cry in the same breath. Her ability to offer comfort and tranquility to others was one of her gifts.

When Beth and I started dating during college, Beth would come home with me, and occasionally, I would tell her I needed to visit Stella. After two of these trips to the funeral home, Beth asked if we could visit Stella at her house instead of at the funeral home. We were home for a long weekend, and I called Stella to see if we could stop by. I told my mom I did not care who else I saw on the trip because Stella was #1 on my list. We sat on the couch with her and talked for hours about everything and nothing at all. She was fighting cancer, but you would never know it based on her energy, enthusiasm, and faith. It was the last time I saw her, but it is a memory I will not forget.

As I anxiously look forward to this season's first basketball scrimmage, all I want to do is yell at a ref in honor of Stella. Unfortunately, this is not an option because of league rules. We have a zero-tolerance policy for yelling at the referees. I considered asking permission from the league coordinator, the refs, and the other coach. Instead, I think a more fitting tribute is to dedicate the season to her.

Stella meant the world to many people in our town besides me. She knew Marty and I always called each other on Christmas morning. Even now, we still call on our birthdays. We tried to call or text a few times outside of birthdays, but it was very sporadic. I like to think one of Stella's gifts she left behind was to reconnect Marty and me on a more regular basis. We have exchanged more texts in the past week than we have in ten years, and we are already planning his next trip to Colorado.

After the funeral, as luck would have it, I needed a place to crash in Lexington to break up my drive to the Louisville airport. Marty invited me to stay at his house, which sounded like a perfect plan and a lot of fun. I relished the opportunity to tell old stories to his children and wife. I told one of his three sons to keep at least one story for when he needs to get out of trouble and needs to make his dad laugh. That is what friends are for, right?

We laughed and reminisced about stories from our youth until 2:30 a.m. We watched college football and basketball, yelling at the players and coaches the entire time. After all, thirty-nine years of friendship is a lot to cover in a short amount of time, but we shared our favorite memories of Stella and our childhood. We might not have been wearing Pittsburgh Steelers and Dallas Cowboys pajamas, but as we sat in his living room, I felt as if we were ten years old again.

We played a wide variety of sports during our childhood, and the result was always the same. I am guessing my record against him is something close to 0-600. I was the Washington Generals, and Marty was the Harlem Globetrotters.

Late in the evening, I half-jokingly challenged Marty to a 3-point shootout. He cackled and said, "Why do you think you can beat me now?" We did not play on the court at his house, but I promise that when he comes to Colorado for a visit, we will find the nearest basketball court to play and I hope the altitude will be my home-court advantage. Maybe I will make one more basket than him and scream at the top of my lungs and pump my arms like Tiger Woods exclaiming, "Victory at last!" Maybe, he still has the smooth Rex Chapman shooting stroke and will beat me ten times in a row like he always did in his driveway. Regardless of what happens, I need to adjust my record by one W, and it has nothing to do with the outcome of a game but more because I was lucky enough to call Stella Preston my second mom.

V Grino

February 2016 ●

One of my oldest friends sent me a note via Facebook, reminding me we have been friends for over thirty-five years, and it was none other than Vincent "V" Grino. We met in kindergarten, standing in the bathroom line. This was 1979, so my Mom let my hair grow close to my shoulders. I had the 1970s Dutch boy haircut, but V thought I was a girl and kindly told me I was in the wrong line. I went home and told Mom there was a kid in my class who had the best suntan in the world. V is Filipino. That day a friendship for the ages was forged, and we never looked back.

Growing up, we were always running around together. V's family drove to Lexington a lot because it was where the closest mall was located. They treated me like a son, and I was always welcome to eat, sleep, and hang out at their house, regardless of the time of day or night. Thank you, Penny, and rest in peace, Juny.

We played hoops together, joined Boy Scouts, and then I gladly took a back seat as V's extraordinary musical talent took form. He could sing anything: gospel, R & B, rock, or country. At high school dances, I watched from the sideline whenever a slow song came on because *every* girl at PHS wanted to dance with V—because he could sing to them. Billy Ocean, Luther Vandross, Boyz II Men, you name it, he could hit every note perfectly.

One summer night, we were out late and decided it would be a good idea to stop by a friend's house and knock on her window to say hi. This close friend of ours, who was more like a sister, always dressed for success and never looked bad. I stayed in the car, and V carefully tiptoed across her yard, crouched down, and gently pecked on her window. Suddenly I saw V sprinting for his life across the yard, and he yelled, "Wrong house, T, wrong house!" V jumped in the car, and we sped off. It was the right house, but he was not expecting Sabrina's lime green face cream, and neither was I. Thirty years later, we would like to apologize to Sabrina Moore's neighbor for scaring them at midnight since they heard V's footsteps as he ran away.

Our next adventure was a Whitesnake concert in Huntington, West Virginia, with Sabrina and her parents. She had left her ticket in V's new Pontiac Transport minivan, so we purchased an extra ticket and snuck her into our section. The best memory of the night is what Wick—Sabrina's dad—did at a stoplight. He backed up and pulled forward to trigger the light to change. He might as well have changed water to wine, because V and I were stunned. We immediately nicknamed it The Wick Trick, and I still say it in front of our kids. Wick would play another role in my life, but I did not know it at the time.

We were in each other's weddings, and I was honored to be in both of his, even though Stacy (Preston) Grino teased me about being the bad-luck charm his first time around. He and his little brother sang at our wedding, and their talent amazed our guests.

V and I are both habitually late for things, but he is worse than me. He told me one time it was a cultural difference and referred to it as Filipino time. When Beth and I got married, I told V our wedding started at 4:30 even though it began at 5:30. True story. We both made it on time, and I think he was even early.

Like most teenage boys, V and I chased our fair number of girls, but the one he could not catch was always his dream girl. She was nice to him, but she dated one of the football stars, and it did not happen for whatever reason. Everyone in town knew how he felt about her, and I joked with him about all those late-night discussions talking about Stacy. A few years back, fate intervened, and they ended up in the same city. V finally asked Stacy out, and they hit it off and got married. Sometimes dreams come true and the good guy wins in the end. Stacy, now you know what we all knew for twenty years: V loves you more than anything in this world and will always be there for you. I am happy for both of you. V, I am thankful for our friendship, and you are the brother I never had.

Sabrina (Moore) Rader

February 2016 ◔

Sabrina and I met in sixth grade and instantly hit it off. We were like brother and sister, meaning we were close and had our disagreements and playful fights, but nothing ever serious. Believe it or not, I was in a few school plays, and one scene called for me to kiss Sabrina on the cheek. I remember saying, "She is four inches taller than me. I'm going to need a stepladder, people!"

We did not know it, but our dads knew each other well, and that would come in handy down the road for me. In high school, Sabrina and I were always talking about who to date, who we liked, and what we wanted to do with our lives. As everyone knows, I am a talker, and I love learning about dreams and what people want to do with their lives. I always knew Sabrina would be remarkably successful in whatever field she chose because she was an extraordinarily talented person. She always pushed me to be better when I felt like slacking or did not have the energy to push through on homework.

In my junior year, I did a stupid thing on Homecoming night and wrecked my car. My close friend Stacy Preston Grino was right there with me. We were involved in a fender bender because we played "Car Tag." Do not ask. All the reader needs to know is that my dad knew what had happened before I came that night. Of course, I was scared to death and lied to my parents about what happened for the only time in my life. Dad let me go for a day or two before saying I needed to go to the police department, file an accident report, and apologize for my mistake. This incident occurred in early October, and Dad told me he was revoking my driving privileges through December.

A few weeks later, my dad and Wick, Sabrina's dad, went to Cincinnati for a conference, and Wick told my dad he should shorten my punishment based on my normal exemplary behavior. I am not certain what Wick said, but Dad returned from the trip and reduced my punishment; thanks again, Wick!

After high school, Sabrina and I both went to UK and hung out occasionally, but it was sporadic. After college, we lost touch, which happens to all good friends at some point. I honestly cannot remember how long we went without talking, but it was probably close to eight or nine years. Then, a few days before Beth and I got married, I received a long, heartfelt email from Sabrina, and it made me smile. The time we had lost was no one's fault, but we both promised to keep in better touch.

Fast-forward a few years, and she and I came together to work on our class reunion plans. It instantly felt like old times. She had a detailed plan with a budget and a list of menu options and prices, while I shared ten different ideas for the party segment. Some things never change. I honestly do not know why or how she tolerated me for twenty-five years.

I have to say working on the reunion with her was special because it brought back splendid memories. Like all my good friends, she had always been there for me in high school and early college, *always*. Little did I know what impact her unconditional support would play in my life a few years later.

Sabrina, I am glad we reconnected, and I can never truly thank you for being there when I was at my weakest point. You have always been and will continue to be a wonderful person and a great friend.

Steve Belcher

March 2016 📀

I mentioned this good old boy in my post about Marty Preston. Steve Belcher is an old friend, both literally and figuratively. I guess you could

WHO WE MEET ALONG THE WAY

say he played a role in my formative years if you count body slams, head-locks, and hundreds of punches. If V Grino was my twin brother, then Steve fit the role of an older brother to a T. He was a few years older than me, and I looked up to him for some crazy reason. As a goofy middle schooler, he was cool because he played high school sports and eventually joined the Air Force. It always seemed as if he had the girls' attention too, but that remains heavily debated. I still wonder how he scored his rock-star sweetheart of a wife, Nicole. On a more serious note, thank you for your service, dear friend.

Steve, if I am ever in a bar fight, I want you on my side—and not because of your military training. We might get our butts kicked, but something tells me you would make us both laugh through the pain. Thanks for being the big brother I never had and for not breaking any of my bones when I was twelve.

Big Mike Williams

March 2016 🌐

Big Mike and I went to rival high schools. He went to Johnson Central High School. The two schools differed vastly in size, and JCHS was referred to as the county school, and we were the city school. It still makes me chuckle, because PHS had 250 students in seventh through twelfth grades, yet we were considered the big city school. Central was 4A or 5A and probably had over 3,000 students. Both schools were known for their both athletic and academic achievements, but, as with most rival schools, each thought the other was inferior. These preconceived notions dissipated after you spent time with someone from the other school and realized they endured the same struggles and stereotypes you did.

In a tight-knit community, you know or recognize almost everyone. Mike and I finally met our senior year but did not hang out until our freshman year at Prestonsburg Community College. It was a melting pot of several local high schools, and I swear Mike knew people from six different high schools. It is difficult to comprehend how our paths did not cross before then, given that we both were extroverts who immensely enjoyed being around people.

I remember cruising the plaza on the weekends, and he had this big smile on his face, and his friends were *always* laughing with him. He is a funny guy, and I always told him he should try to perform stand-up comedy. His one-liners have always been some of my favorites, and his sarcasm is second to none.

Mike's dad owned a TV and electronics store in Prestonsburg, one town over from my hometown. The store was our safe place to go to when we wanted to chill. We spent hours there, wondering where life would take us. The best part was sitting on the oversized recliners in the demo room and watching movies on a 70-inch flat-screen with ten or fifteen surround-sound speakers.

Big Mike is one of the nicest people in this world. I can honestly say not a single person that I know has uttered a negative comment about him. He does not judge anyone, and he welcomes friends of friends with a hearty handshake and a deep belly laugh. He often joked about my high energy level and asked me if I ever slowed down. His running joke was he could call me at 7:00 a.m. on a Saturday and tell me we were building a house that day, and I'd be at his door with my hammer, ready to go, despite not knowing the first thing about construction.

He is an avid music buff and a DJ for a radio station and the Holiday Inn in Prestonsburg. If I ever appear on *Who Wants to Be a Millionaire* and the trivia question is music-related, I hope his cell phone is within reach because he will be the recipient of my phone-a-friend call. He knows details about every type of music and the stories behind the bands and the popular songs.

For a year or two we lost touch, and it was his choice. He did not return my calls or e-mails, but I was persistent and kept leaving voicemails and conveying messages through other friends. He had made a minor decision and was embarrassed because he thought it would upset me for some crazy reason. I reassured him he will always be one of my good friends, and he knows me well enough to remember I do not judge my friends.

A short time later, he called me and explained his actions, which were unnecessary, and we shared a laugh and quickly moved on. I share this part of the story because we all lose touch with friends for different reasons. It is important not to give up or judge individuals for any reason. It is never too late to pick up the phone and talk to an old friend. Life is way too short to hold a grudge or wonder if you should or should not call someone you have not spoken to in years. It is something we all need to do more often, including me.

Big Mike, I told you this a long time ago, and it still rings true years later: You were my friend then, and you will be my close friend until it is my time to leave this earth. Thanks for listening all these years and for always being there for me.

Missy (Osborne) Myers

March 26 🌐

Missy ("Mis") and I met when we were thirteen years old at a high school reunion. Her mom and my mom went to Mullins High School together. I lived close to downtown, and her family lived out in the county. We heard about each other often from our moms, and we would always wave and say hi, but we were not close.

Later in high school, we started hanging out and struck up a great friendship. We became closer once we left for UK and Eastern Kentucky University, respectively. I would always call her when our group of friends headed to Richmond on Thursday nights to enjoy the sights and sounds of The Dog and Cherry Pit, maybe? When I contemplated changing my major for a record-breaking sixth time, I was ready to transfer to EKU and move in with her.

We always got along well and enjoyed hanging out as good friends do. When we were twenty-three, we jokingly made a pact to be each other's backup if we both grew old and gray without getting married. I think we set thirty as our age deadline, and she got engaged shortly after that, and I did when I was twenty-nine. It is okay, Mis, I can take a hint. Ha ha ha.

I look forward to hosting Mis for several days in the future, showing her The Mile-High City and whatever mountain town she wants to visit. She can play with our kids, get to know Beth, and talk about Johnson Central's most famous alum, the Grammy award–winning country superstar Chris Stapleton.

Missy, I hear Red Rocks Amphitheatre has an incredible slate of concerts lined up this summer, and I might know someone who can get you rather good tickets. It is time to check your calendar and book a flight! It has been way too long, and we need to catch up. Love you, pal.

Matt Burchett

March 2016 🌐

I met Matt when I transferred to middle school as I was entering the eighth grade. His dad coached the girls' high school basketball team and taught science, and he remains an avid angler. I remember him coaching us about hoops by breaking down tape of the 1980s L.A. Lakers and their vaunted fast break.

Our senior class was one of the first classes to host Project Prom, and Matt's mom helped organize some logistics. There were fifty or sixty auction items for students to bid on, including mini-fridges, stereo systems, ten or twenty scholarships worth $500 to $1,500, and a canoe.

Matt and I enjoyed the outdoors and decided early on we would combine our casino play money and try to buy the canoe. He lived near the lake, and he could store it. I loved canoeing from my Scouting days. We thought this was a well-conceived plan. We ended up with the highest bid, and I can still see the look on my dad's face when I told him what we bought. He smiled and said, "Out of fifty prizes, including cash for college, you bought a damn canoe?"

Burchett, as we commonly referred to Matt, has a wicked competitive streak, and even though I am not athletically gifted, I do too. One night in high school we played pool at his house, and we started with a traditional best-of-five series, but that was only the beginning. We kept adding on game after game until we had played fifty-one games. When he visited me in Denver, we laughed about it. To this day, he cannot remember who won, but I think it was him. Part of the reason I think so is that we went to the Wynkoop Brewing Company in downtown Denver and shot pool with some of my coworkers. Burchett ran the tables on all of us. It was as if he had a pool table in his optometry office's break room. Can one of his coworkers conduct some research for me?

On the professional front, Matt has been a phenomenally successful optometrist. He will not talk about it publicly, but I can brag about his accomplishments. He has been involved with the Kentucky Optometric Association and has held several leadership positions over the years, including President. He and his business partners own multiple eye care centers in central Kentucky, and they will probably expand again in the next few years.

Burchett and I catch up late at night on Facebook. We share a passion for giving back; if we ever live in the same city again, we could do some cool things together. I don't know if we can top buying a fifteen-foot Coleman canoe, but we will try.

Kristy (Ward) Orem

March 2016 🌐

Kristy is one of my oldest and closest high school friends. I can remember riding everywhere in her cherry red Oldsmobile Cutlass Supreme. I would be lying if I said I did not say a few Hail Marys a time or two, but we survived as we were jamming out to Diamond Rio and Boyz II Men.

Kristy never settled for anything, and she demanded the best from herself and her friends. Her passion and zest for life are apparent and are among the first things you notice when you meet her. We had some great times running on the track team together and being goofy kids in high school. She and Sabrina Moore were two of my best friends. I hated the fact we lost touch for several years, but I realized it happens sometimes. Regardless of how many years passed, I will always treasure those memories and our friendship.

She loves the game of basketball. We would often play pickup games in the gym, and she would run with the guys and not tolerate anyone taking it easy on her. Her competitive spirit helped her walk on at Eastern Kentucky University. Her drive and determination continue to guide her: She recently finished her sixteenth year of coaching high school hoops.

Kristy reached a significant coaching milestone when she earned her 300th win as Head Coach for girls' basketball at Fleming County High School. I feel sorry for the referees in her region—and not because she is rude or cocky, but because she demands the best and expects it from everyone. I have been to many places in Kentucky, but I have not spent a lot of time in Fleming County. From Facebook posts alone, I can tell the entire town and parents support her and appreciate her dedication to the girls on and off the basketball court. She strives to prepare them for life after basketball and makes sure she sets them on the right path for the future. Fleming County is lucky to have her, and I know she appreciates the community support for all FCHS-related activities and teams.

Fundraising is necessary for most high school athletic programs, and it can be a challenge for schools everywhere. I sent Kristy a small donation and asked her for more information on her needs in case I could help somehow. She told me she set up a four-year rotation, ensuring every senior gets something new. One year she bought home uniforms, then away uniforms, practice gear, and finally warmups. She also takes the team to Myrtle Beach every summer for team camp and to Florida every four years.

On a lighter note, I remembered when my little sister, Brittany, told me Kristy was doing well at Fleming County and that she sometimes coached games in heels. I chuckled and told her it did not surprise me. I explained to Brit that, for Kristy, it was not about looking good; it was about being a professional and setting a precedent for her team and the competition.

This past year, she was promoted to Athletic Director. Kristy, I have told you this privately, but I am humbled by your accomplishments and honored to call you a friend. The AD position is not an easily attained job. I know your hard work, dedication, and fundraising expertise played a part in yet another of your success stories. I cannot wait to see what you accomplish next. Good luck next season, and remember, your team will always have a big fan in Denver, Colorado!

Sara Hopson Blair

April 2016 🌐

Sara was like a second mom to me. She lived across the large grassy field that at one time was the site of our town's drive-in theater. If I was not at V Grino's house, then I was at her home, shooting hoops with her son, J.R. I cannot pinpoint where or how my passion for writing came from, but I know I have Sara to thank for pushing me to be a better writer. She believed in me before I had confidence. I can remember typing school papers on her computer with the white type on the blue screen. I think it was a desktop HP or IBM, and it took up half the desk. The printer was a daisy-wheel format. Do you remember those?

The Blairs' house was usually my first stop on my bike ride or stroll through the neighborhood. We played Wiffle Ball there, swam in the pool daily, and shot hoops regardless of the weather. I remember we had a light on a pole so we could shoot late into the night, and it was common for us to play with cracked or bloody fingers in the winter months.

Sara always made sure we had plenty of snacks and Kool-Aid. I appreciated the fact that she looked out for us. She often shared life advice with me. It was lighthearted but straight to the point and unedited, which sometimes we all need.

I always looked up to her because she wrote a weekly column for the Paintsville Herald, and I always thought it was such a big deal. I thought if I could someday write a column for the local newspaper, then I would be a cool kid.

I was lucky enough to see this dream come true in 1993. I was home for the summer, and the editor offered me the opportunity to cover sports as a journalist and, better yet, to write a column. I titled it "The Inside Pitch." I wrote about life, PGA golfer Paul Azinger's fight against cancer, and my grandmother's battle against leukemia. I also wrote columns on the lost art of baseball card collecting, and I expressed my opinions on what I felt was wrong with high school sports and the funding gap at my alma mater. My good friend Calvin Music was a regional finalist in the 300-meter hurdles. Our school had only nine hurdles instead of the standard ten. I always wondered what would have happened if our track team had the correct number of hurdles because Calvin fell on the tenth and final one.

While in college, I penned a story about my first year living in a UK residence hall. It was published in a national magazine, *College Bound*, and I received fifty dollars for it. I was officially hooked and wanted to write in the future in some capacity, whether as a hobby or a side job.

Sara, thank you for your support, encouragement, coaching, and friendship for over thirty-five years. I will continue to find new topics to cover and ways to inspire others, as you did for me.

Brian Hardison

March 2016 🌐

Brian and I grew up in the same neighborhood, and our houses were less than two city blocks apart. We were always hanging out and playing sports together. His dad coached us in football in their front yard. We would play a simple game of defense, one on one. It seemed as if we would play for hours. Basketball, golf, board games, Star Wars, you name it; we played it.

I have always said I was blessed with a childhood and a neighborhood like the ones you see in the movies. It was safe, we had plenty of room to play, and everyone looked out for one another, regardless of how much money your parents made or the size of your house. Every Saturday was a field day for our neighborhood crew. We would wake up, watch a cartoon or two over a bowl of our favorite sugar-laden cereal, then hop on our bikes and head out to round up the troops. We had this one stretch of grass that connected all the streets. Of course, we called it "the grass paths," which was not very original, but a simple trail meant the world to us. There were open fields from the highway to Brian's house, and it was our domain. Over time, urban sprawl made its way even to our little town, and those grassy fields soon turned into new houses. It broke my heart the first time I came home from college and saw the new development.

Brian and I were best buds, and life was good. There was a little store right behind my house, and it sold snacks and candy. We would always visit with fifty cents and come out with a handful of candy. It had weathered wooden plank floors and was tiny. The owner typically loaned us a dime or quarter or two to help pay for our items.

After a few years, Brian moved downtown near 4th Street, and we remained good friends. Shortly after that, his family moved to Florida, and I did not know what to say or do. I remember we threw him a going-away party at my house, and, as middle schoolers do, we wasted time running around, giving each other Charley horses, and playing Monopoly late into the night.

Now and then, Brian would come back to visit, and we would all gripe about the town and how we could not wait to go to college and escape. However, Brian was excited to visit and kept raving about how great the town was and how much he missed it. We thought he had been overexposed to the Florida sunshine. It would take me a few years to realize he was right and how lucky we were to have teachers who cared about our grades, parents with strict rules, and a one-of-a-kind town to grow up in.

Once we went to college, Brian and I lost touch for the first two years. He went to Florida State University. Then one of my Residence Hall Association (RHA) conferences was in Tallahassee, and we reconnected, which was great, and promised to keep in touch.

We both flew back for V and Stacy (Preston) Grino's wedding, and Brian brought his girlfriend, Jennifer. She was and still is a sweetheart with a gentle smile and an enormous heart. The poor girl not only had to hear every story from first grade to sixth and then some, but also had to endure roaming around town for a week seeing where all these stories took place. I knew then that she was a keeper and that it was only a matter of time before they would get married. Beth and I spent a lot of time with them at the Carriage House Hotel the weekend of V's wedding. Technically, it had changed ownership and was now a Ramada, but it will always be the Carriage House Hotel in my mind.

Soon after the wedding, they moved to Boulder, Colorado, and we both were grateful to be in the same state together. We invited them to the cabin for a night, and it was the B and B reminiscence party until the wee hours of the morning. The next day, we went hiking with the kiddos, and Kaden was like his little shadow. I told Brian how great fatherhood is and how I could not wait for him to experience it. Little did we know Jennifer was pregnant! They told us while we were having a cocktail or two around the campfire. (Point of clarification: Brian and I had drinks, not Jenn.)

Brian is one of those friends I can pick up with right away, regardless of how long it has been since we last spoke. It is as if we are still in fifth grade, riding our bikes along the grass paths and searching for our neighborhood pals.

Don Bryson, Jerry Adams, and Johnnie Ross

March 2016 🌐

These three individuals played an important part in my formative years, as they were my Boy Scout leaders at different times.

Don "Doc" Bryson was my first Scout leader, and he was a combination of a motivational speaker and a life coach. My first overnight weekend backpacking trip was memorable from the start. Our parents had packed our backpacks as if the trip were around the world. We had pots, pans, extra clothes for five days, snacks for a family of ten, and who knows what else. Doc lined us up in his expansive front yard, and we were excited and ready to hike. He looked us dead in the eye and said, "Gentlemen, take your backpacks off and empty them." We were crushed because it had taken hours to compact everything and now we had to repack it without Mom and Dad's help. It was not as bad as I thought, though. He showed us the correct way to pack a backpack by walking us through some fundamental practices such as placing the heavy things near the top and balancing clothes to minimize things shifting as you hike.

We were also working on our lifesaving merit badges, which required us to perform specific tasks such as jumping into a pool, swimming to a drowning person, and pulling them to safety. Doc played the role of the drowning person for our test. I went first. As I swam out to him, I thought I would outsmart him, dive to the bottom, and then try to "save" him by swimming behind him. Well, he knew exactly what I was up to. He patiently waited for me to reach for him, and then he grabbed me and took me under the water. Now, the last thing in the world a drowning person wants to do is to return underwater, but he made his point: A drowning person is worried and panicked and will latch onto anything as soon as you get close. I never forgot the lesson, and it is one I plan on teaching both of our children.

People often ask me why I am not scared to speak in front of people, and I always tell them it's because I was speaking in front of my fellow Scouts and leaders when I was thirteen. Doc made sure we developed our leadership skills early on by speaking during meetings. He spoke only during the last minute of the meeting, which was called the Scoutmaster's Minute. I do not claim to be the best public speaker, but I am comfortable doing it, and I enjoy it. I also learned a long time ago to speak from my heart and not to pull any punches. It has served me well at weddings and other times in my career.

Jerry Adams was my expedition leader when I went to Philmont Scout Ranch in Cimarron, New Mexico. Our troop comprised scouts from all over Kentucky, including Campton, Carlisle, and Cumberland. We were all thirteen to fifteen years old, and it was one hell of a bonding experience to backpack 88 miles in twelve days with those guys.

Jerry taught me the importance of enjoying the outdoors and what it means to have guts. He always had a smile on his face, and he had this go-getter mentality. Our trip out west was spent on a charter bus that originated in Lexington and three days later ended in Cimarron, New Mexico. Along the way, we stopped at a fraternity house in Columbia, Missouri, to stretch our legs and throw some frisbee in the parking lot. Jerry was chasing down an errant pass when he ran into a concrete parking guard. The boat shoes he was wearing did little to shield his toes from the impact. I cannot remember the exact words he muttered, but I do not blame him for whatever he said. He carefully removed his shoe, and his big toe was three shades of purple and extremely swollen. We took him to the E.R., and the doctor told him he should probably bag the trip and go back home. Jerry told him he was crazy, and that he had waited twenty-five years for this opportunity and would not miss it over a bum toe. I do not have a high tolerance for pain, but watching the doctor drain the blood from the injured toe was fascinating and impressive. Jerry had to re-bandage it every day and changed the dressings often, but he made it through the trip. Other survival experts may have a TV show, but when all hell breaks loose and I am lost in the wilderness, I want Jerry Adams as my teammate.

On our ninth day of the trek, Jerry suggested we get up at 5:00 a.m. and hike to the ridge and watch the sunrise. Keep in mind he was hiking with one other adult and thirteen teenagers. We all reluctantly agreed and did our part. We broke camp bright and early and stopped on this scenic overlook to watch the sun rise behind the mountains. Jerry, I appreciated the remarkable dawn, and I remember the smiles on our faces, but I am still not a morning person.

Jerry knows an immense amount about the outdoors and spent his career in forestry, which makes sense. He is also a University of Kentucky alum and prepped me with all kinds of hilarious stories as I got ready to leave for college. We might have spent our time on campus twenty years apart, but he was right about several things. The campus is a great place, and the city of Lexington is not bad either.

Johnnie Ross was the Scoutmaster for the Prestonsburg troop, which was our rival. They did not like us, and we did not like them because we competed at every event, but Doc Bryson and Johnnie were old friends, and both made sure we understood what it meant to respect your competitor. We were Troop 851, and they were 877. I made many good friends among those guys and still talk to some of them to this day.

Johnnie and Doc led both troops on a fifty-mile canoe trip down the Big Sandy River. My house was by that river, near a bridge that is now named after the late Kentucky State Police Officer Alex Rubado. I remember all of us floating under that bridge in our canoes. I remember waving at my family and my neighbors, Wassie and Mary Rose Bailey. It was a sunny day, and I was grinning ear to ear. Life was good. An hour later, we encountered a nasty thunderstorm, and it raged for hours. We did not eat dinner because the weather was terrifying, and the rain lasted deep into the night. We ate the steaks for breakfast and tried to dry our clothes and sleeping bags.

Johnnie also led our state contingent to the National Scout Jamboree. Johnnie has a great sense of humor, is a super nice guy, and instilled confidence in all of us. There is always a lot of patch trading at these events, and the most popular one that year was the Malibu patch. It was bright and colorful, and it had a shark on it. The Jamboree lasted several days, and I tried my best to trade for that patch but I could not find one. At the conclusion of the trip, Johnnie handed me one and signed the back of it. He told me always to remember the Scout Law.

When you are twelve years old and your Scoutmaster tries to tell you the value of being an Eagle Scout, you shake your head and move on to the next thing. He also tells you only two percent of all Scouts attain the rank of Eagle Scout, and that if you can achieve the rank, it will follow you the rest of your life. I was lucky enough to earn my Eagle badge when I was fourteen, and I had my Eagle ceremony on my mom's birthday, which was fitting. I added it to my résumé long ago, and people still comment on it. I am proud of this accomplishment, but I would not have been able to make it without the help and support of my parents or Don Bryson.

You always hear from these wise leaders that one out of every one hundred Scouts will use something he learned in Scouts to save either his own life or that of someone else. Again, at twelve, you are like, yeah, yeah, whatever. However, it is accurate. I cannot say I saved someone's life, but my knowledge and experience from Scouts helped transport an injured hiker to safety.

Fast-forward twenty years. Beth and I were hiking on Christmas Day in New Zealand. We were on the Abel Tasman Trail, which is a spectacular trail that follows the ocean for several miles. You can hike, canoe, or kayak to different points, then catch a water taxi for the return trip. We were on our way back, and we noticed a European couple and a friend resting on the trail. The woman had her sock and boot off, and her foot was in a small puddle. I asked what happened and if they needed any help. She said, "Oh, I will be fine. I twisted my ankle." I asked her if she could show it to me. I am not a doctor, but I knew right away she most likely had torn a ligament or two because her ankle was swollen, red, and more prominent than a softball.

I asked them what they were going to do because nightfall was approaching, and she could not stay there on the trail. I explained to the other two guys how we could create a square seat with our forearms and move her down to the beach, where she could hail a water taxi. I showed them how to lock wrists, and we carefully carried her to the shoreline. The only problem was the date. It was Christmas Day. The water taxis were not running regularly. One of their group had a cell phone and called in a request, and it was a few hundred dollars, but they came to pick her up. As we sat trying to comfort her, the gentleman from Germany started playing the George Michael version of "Last Christmas" on his red Samsung flip phone.

To this day, when I hear the song, I smile and think of Abel Tasman and the group of friends we made on the beach. Doc Bryson always told us he wanted us to achieve Eagle Scout rank before turning fifteen and decided it was no longer cool. Shortly after my Eagle ceremony, I hung up the hiking boots and Scout uniform, but I will not forget all the lessons I learned from these three men and all the great guys I met from Prestonsburg to Cimarron, New Mexico.

Jerry Adams is in the front row, fourth from the left.

Lexington, Kentucky

Next on my path was six memorable years of college at the University of Kentucky. I left the Horse Capital of the World with two degrees: a Physical Education degree and a Master's in Sports Management. I headed west to Denver to complete my graduate degree with a summer internship at a mom-and-pop event management company, Summit Sports & Events. Little did I know how much that soccer and basketball company would impact my life forever.

Beth Tosti

February 2016 🌐

I have always said my wife is my best friend. It has been and will be the truth for years to come. I honestly believe this is one major piece of all successful marriages. When asked to say a few words at a wedding, my friends know I usually say something along the following lines: Love is vital in any relationship because physical looks will and usually do change over thirty or forty years. We all gain weight and lose hair with age, but you still want to sit on your front porch when you are eighty and be able to laugh with your better half. That matters.

Beth, our relationship's beginning was not what fairy tales are made of by any means. I thought you were a big flirt, and you thought I was cocky. I remember our first date was at Charlie Brown's, a popular bar and restaurant near UK's campus. It was my favorite place because it was simple yet had some character. The entire seating area was dimly lit with candles. The décor featured old wooden tables, comfy oversized leather chairs, dusty bookshelves, and a fireplace in the corner.

I was coming off a long relationship in which I was sure I had been cheated on, so I wanted nothing to do with dating someone. We went out a few times, and then you invited me to have dinner with your parents in Louisville, and I promptly broke up with you. It scared me to death, and I practically ran for the hills.

I liked you a lot and kept thinking about how awesome you were and how you were such a refreshing change from other women. The realization that I could be happy with someone new scared me, but luckily you were not a sports fan. It reassured me you were not a robot or one hundred percent perfect (I kid, I kid). A few years later, this, too, would change as you began quoting Heisman stats and speaking knowledgably about basketball moves.

We dated for six years and had our share of breakups—me more than you, unfortunately—but for some strange reason, you hung in there and believed in us. Thank you for not giving up on me or us!

Our wedding was an absolute blast, and one of my funniest memories is the Tosti wedding shuttle we organized. Our good friends Brian Tatum and Will Stevens drove a fifteen-passenger van and picked up friends and family who made the trek to Denver. Those two were the perfect entertainers for aunts, uncles, college buddies, and other relatives.

Next was our honeymoon to Costa Rica and, eventually—our last hurrah before kids—a twenty-one-day excursion to Australia and New Zealand. The trip was epic. We packed a ton of activities into each day, and I would not change a thing.

The next significant change in our lives was the kiddos. You have been an amazing mom, and the kids are lucky to have you in their lives. I always knew you had a high pain tolerance, but the fact you almost had Kaden without an epidural and did not have one with Emily still amazes me. Happy Valentine's Day to my best friend and wife!

Tom Williams

February 2016 🌐

"Tommy Boy," as we call him, is one of my funniest friends for sure. He keeps tabs on our group of friends and always knows what is going on with everyone when we talk. He knows how Mike Guelcher's job is going, and that Silletto's baby does not like carrots and is crawling all over the place, and more such knowledge about friends in all time zones.

One year, a group of us drove to South Carolina for spring break and stayed on Kiawah Island. It was an absolute blast. The stories are not all suitable for Facebook, but one that is concerns the day we returned from the beach and found that the power had gone out. The group talked about pending issues such as cooking and the fact that we did not have any flashlights, matches, etc. The first thing out of Tommy Boy's mouth was, "Oh crap, the beer is going to get warm!"

Tommy and I have had some good times together. We have this weird connection, and we have had a few close calls in vehicles for some odd reason. There was the time on spring break in South Carolina when we approached a bridge that had a "swinging" section to make way for boat traffic, and I did not realize it was preparing to turn. I did what any

Kentucky boy would do; I floored it. We made it across in the nick of time. Another time I was in Lexington for work, and we went out for one beer. On our way home, we were three blocks from his house on Maxwell Street when a drunk driver T-boned us and launched us into a tree. We are reasonably sure the cross street was Lexington Avenue, and the tree was ten feet up on the grassy knoll. We were lucky to escape with a mild concussion (me) and a bruised knee (him).

The Lexington police officer kindly gave us a ride home, but he had to put us in the cruiser's back seat. As we parked in front of the house, I reached over to unlock the door, and of course it would not open. Tommy laughed hysterically and said, "Tosti, these doors don't open!" I knew it, but I did not even think about it. It was the first and only time I have spent any time in the back seat of a police car, and I am glad it was not for any other reason.

Tommy's other important title is godfather to Kaden, a role he takes seriously. He always sends a card and a gift and checks in on Kaden throughout the year. The kids call him Uncle Tommy Boy.

As I mentioned earlier, he and I have been on several trips together, and this guy packs for every situation and potential weather-related catastrophe. He does not go anywhere without this gigantic trunk. No doubt, MacGyver would be lucky to have him as a sidekick. If he were traveling to the Sahara Desert, he would pack a winter coat in case a winter storm swept across the area. A bunch of UK friends went to Detroit to watch UK play Michigan State in the middle of December, and I swear Tommy packed a golf shirt in addition to winter clothes. There is no doubt in my mind he would have survived the sinking of the Titanic, because he would have had eight layers of clothes, a few Coast Guard–issued wetsuits, and two inflatable life rafts.

I will close with something Tommy always tells me: He could have gone to college in Connecticut (his home state) or California, and he still would have met me somehow.

Emily (Neer) Iniguez

February 2016 🌐

Emily and I met during college, and it was through the Residence Hall Association (RHA) where I met a ton of outstanding student leaders. She went to Georgia Tech (GT), and she quickly became one of my close friends in the organization. For years, UK and GT shared a close bond, and our group was the next class to pass on the tradition. My UK buddies and I took multiple road trips to Atlanta because it was a cool city to visit, and we got to spend time with Emily.

On one trip, Emily and I went to the Atlanta Braves Opening Day and saw the players receive their World Series rings. It was a cool experience because Dale Murphy was my favorite baseball player. My Mom and I had religiously watched and rooted for the Atlanta Braves when I was growing up. I remember me and Emily sprinted through Atlanta's airport, and I barely made my flight.

A few of us also decided it would be a good idea to visit Emily during the 1996 Olympics. Thankfully, we left Lexington late and stopped in Knoxville to see yet another RHA friend. If it were not for this pit stop, we would have been there when the bomb was detonated. Funny how things happen for a reason.

Public transportation, or MARTA, in Atlanta was jam-packed every day. Emily's little brother was maybe ten or twelve, and he referred to the train stops as "clicks." After the police helped push everyone on the train, there was no open space, and it was easy to get separated from your group. I can remember Emily's mom, Liz, repeatedly yelling our station name to her little brother. His response was, "I know, Mom, two more clicks."

The South Carolina spring break trip I mentioned earlier included a great visit with Emily and her parents. We told her we would cruise through Spartanburg after midnight and would call her to say hi, but she had a better idea. She told us to stop by for midnight breakfast. Sure enough, Liz and Emily welcomed us with open arms and served us pancakes at the ungodly hour of 1:30 a.m. with smiles on their faces. Liz, I hope to catch you on one of your Denver trips.

Two summers later, Emily was selected for an internship in Los Angeles and was looking for someone to ride with her cross-country. My good friend Chad Randall and I jumped at this chance. The trip went smoothly until Emily's little car started burning oil near Memphis. It was a temporary setback, and the mechanic told us we could buy extra oil and keep refilling it every other day. We were young and did not have time to waste in Memphis. We stocked up on motor oil, blind ambition, and guts, and away we went.

Once we made it to Los Angeles, we went to a Dodgers game and stayed up all night because we had an early flight and figured the three hours of sleep was not worth it. Emily gave us a ride to the airport at 4:30 a.m., and I remember asking her if I could lay my head in her lap in the terminal because I was exhausted.

After we boarded, Chad fell asleep right away, but someone asked me to switch seats. I kindly obliged and moved up ten rows. We landed in Chicago, and Chad was wedged between these two gigantic men and woke up in a daze and screamed, "Tosti, where are you, man?" I was comfortably seated ten rows in front of him, laughing hysterically.

We survived the trip, and Chad went back for round two when Emily had to drive home. My advice for anyone making this trip is to do your research on tourist attractions, buy an extra quart of oil, and be sure to stop for dinner in Flagstaff, Arizona, and eat at Granny's Closet, which will provide you with enough food for ten—and it is cheap, too!

Single Moms:
Angie Kretzer, Brittany Tosti Pruitt, Angela Bailey, Amy Clay, Lisa Ainsworth, and Mindy Alexander

March 2016 ◑

This post is a little different, and I hope those who read it understand why. I'm going to introduce several friends, then focus on a common trait they all share. It is a small sample, not a complete list.

Angie Kretzer's older brother and I were neighborhood pals. We knew each other well from those days. She was in Denver for work, and it was good to catch up with her. We reminisced about old stories. I reminded her of the time a neighbor's dog bit me, and I tried to run with the dog attached to my thigh. I was nine years old and was terrified because I had to pull my underwear down in front of Angie's mom so she could apply hydrogen peroxide to the wound. We laughed over beers in Denver, but it hurt like hell, both the injury and my fragile ego.

Brittany Tosti Pruitt is my little sister, and she did not have a choice of putting up with me as a child. Most siblings have stories about beating each other up or surviving a suplex move from the top bunk bed, but I never laid a hand on her. I always told her if she could put up with me, she could put up with anybody. I always tell her she is stronger than me, and I often submit my annual donation to The Gathering Place in her name.

Angela Bailey and I met through mutual friends in high school. Angela is also one of my first friends that said I should write a book. One disadvantage of living in a small town is the small dating pool. Naturally, you branch out to nearby towns, and sometimes you end up with a terrific group of new friends. Angela, I have fond memories of your house and running around Inez, the small town she lived in.

Amy Clay was a senior in high school who took a few other friends and me to lunch when we were sophomores. This simple act was a big deal because we could not drive to the plaza for lunch. She is a brilliant writer, and I enjoy reading her Facebook posts. She is also a widow and writes about the real challenges she faces on her own. One of her posts focused on how she views herself and two daughters as a triangle and not a square, which would comprise two parents. I would say the Clay girls are also like circles. They are resilient, flexible, tough, and capable of absorbing the bumps and bruises of life. Think of the Olympic rings or the Audi logo. When I see those images, I think of strength, a tight bond, and a chain that would be exceedingly difficult to break.

Lisa Ainsworth and Beth have been friends for over sixteen years, and she has always been kind and supportive of our family. This friendship might not be what it is today if it was not for a small yet big misunderstanding between her and a mutual friend, Adam Koski, who she was dating years ago. I can't imagine not having her in our lives. Lisa knew what motherhood entailed and she bravely forged ahead with a powerful and unselfish decision.

Mindy Alexander was our longtime neighbor across the street in Denver and was much more than a great neighbor. Beth and Mindy were both pregnant, which was just one of the bonds they shared. We were always ordering last-minute pizzas or grilling out in each other's backyards, but we picked each other up when we had a bad day. Mindy moved to Nashville the past year so I was excited to spend time with Mindy and her two daughters a few weeks ago when I was in the Music City for a friend's surprise birthday party. We miss you guys!

These ladies all share a few characteristics, but they have in common that each one is a single mom. How they got there also varies, but they are such strong individuals, and I admire all of them from afar. I sometimes think about the little things I struggle with as a dad and cannot imagine having to do it all by myself. It is what these ladies do, and they do it very well. They often wear all the proverbial hats in the family.

These women are not just strong but also beautiful (inside and out), hilarious, sarcastic, passionate, athletic, witty, and fun to hang out with—and they have superhero powers as it pertains to parenting. Much love and respect!

Nels (John) Bjorkquist

February 2016 🌐

As a freshman at Prestonsburg Community College, which was located 20 minutes from my home, I honestly had zero interest in UK. I was really against it, but something changed after a few visits to see V and Charles Lusk at UK. They lived in Blanding Tower, and I knew right away that twenty-one floors of college coeds was not as fun as it sounded. The 2:00 a.m. fire alarms and ungodly wait times for the elevators made a low-rise hall decision an easy one. I would opt for the low-rise hall with only three floors.

After further reflection, I decided I wanted to go to UK because it just felt

right. In my sophomore year, John and I found ourselves as roommates in Blanding 2. The residence
hall had a terrible reputation, but we were new students and figured we could make a difference. John
and I decided we would run for hall president and
vice-president. I was the presidential candidate, and
John was my VP. Our campaign signs were not even
close to being politically correct, but they were hilarious and effective, and our hallmates took notice.

We took our roles seriously and created all kinds of
unique programs. One event was simple yet seemed
powerful. There was a proposed student tuition
hike (shocker, I know), so we wrote and sent letters
to our politicians. I received one from my hometown rep, who listed some
lame excuse about why an increase was needed, and the tone of the letter
was not what I expected. I am usually not negative on Facebook, but that
experience struck a chord with me. Maybe it is why I am stubborn and
genuinely believe we all can make a difference in people's lives. We won
the Hall of the Year in 1994. It was an impressive accomplishment, but the
credit goes to many other friends who helped us along the way.

Back to the story: I often tell people John is the most intelligent person in
my group of friends. His wealth of knowledge is unmatched, and his ability to argue is second to none. Hint: He changed his pre-med plans and
became a lawyer. I feel sorry for anyone who must go against this guy in
a courtroom. His vocabulary was a hundred times the size of mine, and
I tried to learn from him whenever possible. He would be one heck of a
teammate in Boggle or Scrabble.

John is 6 feet 5 inches tall. I remember his feet always hung over the
edge of the dorm bed, and he could never sleep comfortably. His height
provided him one benefit, and it was on the basketball court. We shared
a passion for playing hoops, and his wingspan killed me. He blocked my
shot one time and sent me a photo. Why someone had a camera at 10:00
p.m. on a Wednesday night at the Haggin Hall courts is beside me, but it
happened, and John reminds me of it to this day.

As I have mentioned previously, I was a good kid and rarely got in trouble.
Everything changed when John brought these five-foot Kenwood speakers with XXL bass components to our tiny room. Every day after his 2:30

class, he held an impromptu rock concert in our room and treated the entire building to it. The loud music did not sit well with our hall director. Naturally, we heard about it, no pun intended, and received a letter outlining the next level of punishment if the hall director heard Public Enemy at 200 decibels again.

Somehow, our room became the dance party room on weekends. John hung Christmas lights early in the semester, and it was a famous study-break spot for everyone. There might have been a few banners or signs we borrowed from random places and our road trips.

John's favorite thing to eat late at night was peanut butter and Ruffles sandwiches. He always had these gigantic value-size canisters of peanut butter that he would devour in a few weeks. Like clockwork, his parents would ship him a new box when he was close to polishing off his last canister. He was always super skinny. I figured he was trying to bulk up.

The following year, he transferred to the University of Wisconsin–Madison, and it was hard on both of us. You do not spend close to a year of your life with someone in a 15' × 10' space and not become close friends. John and I kept in close touch and agreed to try to visit whenever we could. We were in each other's weddings, and he is and will always be a special person to me. I cannot thank him enough for his support and friendship. Love you, brother!

Brad Flener

February 2016 🌐

Brad Flener lived a few doors down from Chad Randall and me in the residence hall, Blanding 2. His roommate was David Bevins or Country Dave, as we called him. Dave was from Elkhorn City, near Pikeville, and we went to community college together for the first year before we transferred to UK. His nickname stemmed from his accent but also his well-known country sayings and affinity for fishing.

As we called him, Brad or "Flea" has always been a little shy at first but is naturally outspoken and not afraid to tell the truth like a Bostonian or true New Yorker. He was also a formidable competitor in any sport or activity we played. We played pickup hoops together, and both of us shot three-pointers like Loyola Marymount in the '90s. If we were on, we could hang with anyone, but then a middle school team could beat us if we were off.

One day his competitive fire may or may not have gotten the best of him or me in this case. Brad is a good golfer, and I am not, but we shared the simple joy of hanging out on the course and playing whenever we got the chance. We always played with Country Dave and another friend, Miles. One day we headed out to a municipal golf course for a round of eighteen.

We were goofing off, having a good time, and played bumper cars on the first few holes. I gently bumped Flener's golf cart, and he bumped me back. I must have hit him harder than I thought because the next bump was not gentle at all. I started driving down the cart path, began turning left, and Flea decided it was a perfect time to bump us back. He hit our rear left wheel as I was making the sharp turn and the laws of physics took over, and our golf cart flipped on its side. I landed on top of my buddy, and I laughed harder than I ever had as he was yelling for me to get up. Gasoline was spewing everywhere, and it pressed the seat cushion against our heads. We jumped back up quickly, reassembled the seat, closed the gas cap, and did a quick check to see if anyone saw what happened. We all laughed, we cried and tried to continue playing, but we could not do it. Every time we drew the club back, someone started giggling, and it went downhill from there. The cart was okay, but our foursome called it in for the day.

The other time his competitive nature reared its face was when we were driving to the Fayette Mall. We all had small, old two-door cars which were perfect college cars, but not fit for speed and not a road race. Everything was fine, and then some jerk cut Brad off on Nicholasville Road. I think we yelled at him, and I figured it would pass, but Brad had other ideas. He downshifts his Toyota Tercel and punches it. As we sped by the mall, and he passes the guy, gives him the middle finger, and looks at me, and says, "Now, we can go to the mall." I told this story at his wedding when he asked me to say a few words.

Brad's brutal honesty came to my rescue one time with a girlfriend situation. Someone had dumped me after two years and I was struggling to get over it. One day we were walking to Commonwealth Stadium for a UK football game; he looked at me and said, "Tosti, you need to stop talking about her and move on because she has, and I am tired of hearing about it." I smiled, agreed to move on, and appreciated the tough love from a close friend. He was right. I do not think it would have meant as much coming from someone else, but it made sense. I genuinely appreciated his words.

After graduation, we both were still living in Lexington, and his Mom lived near campus. She had a pool table and an impressive stereo system in the basement. Often, we drank a beer, shot pool, talked about old times, and listened to some Jimi Hendrix and The Rolling Stones. It was our escape from reality, and it never got old.

Chad Randall

February 2016 🌐

Chad and I were roommates in my junior year at UK and for a few years afterward. We were both good old Kentucky boys who seemed to get along well from the start. Our room was simple, and I remember he had this Pamela Anderson Baywatch poster that everyone loved.

There are a few characteristics that define Chad. He has always been a hard worker. He loves to dance. He researches any big purchase a thousand times, analyzing it in different ways. And he is Metallica's number one fan.

Our first year as roommates, I remember he would drive home to Somerset to work at K-Mart on the weekends because he was paying his tuition. He would do that when the rest of us were having fun and wasting time. I always respected him for this attribute. He liked to have a good time and enjoyed life, but work and paying bills came first. Another college job he had was the night shift manager at a hotel, which was always a challenge because he worked from 11:00 p.m. to 7:00 a.m.

Chad is also a superb athlete and is deceivingly quick. In softball, this guy routinely turned singles into doubles; our team won the residence hall intramurals championship. We played outfield together and had fun with our hallmates playing sports.

Chad and I were evenly matched in golf during college, but I had his number one day at Meadowbrook, a short par-3 course. A baby tree or two may have been lost to Chad's golf club–throwing tantrum. We would always wager something goofy, like the loser had to cook dinner for the winner. Bragging rights were not included, but excessive sarcasm and trash-talking were required at the meal. Then Chad got serious about his golf game, read some golf books, and flipped a switch, and I have not finished within twelve strokes of him the past ten years.

We moved from Blanding 2 to Conn Terrace, then Lakeside or Lakefront Apartments off Richmond Road, then to a duplex on Winter Garden, and finally to a townhouse he purchased near Red Mile. This last stop was going to be where we went our separate ways after three years as roommates. I started graduate school in the fall and was looking for one-bedroom apartments, but everything was expensive, and I enjoy being around people. I think he felt sorry for me, but I appreciated the favor and have always thanked him for looking out for me and letting me stay there for a year. I never forgot his generosity.

We both like to have a good time and enjoy life to the fullest. We threw some legendary parties in our day, including an '80s party, a housewarming party, and some classic UK NCAA watch parties.

We had some great times together as roommates. We lived with six guys in a four-bedroom house one summer, and everyone had to label their food with a Sharpie. The two essential house rules regarding food were (1) Do not touch an unopened bag of chips, and (2) If you finish anything, you have to replenish it. Mostly, we all got along and followed these rules. I have been a snacker all my life because of a hypothyroid problem; I eat snacks all the time. Occasionally, I would ask Chad for some of his Little Debbie Snack Cakes or his Pringles.

One day at the townhouse, he and I were in the kitchen together. I saw him carefully replace the paper seal on a can of Pringles before putting the plastic lid back on. I said, "That's weird; why don't you throw out the paper cover if you already have the chips open?" He flashed his big grin and started cracking up. He said, "Tosti, I do it so you won't eat my chips since you think they aren't open."

As I mentioned, this kid loved to dance. We would go to the bars, and he would walk up to a group of girls and ask any of them to join him in the middle of the floor. He would let them know he was not hitting on them, and that he just wanted to dance and have fun. Two seconds later, he was pulling me to the dance floor to reluctantly join the party.

Close friends talk about life, girls, and everything in between. But when Chad started dating Rebecca, he did not talk much about her. I knew then that it was serious. He was so happy; I could tell he was hooked. The ironic thing is I did the same thing when Beth and I started dating.

Rebecca is a rock star in her own right. She can shoot a mean game of pool, and she has a powerful singing voice. These two karaoke fanatics were a perfect match. I am still happy for you both after all these years, and I hope we can catch up the next time we fly into Louisville.

We have taken several road trips to UK bowl games (Nashville and Tampa), golf trips, and quick getaways, not to mention the cross-country tour with Emily (Neer) Iniguez. I always tell him that if one of us wins the lottery, we will play Pebble Beach Golf Course.

Chad knows my dark secrets, short-comings, and faults but still puts up with me through thick and thin. There are times I wish we lived in the same time zone. We both wish we could hang out more often, but we packed a lot into four years. I think I still owe him a few Pringles cans, but do not tell him because I might send some as a surprise Christmas present.

Kenna (Mills) Shaw

February 2016 🌎

Kenna and I met at a regional residence hall leadership conference and quickly became buddies. She went to William & Mary and amazed me at all she accomplished during school. Nels (John) Bjorkquist has the best vocabulary of my friends, but Kenna might have the best brain. She is highly intelligent and always has been.

She and I served together on the regional board for SAACURH and shared a few flights and long work weekends together. Our first flight was from Memphis to Hattiesburg, Mississippi. We had a team meeting in June, and I believe the southern tip of Mississippi might be the closest thing I have experienced to the Amazon in terms of humidity.

I have been on a few puddle-jumper type planes, but this plane had only ten seats. Kenna and I sat in the first row. She grabbed my arm right away and started screaming at me. "Tosti, I can see the freaking windshield, the pilots, their cup of coffee, and all the controls! This is not good!"

I remember walking off the plane and looking for the baggage claim. I looked over to my left, and there was a large metal door. Suddenly, this WWE-sized airline employee with a cutoff T-shirt and jean shorts starts chucking suitcases onto the floor. This is a true story. I think I have a picture somewhere.

A few months later, Kenna came to visit me in Lexington. Our first stop was Keeneland Race Course to bet on the ponies and take in the beautiful landscape of the track and surrounding horse farms. Kenna is petite—probably 5' 4", give or take—and usually shows a serious, businesslike demeanor. We made our first $2 bet, and I told her we could move up to the rail to hear and see the horses better.

I tutored her on the racing terms, what to expect, and how the cash winnings were calculated. The horses took off, and we were cheering softly like everyone else, gently clapping and enjoying the sunshine. The horses made the second turn and started heading down the stretch. Suddenly, my little shy and reserved friend jumps up on the rail and yells, "Let's go #13, you're my horse! Break!#4's leg!" Of course, she was kidding, but her competitive nature came out, and I did not know whether to high-five her, hug her, or run for the car. I enjoyed every minute. I cautiously informed her we had to wait twenty-five minutes for the next race. I could tell she was disappointed and was ready to cheer her favorite horse on again.

After college, we kept in touch for a while, even when she went to Chile for a summer program. She sent me a few letters. One of them referenced Beth, and Kenna said she wanted to give her stamp of approval and expected a front-row seat at our wedding. It makes me smile to think about the power of writing letters and how much fun it was to do as a kid. Our children will never really know how it feels.

Today, this dear friend is still putting her competitive spirit to good use, but now she fights cancer. She is Executive Director for the Institute for Personalized Cancer Therapy at MD Anderson Cancer Center, near Houston.

Rick Hatcher

March 16, 2016 🌐

Rick is one of my mentors. He is a baseball guy to the core; he pitched for Florida State University and the Atlanta Braves in double-A ball. After the minors, Hatcher was a pitching coach at Georgia Tech and at the University of Tennessee. My favorite recruiting story was when he went to a town to scout this senior all-star player. Rick came back to his boss and said, "We needn't worry about the senior. We need to sign the freshman first-baseman. He's a can't-miss prospect, and he'll be in high demand soon." Todd Helton— perennial All-Star for the Colorado Rockies, and Peyton Manning's backup QB at Tennessee—was that player. Rick also coached Nomar Garciaparra while he was at Georgia Tech.

Our paths crossed when I was in my last year of graduate school at UK. Rick visited our Professional Sports Marketing class and spoke to us about the sports industry. The end of his speech caught my attention because he closed by saying, "Here is my business card. Please call me if I can ever help any of you." As my mom says, "Do not become friends with my son unless you want to be his friend for life." This was the fall of 1999. Fast-forward to the summer of 2000, and I completed my internship in Lakewood, Colorado, with a small event company called Summit Sports and Events. I was handling our national sponsors, but I do not like to settle for whatever task I am assigned. I like to grow and advance in whatever job I have. I asked if I could sell basketball and soccer tournaments in new markets.

Rick was the first person I called because I knew Lexington was a hotbed for basketball and youth soccer. I sold my first tournament to Rick and the Lexington Area Sports Authority. He also opened other doors for me, which allowed me to sell a basketball tournament to the city.

I had some other sales successes in Fargo, North Dakota, and some other small markets. Rick told me about the National Association of Sports Commissions and their annual conference. The year I attended, the conference was held in Richmond, Virginia. He said it was an excellent opportunity for an event owner because we could meet with sports commissions of all sizes. It was a significant step for our little company to attend a conference where cities competed for events and it opened doors and more networking opportunities. I cannot tell you how many jobs stemmed from that one conference, but it is a central focal point of my networking speeches when I am asked to speak to college classes. I refer to it as "the Stevie D story." At that conference, Rick introduced Matt Stoll and me to Steve Dupee. I kept in touch with Steve, and he eventually hired Matt and also Tiffany Baird, my intern at the Sports Commission. Several years later, Tiffany hired my good friend Brian Tatum. Funny how it works considering those relationships began in 2003 and continue twelve years later. I have said it before, but networking is the most critical career skill you can develop.

Another lesson Rick taught me was that it is okay to have fun at these conferences, but if you stay out late, you need to be the first guy in the group meeting area the next morning. There is no time for laziness at conferences, because you have work to do, and people take notice of who is late for appointments or is moving slowly in the morning.

Eventually my internship at Summit Sports and Events became a permanent position. Two years later, though, the parent company closed the Denver office. Rick helped me land an interview with the Metro Denver Sports Commission. After my time there ended, he continued to help me evaluate job opportunities, often calling me and recruiting me to come work with him or his friend in another state. I always thanked him for looking out for me, but I never had the chance to tell him how much it meant to me, but it was something I will always remember. The sports industry is a nasty animal. To have someone looking out for you even when you are content is a blessing.

As my career weaved in and out of success and failure, Rick's support never wavered, and I still call him before I make any major career decisions. He has a rational mind, does not skirt important issues, and is a genuine person. I left the sports industry to focus on our family and regain some nights and weekends. I am happy with my current job, but I know Rick would be the first person to call if I ever return to the sports world—only if he has not called me with a job offer first.

Matt "Miller" Millar

March 9, 2016 ⊗

Matt and I met at UK when I was the Student Ministry Leader at the University of Kentucky Newman Center. He might be the biggest Cincinnati Reds fan I know; his rants, musings, and celebrations on Facebook are hysterical and legendary. I do not watch baseball on TV much anymore, but Matt's angry outbursts make me laugh every time. He does not have a filter when he comments about his favorite baseball team. Consider this a warning if you follow his posts.

Matt's nickname is "Miller." We anointed him this name because of a Lexington judge who mispronounced his last name. When Matt corrected him and said, "Your Honor, it's muh-LAHR," the judge smirked and said something like, "Okay, whatever, Mr. Miller." From that day forward, we called Matt "Miller."

Miller's sister attended Notre Dame, and we took full advantage of this by attending a home football game. I have been to several college football stadiums, including Michigan, Nebraska, Tennessee, and Georgia. The game-day experience at Notre Dame is unique and unforgettable. The pep band lines up and marches across campus, stopping along the way for some drum performances and small victory cheers. We took the obligatory picture of Touchdown Jesus and saw the golden dome.

After college, a group of friends started an annual golf trip called The Bogey Makers Open. I have been able to make only four of the eleven trips, but it is always a blast. Miller is intense on and off the course and can get a little fired up. We all have fun, but he owns the unofficial record for tossed clubs. Thankfully, he has not hit anyone or broken a club yet.

Last, Miller taught Beth and me how to ski at Paoli Peaks in Indiana, which is the equivalent of skiing down a hockey rink at a 45-degree angle, but you have blue jeans and six layers of clothing on. Yes, Colorado friends, Beth and I committed the biggest skiing faux pas once or twice during our college days. I guess I should not snicker at all those Texans in jeans on our world-famous slopes.

Leeann (Aylor) Smiser

March 18, 2016 🌐

I met Leeann—or Aylor, as I often called her—at UK. I was recruiting student leaders for the Residence Hall Association (RHA), and she had volunteered for her building, Donovan Hall. We traveled to multiple campuses for conferences and relished staying up way too late talking about life. We struck up a special friendship and kept in close touch during the years we were on campus.

She and I played tennis, went to Mass together occasionally, and, of course, shared a beer now and then. One time we might have talked a little too much, because the priest pulled me aside and let me know he noticed us talking excessively during Mass. Let it be a lesson for all my Catholic friends who have ever assumed the priest doesn't notice what everyone is doing during the service. In case you were wondering, yes, it was Father Dan.

In my junior year, Leeann helped me run the charity softball tournament I created, Hit the Halls. After I moved to Denver and she moved to Chicago, we kept in close contact. I stopped in Chicago to see her while driving a Sunny Delight truck from Denver to Louisville for my company's 3v3 soccer tournaments. The only problem was having to park a gigantic 15-foot Budget rental truck in the middle of Wrigleyville.

Leeann was one of the UK friends brave enough to join me for an Apple Festival excursion. My mom enjoyed meeting the friends I brought to the festival, but she seemed disappointed when I only brought one or two instead of a small army. One was from Queens, New York, and there were others from big cities who had never been to a tiny town and loved every minute. The Apple Festival has a ton of activities and events, and my dad has volunteered as its director for over thirty years. The festival always starts on a Tuesday, runs through Saturday night, and culminates with a country concert.

Leeann was not a fan of country music, but she was a good sport and went to the show. I did not think much about it. For years after, my mom referred to her as "the cute little blonde who didn't like country music."

Leeann and I do not get to talk as much these days, but it is for a good reason. She and her husband have three boys, and the youngest two are twins. Life is busy for all of us. When we talk on the phone, it seems as if we are back on campus, worrying about the next stage of our lives and what the future may hold.

Alisha (Colyer) Wilson

April 3, 2016 ⊗

Alisha and I spent one year together on UK's campus, but we packed great memories into those two semesters. She hailed from Columbus, Ohio, and was an ardent Ohio State Buckeyes fan. Another thing I remember is her family's affinity for Jeep Wranglers. She and I were like brother and sister.

She always knew which girls were trouble, and she spared me a few head-aches because she always told me which ones had her seal of approval.

Lish recorded the popular TV shows *Friends* and *ER* on her VCR for our viewing pleasure. We both liked sports, and Dr. Pepper was our drink of choice. She always had Dr. Pepper and Twizzlers as snacks in her room. I think this was 1995.

Fast-forward to 2002. I graduated and moved to Denver and had knee surgery that fall. Instead of a get-well card, Lish sent Beth a check to buy me some Dr. Pepper, Twizzlers, and Kudos granola bars. This was also the first time I had taken any kind of powerful painkiller. Vicodin was not my friend. I wolfed down a Kudos bar and a few Twizzlers only to get sick immediately. To this day, I can occa-sionally eat a Twizzler, but rarely.

I visited Lish's family's house several times for fun and work. Her dad made the *best* homemade pizza in the world. It was a thin crust, and I think his secret ingredient was salt for the crust, because it was tasty.

Diana Colyer, thank you again for always letting me crash at your house when I was working in Columbus instead of staying at a hotel for a week. Lish always joked about Diana liking me more than her, which we all know is not true at all. We chat now and then on Facebook but sadly have not seen each other in seventeen years.

Jeff Johnson

March 26, 2016 🌐

Jeff and I met through a mutual friend at a Campus Recreation and Intramurals conference in Kansas City. The friend introduced us via email and suggested we split a hotel room to save on travel costs. The first thing I noticed about Jeff was how much he resembled Cal Ripken, Jr.

After a night or two at the conference, we ended up at a casino. It was my first time gambling on a riverboat. I always remember one piece of advice

Jeff gave me. It was simple, accurate, and powerful. He told me to take out $40 from the ATM for my play money. It was my gambling money, and once I lost it, I was done for the night and should not return to the ATM under any circumstances. I have been to Las Vegas several times since then, and I only stop by the ATM one time, and the dollar amount is always low.

He and I kept in touch after the conference. I admire him for his ruthless honesty with every aspect of his life. He has always maintained high standards for himself and those around him, whether you are a friend, a boss, a family member, or a vendor. I wish I had half of his tenacity. He is also highly intelligent and owns a few higher ed degrees.

I call Jeff both a friend and a mentor. He is who I call when dealing with a challenging boss or a tough career decision. If I were a professional athlete, Jeff would be my agent because I know he is a fighter and does not like to lose. I wish I could share some of his comments about former bosses, but my mom might read this; I had better use my discretion.

Jeff has always been in great shape, and he worked as a personal trainer. Several years ago, he suffered a stroke and a heart attack. He died on the operating table, but the medical team resuscitated him. Next, his doctor discovered cancer, and Jeff is still battling this stupid disease. He is one of the strongest people I know, and I am glad to see him return to work as a personal trainer. He counts his blessings and has faced each setback with fierce determination and a level of intensity that would make anyone command his respect.

During my senior year at UK, I had an early Kinesiology class. The professor locked the door at 8:00 a.m. sharp; if I woke up late and looked at the clock and it was 7:55, I would roll back over and not even try to race to class, even though it was a mere 200 yards from my residence hall. This drove Jeff crazy. To this day, he still aggravates me about it and questions how I earned two degrees from UK. In all honesty, I probably only missed two or three classes, but who is counting?

A year ago, Kaden's class had a postcard project where the kids tried to collect postcards from as many different states as they could. Jeff sent him multiple postcards from Jackson, Mississippi, along with historical pamphlets and a travel brochure. He also included one of his favorite childhood books, which I thought was cool. Ironically, he knows everything about Beth and the kids even though he has never met them. Keep fighting, pal!

Denver, Colorado

The last stop on my path turned out to be the Mile High City. My dream had always been to move out west, and a graduate-school internship made the dream come true. Twenty-one years later it is still one of the best decisions I have ever made. Little did I know that the people and experiences would impact my life in ways I could not imagine.

Kieran Cain

February 29, 2016 🌐

Kieran and I worked together at Kroenke Sports—specifically, Dick's Sporting Goods Park and the Colorado Rapids. His creativity and ideas are legendary. I cannot remember all the unique events he created, but the Lucha Libre Mexican wrestling match after a Rapids home match was my favorite. He spent close to fifteen years with the team, which meant he saw all the uniform changes, players, and coaches moving in and out, but the best part was when he was in the stands to witness his team hoist the MLS Cup trophy in Toronto.

I am not a soccer guy and probably never will be, but I was genuinely excited for Kieran and Marisa Colaiano because I knew what the team meant to them. I have a picture of them at the championship game with enormous smiles on their faces, a single tear trickling down each one's cheek.

When I started my nonprofit, Kieran was one of my first friends to jump on board, literally and figuratively. He served on the board of directors for several years and made the trek to New Orleans for a few volunteer trips. He always managed our marketing and PR efforts, including social media.

In the early stages, we were still working on a logo, and he designed and bought ten T-shirts for all of us to wear on the first volunteer trip. It was a simple black T-shirt with a white font. The back said, "I helped rebuild New Orleans." It is still my favorite T-shirt.

When it comes to food, I am picky and a germaphobe. I am cautious of certain restaurants. I'm also leery of some mobile food trucks—not the nice ones, but the ones with campers on the back that cruise around construction sites. You know the ones I am talking about. I should have known I was in trouble when Kieran convinced me to eat shrimp in Commerce City. He needs to hang out with Andrew Zimmern and Anthony Bourdain for a long weekend, because he is not afraid to try anything. He is *fearless*.

Kieran Cain is one of the hardest-working guys in the ski industry. When he moved to Breckenridge, Jeff Mathews and I both laughed and shook our heads. We knew the laid-back mountain attitude would not fly with Mr. Cain. He can relax and have a good time, but he is a hustler—in a good way—and a hard worker. I hated to lose a good friend to the mountains, but I was traveling the state for Ihigh.com. I was on I-70 a fair amount and got to see the Cain family a few times. I always called him as I was passing through the ski towns. He always offered me a place to crash or a hot meal.

After Kieran's first year in the marketing department, the resort won an award for social media excellence if I am not mistaken. He has since been promoted twice and has not slowed down. Vail Resorts hired a rock star, an avid snowboarder, and the biggest soccer freak in the world. I am in awe of his accomplishments, and I am glad to call him a friend. Now if I could convince him to watch a basketball game or two with me during March.

Walt Reisbick

March 14, 2016

There are certain decisions we have a say in or control in life, such as choosing a career, a significant other, and friends. One choice not in our control is our neighbor(s). Walt is our neighbor. He is in his late 80s and has lived in his house since 1951. He paid $12,000 for the home and raised three children in it.

Walt is one of a kind because it is rare for homeowners to stay in the first house they buy. He has looked out for us for the past twelve years. Walt's encyclopedic memory of the families who have lived on our block is unbelievable. Even better is the fact he knows every detail about our little house. If we ever had a question of what someone did to our house, he knew the answer. His knowledge has saved us money and a lot of stress.

Walt has many stories about life in Colorado. My favorite is about the days when Vail Mountain was first developed into a ski resort. He said they were offering an acre or two for $5,000. It was a lot of money back then. He mentioned people laughed and said, "What in the hell are they going to do with a big mountain?" Today a one-bedroom condo goes for $400,000 or more. I cannot even imagine if someone had purchased ten acres and sat on it for forty years.

Walt loved woodworking and has forgotten more about woodworking than I will ever learn in my lifetime. His garage is full of every important wood-working tool you would ever need. He often joked he had every device the guy on *The New Yankee Wood Shop* used, except he had to pay full price for all his equipment. Walt built this beautiful oak bed. The materials were $700, but similar beds were priced well over $3,000 in the stores. The spindles on his front porch were also made by hand. The man has two of every essential tool and would always let me borrow something for as long as I needed it.

Unfortunately, Walt's health took a turn for the worse. and he was admitted to hospice. I went to see him and did not know what to expect. I tried hard to prepare myself mentally and think about what to say and talk about during the visit. As people know, I am never at a loss for words, but this was tougher than expected. He is not coming home, and he understands it, but it does not make it any easier.

He has lost a lot of weight but looked like himself, which provided a small bit of solace but not much. Once I spoke, he recognized me, and we talked briefly. I wore a mask, gloves, and a hospital gown to prevent him from getting sick. I tried my hardest not to cry in front of him. Thankfully, the flimsy paper mask concealed my puffy red eyes and the tears slowly streaking down my face. I was doing okay, and I thought I was ready to shake his hand and tell him I loved him and appreciated everything he has done for our family. Before I could say anything, he looked at me wide-eyed and told me to tell Beth and the kids he loved them more than anything and to remind the kids never to forget their grandparents. I bit my lip, took a deep breath, shook his hand, and gave him a gentle fist bump, and walked out sobbing like a little tyke who lost his favorite toy.

Walt, you taught me a lot about this thing called life. You always reminded me to make sure Beth knows how much I love her and to treat her right. You talked to me about enjoying the kids while they are young and always being there for them. You might be the world's best neighbor! I am thankful you were part of our family for the past twelve years. It is one choice I did not make, but I will always be grateful for the memories for years to come.

I wish you peace, tranquility, and a dinner date in heaven with your wife, Ruth, whom you lost way too early after her retirement. (He tells everyone there is not a day that goes by when he does not miss her.) You will soon be reunited, and, as much as we hate to lose you, I know it is for the best.

Jane (Koski) Bartine and Chris Bartine

TURKEY DAY, DENVER STYLE

March 17, 2016 ◉

It all began with a simple invitation. It was Thanksgiving week sometime around 2001 or 2002. Beth and I were not married yet, but we were invited to stop by Adam Koski's sister's place for Thanksgiving. We barely knew Jane and felt kind of awkward showing up at a major holiday gathering at her apartment. Adam was my friend from work, so we took a chance. Looking back, I think he invited our entire office.

At the time, most of us worked together at Summit Sports and Events, loving every minute of our jobs but not saving much money. The downside of making a low salary is you sometimes have to make meaningful choices, such as picking which holiday to travel home for the holidays. It was too expensive for us to fly home for both Thanksgiving and Christmas. We stuck around for some turkey in Denver. Keep in mind we were all between twenty-three and twenty-five years old and clueless when it came to massive meal preparations. Heck, Boston Market sounded fairly good for a Thanksgiving meal at the time because none of us knew how to prepare a turkey.

Jane was our saving grace, and everyone appreciated the food, the multiple desserts, and her motherly instincts. No doubt, we all missed home, but Jane made you feel you were part of her family. As our super chef moved from a condo to a rental house to a new home, the group followed the turkey trail.

Hailing from the great state of Kentucky and the Deep South, as some of my Ohio friends might say, I know comfort food when I see it, but Jane's cheesy mashed potatoes deserve a select category. They were scrumptious and full of flavor, and they melted in your mouth. One year, I made the mistake of watching Jane prepare the potatoes in a mixing bowl the size of a small UFO saucer. I stopped counting after the sixth stick of butter and ran off as quickly as I could. I am not a health freak, but I try to eat somewhat healthy mostly, and this was too much for me to take. To this day, I only eat one serving of those bad boys as Jane giggles, trying to lie and tell me she used less butter in this year's version.

The best thing about the event was the duration. It was never the wrong time to stop by and celebrate with this group of friends. Some people showed up at 11:00 a.m., while others would appear at 11:00 p.m. to have a drink and a second plate of dessert and to partake in the late-night shenanigans.

We played every type of game you could think of, including Catch Phrase, Guesstures, Spoons, and Name That Tune (this was before Pandora or Spotify). One year we even had a food fight with Laffy Taffy. I am not sure how it started, but I am blaming Lisa Ainsworth because she asked someone to throw her a taffy piece, and the next thing you know . . . Another year it was the arm-wrestling matches for the fellas. And how can we forget the Senator Obama debate until 3:00 a.m.?

This year's edition will be the last installment of this one-of-a-kind holiday gathering for this large group of special friends. On behalf of our crazy and beloved crew, I want to thank Chris and Jane for being such wonderful hosts for many years, and for reminding us that, while the South might be known for its hospitality, a couple of farm kids from Wisconsin and Iowa know a thing or two about it also.

Certain married couples seem to fit together perfectly, like chocolate chip cookies and milk or peanut butter and jelly. Chris and Jane Bartine are both sarcastic, caring, unselfish, and plain ol' down-to-earth people. I am convinced their parents did a superb job instilling strong midwestern values, along with a few doses of sarcasm and humor for good measure. They have hosted our orphan Thanksgiving dinner for close to fifteen years, and, sadly, 2015 was the last one.

Jane is a nurse and is the best dessert chef in Denver. I always joke with Chris because I do not understand how he has not gained 75 pounds. She can bake anything: cookies, pies, candy bars, you name it. The delicacies are all nonfat, non-GMO, and low sugar, of course. I always tell her she should open a bakery.

She visited us in the hospital shortly after Kaden was born, and she showed me how to change a baby's diaper. She said to grab the baby's legs like two turkey legs with one hand and wipe with the other. This was a big deal for me because I am an exceptionally clean person and a germaphobe. Of course, Kaden peed on me on cue, and we have a picture of the three of us and my wet sweater. Jane deals with all kinds of crap, literally and figuratively, daily. I have a lot of respect for nurses because the people you are dealing with are not only sick but also tired, in pain, and anxious to get home. I have a feeling all nurses share a similar sentiment.

I routinely call or text Jane with medical questions. She was the one we called when Beth thought she was starting the early stages of labor with Kaden. Sure enough, Jane was right when she said it could happen early in the morning or in the next day or two. Kaden arrived a week early. The best part is Jane does not charge me a copay, and she talks me off the ledge—unlike WebMD. God, that website is pure evil.

Chris has a sarcastic streak, and it always serves him well with friends. He has a one-liner ready for any occasion. On a more serious note, he is an incredibly talented individual who is always doing home projects and building things. He has done a significant amount of work on their house, and I think the only thing he cannot do is electrical wiring. I struggled to build a tiny two-shelf bookcase from Ikea. This guy finished his basement with a bedroom and bathroom suite that Four Seasons would envy. Did I mention he has also renovated their kitchen and master bathroom?

When Beth and I bought a fiberglass storage shed, we called two people: Brian Tatum and Chris. Chris served as our project manager and helped us stay on track and complete the job in four hours when it would have taken me four days, and the door would not have worked properly.

These two and their adorable daughters have decided to move back to Wisconsin later this summer. We are excited and bummed. I understand why, but, selfishly, it stinks. We are losing much more than our Thanksgiving cooks and hosts: the Denver crew is losing great friends whom everyone loves. Thanksgiving will never be the same for us, but my arteries might be a tad bit happier without those Iowa and Wisconsin butter-infused cheesy potatoes.

Kristen Kelly

March 21, 2016 🌐

Kristen and I met in 2003 when I interviewed for a job with the Metro Denver Sports Commission. The projector and screen I was using for my presentation were not working correctly. Kristen was asked to see if she could adjust the controls and fix the problem. She and two IT employees tried multiple things, but nothing worked. I had memorized my presentation and finished it with no tech assistance. I was not nervous and have always felt comfortable speaking in front of people. I kept talking and reviewed my marketing plan and the concepts' remaining details. After the presentation, Kristen commended me for my poise and for not being rattled. Shortly after that, we quickly became friends.

She is a friend who knows a little bit about everything and could give MacGyver a run for his money with her creative skills. She was my go-to resource for everything from engagement ring advice to correct margins and spacing on a Microsoft Word document to what suit-and-tie combo looks good for an interview. She might be little in stature, but she has an enormous heart. One day we talked about my family, and I mentioned my little sister had recently gone through a divorce and had an infant at

WHO WE MEET ALONG THE WAY

home. The next day Kristen came to work with this big box of baby clothes and asked for Brittany's address. She is and always has been a great friend and a good-hearted person, to me and countless others.

Another time she offered to babysit Kaden to allow Beth and I to escape for a few hours. Keep in mind she lives about forty-five minutes from our house. She told us to take our time and enjoy a nice dinner. I remember she texted us this cute photo of him smiling and said, "Don't worry, Mom and Dad, I'm fine." Kristen also told me to read Kaden multiple books when he was a baby because it was beneficial for his development. We do not know if it worked, but he started reading at age three and a half and has not stopped. Thank you for the advice!

Kristen has worked for the same company for twenty years and has a great group of office friends who religiously go to lunch together. They know the ins and outs of every mom-and-pop restaurant within a ten-mile radius of downtown Denver. If I ever need a recommendation for an excellent lunch spot, Kristen is my first call. She can tell you critical details such as what to order, what not to order, and the busy times to avoid. We met last Friday for lunch. I mentioned Sam's No. 3 because they serve Colorado's honey-smoked salmon. After all, there is a limit to how much cheese pizza a Catholic can take on Fridays. Sure enough, she told me we should go to Wazee Supper Club because Sam's is packed on Fridays. I walked by Sam's on my way to the 16th Street Mall; sure enough, there was a line out the door at 11:30.

She and I meet sporadically for lunch to keep up with things and touch base. I always know she is missing lunch with her standard group when she agrees to meet me. Sometimes she invites me to tag along with the club since I know them from having worked in her office. The ironic part of our lunch friendship is that I am a Plain Jane when it relates to food. On the other hand, she will eat anything. She has taken me to a pho restaurant on Federal Boulevard as well as a great hole-in-the-wall Mexican place and, of course, Tom's Diner. Tom's is closed now, but it served southern delicacies, and they sold lunch until they ran out of food. It was one of Denver's best restaurants and the closest thing to the South this Kentucky boy has experienced since leaving the Bluegrass State sixteen years ago.

When Beth was sick, I could tell Kristen was worried about Beth and me. I did not have to reach out to her or ask her for support because she started calling me to set up lunches every two to three weeks. I knew this was odd, but I realized it was her unselfish way of being there for me. She always gave me two big hugs and knew when to ask questions about chemo and when I needed to chat about nothing at all. It meant the world to me. I appreciated it more than I ever can put into words. I told her then, and I am repeating it now: THANK YOU. Thank you from the bottom of my heart. There was not a day that went by when my mind was not racing, and I needed many friends to help me fight through the fear and stress of my wife's fight against breast cancer.

Thanks for putting up with my vanilla taste in cuisine, my endless jokes about your age (even though you are only a few years older than me), and my Chicago Cubs jokes. You have always been there for my family and me. I hope you know I will gladly be here for whatever may come your way. Please never change.

Suzanne Fischer

March 27, 2016 ⊙

Suzanne and I met because she and Beth worked together several years ago. Our family calls her Suz, Fish, and Aunt Suzanne, and Emily calls her Suzie. She is a high-energy workout fiend, a sports nut, and a super Iowa Hawkeye fan.

She played soccer in college, and we were looking for extra staff to help us manage Dick's Sporting Goods Park at night. Suzanne did not need the money but wanted to be around a sports facility and soccer. One night she and I were riding a golf cart checking on fields, and she asked me about getting a marketing job. I was stunned because I was in the sports industry field, and I thought she was an engineer. Keep in mind we had known each for five years and I assumed she was an engineer because she worked with Beth. I wondered how she would transition from being an engineer to working in sports. After thinking about it for a moment, I asked her how I could help her and why she would want to switch careers. She laughed and said, "I'm not a damn engineer; I handle the firm's marketing efforts. I'm a marketing gal."

We both had a good chuckle. I told her it made sense because she had such a fun and outgoing personality. I always joke with Beth about stereo-types and engineers. I knew Suzanne was too cool to be an engineer.

My best memory of her is the year I formed a team for the Make a Wish kickball tournament. They held it at DSGP. The night before, she ran into an old friend, stayed out later than she had expected, and did what we have all done in our lives: She had an extra cocktail or four. We called to tell her we were on our way, and I could feel her headache through the phone. We picked her up and headed to the park to meet the team because we had the early game at 8:00 a.m. As luck would have it, Tatum told her to kick leadoff since she had a good leg and had some speed. Suz got a base hit and then ran the bases on the next kick and scored our first run. I high-fived her, threw her my office keys, and told her to take a quick nap. She woke up and was rejuvenated after a twenty-minute snooze and helped lead us to the championship game.

Fish is now running the marketing program for an engineering company once again, but this means she must travel a few days a week and some-times two weeks at a time. This leads to another benefit of our friendship. If she leaves her curling iron on or a snowstorm rolls in unexpectedly, Beth and I run over and make sure her house is in one piece. I always shovel her driveway. We also pick up her internet shopping purchases and FedEx packages. In return, she watches our kids, which saves us money and sanity. The kids adore her and love going to her house because she lets them eat extra cookies. Suz matches their energy level for an hour or two, which is impressive.

This past week, she came to our rescue once again. Wednesday morning, I woke up the kids, fixed coffee, and toasted some bagels, and then the power went out. We immediately called Xcel Energy. I expected the power to be out until Thursday at 6:00 a.m., so I sent Fish a text to see if she had power, hoping we could run over to eat and sleep if needed. She replied, "Come on over! I have power, plenty of food, and hot cocoa!" I woke up the next morning, and there were five cereal boxes on the table and a massive skillet of scrambled eggs and toast on the counter. I thought I was at a four-star hotel. It was such a gracious gesture and much appreciated.

She worked from home, and due to the power outage, the schools were closed for a second consecutive day. She offered to watch the kids once again for us. Aunt Suzanne to the rescue. She has always gone above and beyond for our family, and we appreciate her for all of it.

Last, she is a superb cook and has this uncanny ability to invite us over for dinner when we need it the most. Sometimes she delivers the meal to our house, drops it off, smiles, and runs out the door. She is a friend everyone needs and just knows when you need a pick-me-up.

Josh Gross

March 28, 2016 🌐

Josh and I worked together at Kroenke Sports Enterprises. We worked in the basement of the Pepsi Center Annex. He and I created an unofficial bring-your-lunch club that met on the upper concourse. We had interns, full-time staff, and anyone else who was interested in sharing lunch with us. The only rule was they had to tolerate our crazy lunch hour, which was often a cross between a talk show and sitcom. We were loud, we told jokes, and we shared opinions and comedic rants on what was wrong with the world.

Josh worked as the play-by-play announcer for the Colorado Mammoth. I thought that was cool until I had to share a hallway with him. He has a ticket-sales background, but his emcee voice is first class, and it carries in a wide-open room such as a basement. I felt like I was entering the ring for my own WWE match.

I joke about it, but he is a professional, and he took his position seriously. If it was a game week, I knew not to call or ask him to hang out because he was studying three or four hours a night for multiple days in a row before the game. At first, I thought he was focused on pronouncing the Canadian players' last names and hometowns correctly. Then, I asked him why he must study for hours, and he said he wants to be the best. During a live sport broadcast, there are many moments where the announcer can make or break the dull moments or the historic ones. Josh knew the other team's MVP liked alfredo sauce instead of marinara, preferred Chevy trucks over Ford, and had a pet iguana named Charlie. I gained a lot of respect for Josh after he explained this to me. Sure, he could probably make something up and cover his tracks, and few viewers would know, but his drive and determination impressed me the most.

He is silky smooth on the microphone and poised in front of a camera. When we organized our sports equipment distribution day at North High School, he was the first friend I called. He emceed the event and treated it like a National Lacrosse League game. He was peppering me for information about the coaches, the players, and their records. Keep in mind this was a celebration because we were donating $10,000.

This was not the first time he had donated his time and expertise to help me with my charity. He also stopped by South High School and helped me interview the lacrosse coach and several players when we donated some lacrosse gear. Instead of a home movie with a shaky camera appearance, I had a professional sports broadcaster making us look like pros.

I always joke that Josh's only fault is that he is a Syracuse alum. He made the mistake of showing me a middle school photo, and he has a 1980s multi-colored tank top and huge glasses like we all had back then. He is standing with Donovan McNabb. His smile was a mix between sheer disbelief and a star-struck fan. I took one look at it and said in my geekiest Steve Urkel voice, "Hiiiiiiiiiii Donnnnnnnnoooooovan!" We still laugh about it.

Last, Josh is a competitive guy, like most people I know. He came to our Kentucky Derby parties and had one mission: to win our hat contest. This guy did not mess around, as evidenced by his first-place finish for multiple years. The best one had this vertical plastic game board that listed the horses, and he stapled it to a baseball hat.

I would be remiss if I didn't mention his hilarious wife, Natalia Swalnick. We were chatting one time about something funny and being married, and she grinned and said, "Tosti, Josh knows you don't cross this," and she pointed at herself. On a more serious note, she went out of her way and delivered multiple meals when Beth was sick and a bottle of wine to celebrate the end of her chemo. Thank you, Natalia!

Brian Tatum

March 29, 2016 🌐

Brian Tatum and I met as Summit Sports and Events interns in the summer of 2000. The company produced the country's largest 3v3 soccer tour, which included sixty-five cities. He was a roadie, and I was in the office for most of our event season. We did not meet until late in the summer. I had heard all the stories about him and thought, great, all I need is to meet another truck-driving, cocky Texan. Sure enough, he had a big Ford F-150 with Yosemite Sam floor mats for mud flaps, but it was because he went to Texas Tech University. I was thinking, I am sure I will not like this guy at all. Funny thing, I ended up rooming with this fool who epitomizes the term "best friend" to MANY people.

We often refer to him as the glue guy for our Denver group of friends. Tatum was always organizing get-togethers and keeping everyone posted on the whereabouts of everyone well before Facebook existed.

As our internship ended, he and I accepted full-time jobs at Summit Sports and Events. We barely made $24,000. This meant our housing budget was low and firm. We looked at a few overpriced options in Washington ("Wash") Park (funny how it has not changed) but settled on a mini attic apartment near 12th and Lafayette for $725 a month.

This humble abode had two bedrooms, a tiny quarter bath that resembled an airplane lavatory because you could not turn around in it, and an efficiency kitchen. The house had seven or eight small apartments inside it, and we were the last ones to receive hot water and sometimes any water at all. It only took one time for us to figure out a solution for when the water ran out during a shower. We filled up two 7-11 Big Gulps with hot water and set them on the edge of the tub because it was inevitable the water would run dry as soon as you put shampoo in your hair. The living room was probably 8' × 10' on a good day. We only lived there for half the year, but we had some good stories during our brief stay.

Tatum is also known for his sharp sense of humor and uncanny ability to tell interns' biggest whoppers. You would not believe the number of our company's interns he convinced I grew up on a farm with covered wagons, no electricity, and no running water. The hard part is he somehow can keep a straight face, even as the tall tales gain more traction. I have watched him pull this trick on countless people; it never gets old.

He is also the unofficial gambling commissioner for our group of friends. Whether it is fantasy football or March Madness, you can count on a sarcastic email announcing the league or the pool. God help your soul if you are late with payment, because the sarcastic cheap shots do not stop, and with every email the jokes worsen. Speaking of which, I need to send him a check for my bloody bracket. Stupid Sparty!

I can joke about many things with this guy, but he is a darn good cook. He would make The Tatum Special: spaghetti covering the plate from one side to the other, a few pieces of garlic bread, and two Coors Lights. This was a staple for the longest time. We did not have a grill, but we survived on microwave dinners and ate a lot of pizzas.

He was the first friend to see us in the hospital with both kids. He was excited and told me he would not finish second to anyone else. It is one of the many reasons our kids call him Uncle Tatum or Uncle T. He would have been a godfather for one of our kids if he were Catholic.

We have shared some great memories through work. One fall, he and I drove to Provo, Utah, to run the BYU 3v3 Soccer Shootout. Tatum sported a goatee of Viking proportions, and I wondered why everyone on campus was staring at us. Then I remembered facial hair was not allowed on campus per religious beliefs.

We stayed at a Marriott property where they serve chocolate chip cookies. When we arrived, the plate was empty, and we assumed we were out of luck. However, the front desk employee started a conversation with Mr. Tatum and invited us to a party but mentioned it might not be our type of party. We did not go, but she delivered fresh-baked chocolate chip cookies to our room. I am sure she had her eyes set on T, but sometimes politics and religion can intervene. Damn that Viking goatee!

Tatum is a big softie, and the women in our group of friends have praised his manners and kindness for years. One of his most impressive character traits is that he never leaves a friend in need. He does not have kids yet, but he always takes care of his friends and makes sure everyone gets home safe, regardless of what time it is or what mode of transportation it takes to arrive safe and sound.

We have one more event to spend together with our group of guy friends. It will be a brief excursion to Sin City. I kind of hope we run into Mike Tyson, minus the knockout punch and lost tooth. We are too old to get into much trouble these days, but it will be fun to rib him with all our married-guy jokes. This guy has been in so many weddings, he should have bought a tux years ago. He presided over two weddings, if I recall correctly, and asked to speak at other ceremonies. The good thing is he charges a nominal fee. Tatum has graduated from barbecue brisket and a six-pack of Coors Original to a New York Strip and a nice bottle of wine.

On a serious note, he was the one friend who regularly checked on Beth and me during her cancer battle. I have said this before, but he knew what to say and when to remain silent and let me babble. He asked about the acronyms, the health lab results, and the endless numbers that accompany a cancer diagnosis. He was also the first friend in our group to organize a team in the Susan G. Komen race in Beth's honor. I am surprised he did not show up with an oversized plate of spaghetti and a Coors Light.

Now it is my turn to return the favor as Tatum's dad faces his second battle against cancer. Beth and I make sure to check in on him and his wife, Nena, often. We might have sent some cookies along the way. Keep fighting, Glen!

Tatum always jokingly (I think) reminds me I married out of my league. You are right as usual, T, but I think the same can be said for you regarding your friendship with me, not to mention several others. Thanks for everything, brother.

Nate Baldwin

February 12, 2016 🌐

Nate and I met while I was working at Dick's Sporting Goods Park. He ran a small recreational sports company out of his basement called WASA, which stood for Western Alternative Sports Association. At the time, he was my smallest client in terms of field rental and revenue, but it did not matter to me. I reminded my team daily that while we might have been the most prominent sports complex and the most admirable one in Denver, our clients still had a choice. I wanted us to take care of the little guy in town as well as the big soccer club.

When I first heard about WASA, I thought this guy's wife must be making a lot of money if she is letting him run an adult kickball league as his full-time job. I was jealous because I am an entrepreneur at heart and knew Beth has always supported me with every business venture, but an adult kickball league might be a stretch. I did not realize how creative and intelligent this entrepreneur dad was until we did business together.

Another business friend of mine had built the most extensive adult recreational sports league at the time, and I wondered what Nate's competitive advantage would be. Every other company organized its leagues in or near downtown. The central location allowed people to run over after work, grab a beer, and play some kickball or dodgeball.

Nate lived in the suburbs and liked to have a beer with friends as well. He realized suburban parents wanted and needed a break from life just as young professionals do, but the downtown location was a significant hurdle. Nate's brilliant solution was to host sports leagues in the suburbs and provide the opportunity for moms and dads to play in their neighborhood parks instead of trying to stay downtown after work.

It was a brilliant move, and it was only the start. Nate also realized that not everyone is super athletic, and they do not want to deal with the high-school jock who takes every sport way too seriously. Nate not only created new sports, he also did something that to this day still amazes me: He created a culture, not just a company. Do you realize how difficult it is to pull this off? Mom-and-pop startup companies are not known for this capability. Global behemoths like Under Armour, ESPN, and MTV created cultures.

WASA players were laid back, loyal and could not get enough of the fun new league. The next step was to create some distance between the other leagues by adding simple playground rules. If there was a disputed call at first base, the two team captains met and played rock, paper, and scissors to decide the call—no yelling, fighting, or arguments. The leagues grew exponentially. The next smart move was to create an end-of-season Golden Keg Tournament, where each suburb's leagues would compete against the other WASA ones; after this came theme nights, which became more popular than anyone could have imagined.

Keep in mind Nate's operating expenses were a $10 rubber kickball, a $20 set of rubber bases, referees, and field space. As the popularity of WASA grew, subsequently the expectations for more sports did, too. Nate added inner-tube water polo, capture the flag, and WASApalooza. This was a shorter league for WASA fans who could not get enough. It ran in the summer, and each week the teams showed up not knowing what game they would play until Nate announced it. They played all kinds of goofy playground games, but people loved it.

Other groups noticed, and Nate was asked to join the Make a Wish Young Professionals Board. The group brought Make a Wish's kickball event to Dick's Sporting Goods Park. He helped them streamline operations and increase revenue, taking the event from a $30,000 fundraiser to close to $80,000 if I am not mistaken. Those numbers were not too shabby for a one-day, eight-hour kickball tournament.

As his business prospered, he rented more field space from me, and we started meeting more often and struck up a friendship. We were both young fathers, and we shared the same business principles: creativity, excellent customer service, the need for constant improvement, and giving back to the community.

Nate made the tough decision to sell WASA after ten years and moved his family back to his home state of Wisconsin. There he started Red Ball Nation, a WASA version for youth sports. He tackled everything wrong with youth sports. The program was an instant success, and the local parks and recreation department noticed that someone else was doing a better job. Red Ball Nation provided a plan for all ages and made the sport of kickball fun and easy to learn by implementing step-by-step processes that allowed the kids to develop over time and at their own speed. Once again his ingenuity amazed me.

To this day, Nate and I talk and dream about starting an event consulting company. We dream about hosting a sports podcast to talk about hot-button sports issues because we think it would be a lot of fun. He might have a different address and ZIP code, but we still call each other regularly and chat about life, fatherhood, business, and the power of positive thinking.

New Orleans, LA

Mack McClendon

March 30, 2016 ●

I met Ward "Mack" McClendon on one of my first scouting trips to New Orleans when I identified potential volunteer projects for Sports for a Cause. Mack was a lot of things to many people. He grew up in the Lower Ninth Ward in New Orleans. After Hurricane Katrina, he made the unselfish decision to forgo rebuilding his lovely house to focus on helping everyone else in the neighborhood, but particularly the kids in the area.

He stayed with a friend and invested his own money, time, and effort in refurbishing an abandoned warehouse, which he called Lower Ninth Ward Village. He did not have the time or money to return to his house, which was two blocks away from the Village. Yet he was not worried or concerned because he wanted to help others first and did so with a smile on his face. The house was structurally sound, but the interior had suffered a significant amount of damage.

Mack was a source of hope for the entire neighborhood where he lived. He had a mental list of small repairs and all sorts of other projects for the older adults in the area who needed help. Our group was fortunate enough to rebuild a staircase for "Miss Tish," and she insisted we stop by when we were in town because she would always make us red beans and rice. Mack created an evacuee program called Where's Your Neighbor. All he wanted was to bring residents back home. He would gather kids and have them mow the lawns of the abandoned homes. The goal was to ensure the empty lots did not look unattended.

Mack's resilience and positive attitude were among the reasons I wanted to help him however I could. In my heart, I hoped to return to New Orleans as often as possible. I always said he should be on CNN, not the looters. Mack chose to *do something*, because sitting around complaining about what the POTUS and FEMA did not do right would help no one. They always told me that if they sat around whining, no one would care, and the volunteers would not travel to help the city rebuild.

At first glance, the Village was a little rough around the edges. It needed a fresh coat of paint or two, a lot of basic woodwork inside, and some other necessary cosmetic repairs. It was an abandoned warehouse, but Mack had a vision and a dream to refurbish it as a cultural and recreation center for the neighborhood. He had excellent ideas, and he was determined to bring those dreams to fruition. Some of his ideas were to create a music studio for recording and piano lessons, a garden for the neighborhood to show the kids how food is produced because of the well- known local cuisine, and finally, a computer lab. Several friends of mine helped paint the interior, performed some major landscaping around the building, built a chicken coop, installed new doors, and did countless other minor projects. Over time, Mack found some old Mac computers for the makeshift computer lab.

Another Mack story I want to share is how the entire experience affected my father-in-law. Joe is one of the handiest people I know and can build anything from scratch. He was instrumental in our success with the basketball court project and made sure everyone knew what to do to accomplish the various tasks. He can be a little impatient for those who don't know him, and he is antsy like me. On Sunday morning, I told the group I wanted to take them to the Ninth Ward to meet Mack and take his unofficial Ninth Ward Tour. Joe had joked with Beth earlier in the trip how I could talk to anyone, even if he or she were a stranger.

As we left the hotel, Joe expressed to me that he needed to get on the road home to Indiana by a specific time, and I told him it would not be a problem. I could tell he was not crazy about the tour, but he went along for the ride with no complaints.

The tour was mandatory for anyone who accompanied me on a volunteer trip because Mack tells a story about each house and knows everyone in the area. He honks and waves at someone on every block. Mack also drives by four or five houses to show the holes in the roof where people hacked through with butter knives to escape the rising waters, where some made it and some did not, because most of the citizens could not swim once they reached the rooftops.

He drove the volunteers to the levees to provide the opportunity to stand and look out over where hundreds of homes once stood, which I have done myself, and it is an immensely powerful and humbling experience. As the volunteers returned and departed the van one by one, I waited for Joe to exit and expected him to say a quick goodbye and get on the road. Surprisingly, he left with this massive smile on his face and thanked me for introducing him to Mack and for suggesting the tour. He enjoyed it and said the three days were eye-opening for him. Now he understands why I work hard for Mack and his neighbors. Joe, your comment and actions made my trip.

On Saturday night, after two long days of work, we were guaranteed two things. First, Mack would prepare us a homemade tasty crawfish boil feast. Second, Mack would line everyone up, shake each person's hand, and hug them as he graciously thanked them for spending their vacation time and money to help the Ninth Ward and New Orleans city.

A hurricane did not break this man's spirit, and neither did cancer. Cancer spread to his brain, kidneys, and lungs. The doctors told him he had two to four weeks left on this earth. I was lucky enough to talk to him for a few minutes the last week. Mack laughed as only he could. We talked about life, what a blessing he was to other people and me, and how he would fight cancer as long as he could. Mack left this Earth on Valentine's Day, which I thought was fitting based on the size of his heart and love for his neighborhood.

Mack was an amazing person and a great man and will be missed by everyone. The word *unselfish* does not describe what he did for an entire neighborhood. The man might not have had many material possessions, yet as I look back on the time we spent together, I realize he had everything. He had one of the world's biggest hearts, and one cannot put a dollar amount on something so valuable. His contagious smile, his ability to dream bigger than anyone else, and his positive attitude to keep fighting for the neighborhood he cherished are what I will always remember. I am proud to have called him a friend and glad our paths crossed because I am a better person for knowing him.

Some people dream and talk about changing the world or helping others, but Mack truly lived this philosophy for years after the storm. It is safe to say he touched hundreds of lives in a few short years. Cancer stole Mack from us, but I refuse to let it take his spirit and determination to make things better for others.

Someday when I return with my family to show them Mack's neighborhood, I hope the welcome sign says, "You are entering the Lower Ninth Ward—Mack's Ward." Often we name buildings after wealthy individuals or sell sponsorship rights to a family foundation, which helps offset construction costs or operating debt. To have a street or building named in your honor is a powerful gesture, but Mack deserves more than a street or a building. He was the face, heartbeat, and voice for his community for years after Hurricane Katrina. Mack was wealthy, too, but in the best way possible: he was rich in life, and he lived it every day. I will never forget my favorite New Orleans saint.

My family with Mack outside Lower Ninth Ward Village.

A.C.

February 11, 2016 ⊗

A.C. and I met soon after I started my nonprofit. He was one of the first people I spoke to by phone when I was still in research mode and determining what the schools needed. I think neither one of us knew what would happen next. Maybe he thought I was a flash-in-the-pan from Colorado, but he soon found out I was in it for the long haul and would not give up or walk away.

A.C. worked for the Recovery School District in New Orleans and practically carriedthe 130 schools on his back. He worked like hell for over six years ensuring every school was taken care of, whether the need was a handful of used desks, musical instruments, pencils, sports equipment, or a fresh coat of paint.

He worked six days a week, and his energy level was always off the charts. No task was too big, and no classroom was too small. The most amazing thing was that he had the inventory list of what twenty or more schools needed in his head. I think he took part in over a hundred playground builds.

Everywhere we went, everyone adored A.C. and welcomed him with a bear hug or a hearty handshake. Teachers gave him high-fives, and students would run up to him with smiles and hugs. You must understand A.C. is close to 6' 5" and has a few tattoos on his calves.

We spent a lot of time together during my seven volunteer trips, and he always inspired me to do a little more. When I have a terrible day, I take a second and think about what my friends in New Orleans went through and quickly realize a bad day is not as bad as I might think.

On my first trip, A.C. got angry when I told him I would get a rental car. He insisted on picking me up in this gigantic, oversized Ford F-250 truck. He took me on a tour of the hardest-hit areas and Brad Pitt's project. We drove, talked a lot, and bonded. He was also nice enough to treat me to a Hornets game and a Saints game, which was an incredible experience. He is a season ticket holder and a huge Saints fan.

During the first trip, we also built a playground together, and I was hooked. I have told the stories about how people from the community came together, and it did not matter what color your skin was, what label was on your clothes, or how much money you had. It is how society should be.

A.C., I have told you this before, but please know you will always have a room at the Tosti house for as long as I live, brother. I genuinely hope to see you and your wife in Denver sooner than later. Beth and I often talk about bringing the kids to New Orleans, but I could not fly there and be a tourist. I would grab a shovel or a paintbrush and work on some projects with you.

Denver might not have the famous Cajun cuisine and history of New Orleans, but I promise you there are more than a few of my friends who want to buy you a cold Colorado microbrew or two. God bless you and your wonderful city.

His name was changed because I lost touch with him and was not able to collect a waiver.

Lent Challenge Day 40

March 31, 2016 🌐

When I started this project, I had no idea if anyone would take time to read a post or if it would make a difference to anyone. The messages moved me, and I appreciated the support I received. Thank you to those who read one post or all of them. It is difficult to catch someone's attention for more than a minute or two in this day and time.

When you strip the multiple layers of life down to the core, you realize it is a beautiful thing and quite the gift. The ups, the downs, the challenges and obstacles we all face one way or the other define us. Some days you fight, others you pray and try to appreciate everything around you. It is about chasing dreams, true love, and discovering a passion in life that makes you smile.

The common thread we all share is the bond of friendship. Too often, our society labels everything, especially people. We may label people rich, poor, black, white, gay, straight, or even the oldest one, Democrat, or Republican. What if we removed the labels for a second to reflect on what friendship means and why it is important in life? A good friend appreciates you for your finer points, your faults, and everything in between. He or she embraces you for your spirit, quirks, and dedication. A loyal friend accepts you for who you are and what you stand for and respects your beliefs even if they differ from your own.

The people from the following posts have influenced me on some level and helped me understand why I love life. As I prepare for my next forty years, I look forward to spending time with some friends, old and new.

Chad Randall's post

> *My good friend and my longest-tenured college roommate, Chad Randall, asked me to include his version of Focus on Friends here.*

April 1, 2016 🌐

Okay, given all the hard work and commitment Brandon put into his Lent challenge, I figure we owe him one too. So here is my attempt at a Focus on Friends response to my friend, Brandon Tosti. Hopefully, I can express how special a friend he has been to me, and I bet to many others he has graciously written about on Facebook.

I have had the honor of being Brandon's friend since I started at the University of Kentucky back in 1994 (Wow! Twenty-two years!). We became friends while living in the same dorm for my first year and then shared a dorm room in my second year. As Brandon stated in the post about me, I worked all the time. I did work too much and almost missed meeting my future wife, even though she lived in the same dorm as Brandon and me. She was friends with Brandon, but heck, everyone was his friend. Brandon and I ended up living together for three more years in a variety of places.

Brandon would cut inspirational quotes and pictures out of magazines and post them all around the dorm room. I thought it was the coolest thing. He was continually surrounding himself with positive reinforcement, such a small thing yet so powerful. He is such an eternal optimist and so positive, you cannot help but feel good around him. Something else I learned living with him in a dorm room, he is also a snack bandit. He would not open something or eat the last item in a container, but it was fair game if it were already open. We devoured countless boxes of Ritz crackers, Cheez-its, and Mike and Ike. That is when I learned not to tear off the vacuum seal on the top of my opened Pringles cans. It took him a couple of years to figure out my trick.

I quickly learned Brandon knows everyone; you cannot take him anywhere without him running into someone he knows. Frankly, everyone is Brandon's friend. He continually amazes me how he can maintain so many "best" friends, and we all consider him our best friend. He has a genuine interest in people and loves being around others. We always joked he was going to be a politician or a sports agent. When I first watched the movie *Jerry Maguire*, I thought, that is Brandon.

Another funny trait is that this guy uses so much energy and is always moving. He unavoidably falls asleep when he finally sits down, even in the middle of a conversation. I cannot count the number of times he has fallen asleep while telling me a story. I got used to it after four years of living with the guy. He will be up in twenty minutes, ready to go again.

Brandon is what I would affectionately refer to as a dreamer. Not always great with the details and hard to keep tied down, but what great ideas and vision. He can make anyone believe in themselves and do more. He is such a great leader. Therefore, I think Beth (his brave and lovely wife) is such a great match. She keeps him grounded and on task and complements him so well. This is also the reason, though, that I always get my rental car when I visit him. He will agree to pick you up at the airport, but inevitably see an old friend, get distracted, and you are not exactly sure when he will be there.

Let me explain why this is genuine and we all forgive him in an instant. Brandon was passing through Louisville recently to pick up his wife and kids at the airport for a trip home to see the family. He had already spent all day seeing other people, and he called me at like 8:00 p.m. on a week-night. He said, "I have about fifteen minutes to spare if you want to meet up somewhere"—typical Brandon. So, without hesitation, I said, "Sure." We met and reminisced for about twenty minutes; it was cool and a great opportunity to see my friend. He was already tired and now running late to pick up his family, but it was important to him we met even for only a few minutes. He makes everyone feel this special.

Brandon inspired me to be spontaneous and to enjoy the experiences in life. I have many fond memories of our road trips. Most I learned about only a few hours before departure, like our trip to Detroit and Ann Arbor, Michigan, where we snuck into Joe Louis Arena after a Red Wings prac-tice. I still have the hockey puck a security guard gave us. On the same trip, we also slipped into the Big House at Michigan and walked on the field until we were asked to leave. We caught a baseball game at the old Tiger Stadium, special to a baseball fan like me. Last, we slipped into Canada for a little casino action.

On another trip, we drove cross-country on I-40 with Emily in her Sentra, packed to the ceiling. We stopped at every memorable spot along the way: Beale Street, Oklahoma City bombing site, Cadillac Ranch, Painted Desert, Meteor Crater, Grand Canyon, Vegas, across a deserted highway to go to Joshua Tree, Rose Bowl, Hollywood, Dodgers baseball game, Manhattan Beach, and I was even offered drugs at a Ralph's grocery store in South Central L.A. This was only two trips; I could go on and on. I would have had none of these wonderful experiences without my friendship with Brandon.

If you ever meet his parents (Ray and Linda), you will understand where Brandon gets it. I have only met them a few times, but I truly feel like they are family. To wrap this up, I want to say thank you, Brandon, for being such a great friend, and I am truly honored to be one of the friends you selected for your Lent Challenge Focus on Friends. Keep dreaming, keep inspiring, keep enjoying life! Happy belated birthday, too!

Chapter Four

Leave a Mark

Some friends join your path for a short time or maybe even a year or two, but a few of them leave an indelible mark in your heart, long after they unexpectedly leave your path. True friendship transcends race, gender, religion, and politics, which are topics that typically divide two people.

You make memories with friends. You laugh, you cry, you play a part in each other's weddings. The stories range from simple to outlandish, but retelling them never gets old. Chances are your best stories were ones shared with your closest friends.

Marisa Colaiano

Spring 2011 ◑

In November of 2005, I started a new job at Kroenke Sports Enterprises. One of the first people I met during my first few weeks there was Marisa Colaiano. We quickly became good friends. I am not sure if it was because we shared Italian heritage or that our favorite candy was gummy bears. Our mutual admiration for sarcasm solidified our friendship.

I changed jobs last May and dreaded telling her more than anyone else at Dick's Sporting Goods Park or Pepsi Center. This was because I knew the days of walking across the stadium to talk to my buddy about everything would no longer be an option. Last-minute lunch runs to Anthony's Pizza or Noodles & Company would now have to be scheduled in advance. The discussion topic was always changing. One day we would talk about life, sports, or whatever was going on in the world. Other times, the Italian temper gene would make an appearance; we would jokingly yell at each other. At first, people thought we were furious at one another until then they realized it was how two good friends communicated.

She is my pal, my teammate, and an adopted sister of sorts. I know other people can say the same thing, which is an example of why many friends, coworkers, and clients are pulling for her. We would joke about life, whatever was aggravating us. Like a true friend, she always listened, but she was also honest with me and kicked me in the butt when necessary. She would routinely ask about my wife and kids. That is the person she is: extremely unselfish, caring, and always wanting to hear about other people.

Marisa is a quiet person unless you are talking about her favorite team, the Chicago Cubs. When spring training entered daily conversations at work, she smiled more each day and had a little extra pep in her step. Our boss would conduct staff meetings, and regardless of how stressful the office environment was, he would ask Marisa the number of days until pitchers reported to camp. Without hesitation, Marisa would smile and answer with the exact number of days. She might have even mentioned hours and minutes a few times.

Marisa handled her multiple sclerosis (MS) diagnosis like everything else in her life: with determination and resolve. My only experience with MS was an MS charity bike race my wife and I volunteered with that went through the mountains. I understood the basics of the disease and how unpredictable it was, but now it had hit close to home, one of my dear friends.

I made it a point from the day she told me about her diagnosis not to let it affect our friendship. I assured her that there would be no topic we could not discuss. My goal was always to be available to talk about her good days and bad ones. I asked questions about her different medication types, the new yoga classes, and how her body accepted all the changes. I wanted to understand as much as I could so she would have someone at work to talk to about the unpredictable roller-coaster ride MS is for patients. She had been such a great friend to me, and I wanted to try and return the favor.

A while back, she told everyone about her total blood transfusion and the mandatory four-day hospital stay. I stopped by to see her for a bit over the weekend. The thing I remember is that she smiled and joked with me and two of her girlfriends. During the last few weeks, like all her friends and family, I have worried a lot about her, but the thought of her tremendous smile during the hospital stay is what I try to think about the most.

Marisa, you are one tough cookie, and you have an army of friends and family praying for you during this challenging time. I promise to visit you soon, pal, but I know now it is not the best time. As always, I will bring you some gummy bears.

Love ya, kid.

Tosti

July 16, 2012 🌐

Marisa,

(Jeff) Mathews and I had lunch, not to catch up, but to talk about you and share our grief to make sense of what you are going through. Our usual sarcastic rants were few and far between, mainly because we missed our partner in crime.

We talked about you a lot and smiled when we thought about how mad you would be about these wonderful people talking about you and sharing your life's accomplishments, mainly how many lives you touched by being you.

Thank you for being such a great friend. We all miss you, pal.

July 17, 2012 🌐

If you were close to Marisa or worked in the building with her, you knew that her favorite baseball player was Mark Grace, the first baseman for the Chicago Cubs, who wore number 17. Anytime the opportunity to choose a number presented itself, Marisa took full advantage of it and chose number 17 whenever she could. It was much more than a number to her.

Once we realized that her days on this earth were numbered, someone commented that she would leave us on the 17th. By this point in time, her body had failed her, but her heart and mind still had some control.

This morning, my best friend Marisa Colaiano left this world and is in a much better place and free from MS's pain. I will miss you so much, buddy, and I thank God for your friendship. My heart is broken, and we will all be praying for you and your family during this time. Love you and miss you a ton already.

February 2013 ⊛

Today would have been my friend Marisa's 36th birthday. I have thought a lot about her lately because I knew this day on the calendar was slowly creeping up and because baseball pitchers were reporting to spring training. She was a huge Chicago Cubs fan and would always let everyone know spring training was starting soon. I try to think of all the good times and funny stories we shared.

It is well known that there is no handbook on dealing with the loss of a loved one or a friend. Everyone deals with it differently, and there is not a right or wrong way to handle it. I hate the fact we lost her early in life, but I try my best to reflect on the power of her friendship during those seven years.

I did not get to tell her goodbye officially, but the last time I saw her, she had a smile on her face because I brought two bags of Haribo gummy bears to the hospital for her. Those were our favorite gummy bears. I gave her a big hug, told how much I loved her, and kissed her on the cheek. I did not know it would be our last time to speak to one another, but her big smile is how I will always remember her. She made me a better person and a stronger one.

July 2013: One year later . . . ⊛

This time last year, we were mourning a loss of a daughter, a sister, an aunt, and a friend to many. Marisa, I try to think of the good times and memories that make me smile even though you are no longer with us. Here are just a few of them.

Lunch at Noodles & Company: You would always ask if I wanted to split one of those damn gigantic snickerdoodle cookies, and I would say no, even though we both knew I would devour my half as soon as you opened the silly thing. I still smile when I see those cookies.

MLS Championship—Toronto Trip

I remember how you convinced me to go when I thought it would be best to stay home. I will never forget watching the tears stream down your and Kieran's faces as the final whistle blew. Those were true tears of joy, and I knew what the team meant to both of you and the hard work that went into getting to that point.

Charity: I remember how I never had to ask you for a donation for Sports For a Cause. As soon as I mentioned the fact that we were returning to New Orleans for another March volunteer trip, you would immediately reach into your purse and hand me $50. It could have been $5 or $500, but the fact that you cared enough to support me without my asking spoke volumes about your character and friendship.

Gone but not forgotten: I have taught a Professional Sports Marketing class for five or six years at Johnson and Wales University, and I always start my first class with a brief overview of the sports industry and two of the most influential men who helped shape the industry. This past fall, I decided to add one more name to my course outline. My students will never be able to meet you, but I wanted to make sure they knew your name, what you stood for, and what kind of impact you had in Community Relations. I told them about your World Cup of Wines and Beer event and how other MLS Community Relations employees would call you for advice and ideas. You became known as a trailblazer for new concepts and programs, but you always downplayed the praise and credit.

A lot of us get into the sports industry because we want to experience the rush of planning a major event to entertain thousands, or because we want to play some small part in representing the city that we live in. However, not all of us get to the level where you were, even though you would never admit it. You could have very easily sat back and managed the traditional community relations events that are successful, generate a lot of money, and garner some solid PR, but that wasn't good enough for you. No, you were never one to settle, and you tried to be better, day in and day out. Marisa, in the end, you didn't just play the game well, you changed it—along with many lives, including mine.

Flying the W Flag in Heaven

October 2016 🌐

For decades, the flagpole above Wrigley Field's famous scoreboard has been used to let passengers on the nearby elevated trains know the outcome of each Cubs home game. When the Cubs win, the team hoists a white flag with a blue W.

I am happy for my friends who are Chicago Cubs fans, but the biggest Cubs fan I have ever known was cheering and yelling from heaven tonight. Marisa Colaiano, I know your family and friends have watched the postseason a little more closely than usual this year. We are happy and sad because we want to hug you and jump up and down in celebration; instead, we are telling old stories and appreciating your passion for your favorite baseball team. Do us all a favor and tell the big man upstairs to let you fly the W flag tonight!

You may no longer be with us in person on this Earth, but I promise you are not forgotten, my dear friend. You are missed and loved by so many people.

Adam Koski

It is never easy to watch a close friend fight for his life in a hospital room. Our dear friend Adam Koski faced such a fight in 2015. It was a rough week for a close friend and for many people here in Denver and Wisconsin. I wrote this note for my friends, his family , and anyone else who had encountered our Denver group of friends, otherwise known as the "crew." God bless you, AK, and keep fighting, brother!

July 2015 🌐

In August 2000, I turned down a recruiting coordinator job with the University of Kentucky football team. I took a chance with a small sports events company based in Lakewood, Colorado. Summit Sports and Events was the company name, and their grassroots soccer tour was the nation's largest and most popular program. Time flies because it was fifteen years ago, and little did I know the people I met during my graduate-school internship would be lifelong friends.

The office was full of energy, sarcasm, humor, and a can-do attitude such as I have never experienced at any other company. We were broke—I do not think any of us made more than $26,000—but we were passionate about our jobs. We were young, and we were on the road in some way, shape, or form from April to September. We enjoyed every minute of it. We had many stories from the road and what occurs when you run a 65-city national tour concluding at Disney World for the World Championships.

This group of friends came together through a sports company and expanded through roommates, significant others, and high-school buddies. Some of us started as work friends, but this deep connection has been there from day one. I cannot pinpoint why we bonded or why we love one another so profoundly, but ask anyone in this circle, and you will be greeted with a devilish grin and a loss for words. Maybe it was the fact that we were thousands of miles from family, but I think it was something more profound than geography or missing home.

We hosted annual parties such as the Super Bowl Chili Cook-Off, the Kentucky Derby Party, gut-busting and epic game nights, and Thanksgiving slumber parties. The latter was because none of us could afford to fly home for both Thanksgiving and Christmas. It all changed when Jane (Koski) Bartine invited *all* of us to her condo. She did not want anyone to be alone on this memorable holiday. Jane baked the turkey and mashed the potatoes, but the rest was up to us. Since then, the tradition has moved to her house, and she has only missed one Thanksgiving in fifteen years.

We have fought cancer together, lost jobs, started our own companies, and endured divorces. We have been in each other's weddings, even presided over a few, and were the first friends to visit the hospital when children were born. Our parents know all the nicknames and always ask about the group and how everyone is doing. Many of the parents have joined us for cookouts, parties, and many other holidays. My mom beat a buddy and me in bocce one time, and it was not even close!

One of our friends fought an extremely tough battle, and as soon as word spread, many of us dropped everything and were there in a heartbeat. One by one, the waiting room at the hospital filled up with various members of this group. Friends rearranged personal schedules, made plans to work from home, and even worked from the hospital. This group always hugs each other when it is time to go home, but this time was different. There were lots of tears, and the strong bear hugs meant a little more this time around. Meals, snacks, gift cards, and airport rides were quickly provided for the family and anything else they might need during this challenging and incredibly stressful time. It was a revolving door of friends, and we all took shifts stopping by. We frequently texted each other to know who was stopping by day and night. Our friend is still battling, but things are slowly trending upward. This incredible group of friends will continue to pray and provide support however we can.

We all live busy lives and call different suburbs home, but we all jump right in with no questions asked when one of us falls. I always knew how wonderful these people were, but the past week's events have reminded us of how special this group is and what true friendship looks like. This circle of friends is a wonderful, remarkable, unselfish, and loving group of individuals who support each other like family. I am both proud and blessed to call each of them a friend.

Goodbye, Dear Friend

August 4, 2015 🌐

Monday morning started with a phone call no one wants to receive. My buddy Brian Tatum called me to let me know our good friend Adam died late Sunday night. Adam, I remember the good times and the countless memories we shared with you, whether it was camping, playing hoops, running soccer tournaments together, or hanging out at someone's house on the weekend.

You were the guy friend at the bar—you know, the one a girl would approach and ask who our cute tall friend was standing in the corner. I wish I had a dollar every time it happened to me, because I could retire at fifty.

You were the friend I would want on my side in a bar fight, even though you never looked to start trouble with anyone.

You were the friend everyone wanted on their basketball team and the friend everyone hated when you were guarding them. Damn your wingspan.

You were the friend who always had the funniest fantasy football team names and who talked the most trash, especially when you had a terrible season.

You were the friend who opened his Rolodex for me when my sports career switched from the pro ranks to the high-school level. High-school athletic directors receive fifty sales calls on a slow day, but you told them it was okay to take my call because I was a good friend.

You were my friend who handed me a thank-you card on my birthday because it was the only card you had at your house, and you wrote in the "Happy Birthday" part. It is my favorite birthday card.

 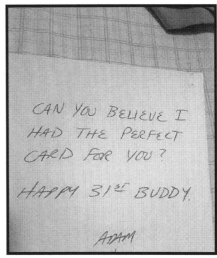

You were the friend everyone stopped by to check on at the hospital. We held your hand, gave you pep talks, and checked on your mom and dad as if they were our own. I hope and pray you knew how many people cared about you.

You were the friend who greeted everyone you met with a genuine smile and a hearty handshake. It must have been your Wisconsin farm-boy background.

You were the friend who *always* helped people move, not because you had a truck but because you were a damn brute, and everyone knew it.

You never said no when it came to helping a friend. You and Tatum helped us move into our little house on a snowy New Year's Day eleven years ago.

You were the friend who could always cheer someone up with a sarcastic remark, a funny joke, or a bear hug.

You were my only friend who knew what it felt like to watch your best friend and wife battle breast cancer. You were a rock for your wife and supported her at every turn.

You *are* a great friend, brother, son, and uncle who will be missed but will not be forgotten.

Jane (Koski) Bartine

A LETTER TO A FRIEND

We all have one friend whose job is to take care of everyone in the group. She is lovingly referred to as the Mama Bear or Mother Hen. She does not judge anyone, regardless of how screwed up the situation seems to be or how much trouble the friend has stirred up. She is there to listen, help, and coach you through it, even if it is a dose of reality and not what you want to hear. I can count on one hand the people in my life I can talk to about *anything*, and Jane Bartine is one of them.

Since last January, our dear friend Jane has been fighting kidney cancer and continues to fight it with an extraordinary level of poise, strength, and calmness. I have prayed for her and the family. I have cussed and cried, talked to my Mom over and over, and even leaned on my neighbor's shoulders when I was really upset or needed to tell a story about her.

We flew to Madison to spend some quality time with her. We talked, we laughed for days about old times and held her hand often. We wanted to let her know we will always be here for her, Chris, and the girls.

Cancer might be waging an unfair battle against her body, but the one part that remains intact and unchanged is her heart, which is fitting if you know this remarkable woman. Jane grew up with three brothers on a large farm in rural Wisconsin; I often refer to her as "country strong." She is a daughter, sister, wife, mother, aunt, *great friend*, and unofficial Mother Hen to more than twenty crazy friends in Denver, Colorado.

To say she has been there for my family and me is an understatement. She has always gone above and beyond the call of friendship and expects nothing in return except a good one-liner to make her laugh, and the more sarcasm, the better. She helped me change Kaden's first diaper in the hospital and helped us during Beth's breast cancer battle in various ways. Jane was the one I frantically called in tears when I honestly thought we might lose our friend, Tatum. She calmed me down and firmly told me it was not his time yet, and I believed her.

When you fight cancer, all the numbers, statistics, and acronyms over-whelm both the patient and caregiver. Each doctor visit includes blood cell counts, dizzying reports, and more medical charts than one knew were possible. The debrief can exhaust everyone, and both parties could use a nap after they leave the doctor's office or chemo ward. Over the past eigh-teen months, Jane has endured scans, X-rays, chemo, and immunotherapy. Every time I talk to her, she is still upbeat, laughing, and facing each chal-lenge one day at a time. It reminds me not to take everything too seriously because our time with family and friends is really what matters the most.

Jane, I want you to know you made a difference in countless lives. Your enormous heart and generosity forever changed the way I view Thanksgiving. Sometimes in life, we measure impact and success based on money, titles, or other shallow criteria. You and Chris opened your hearts and home every year for over a decade to friends, girlfriends and boyfriends, coworkers, and even our parents if they were in town. By my inadequate and unrealistic mathematical estimates, you two probably hosted over 500 people over time.

I often think about future Thanksgivings and how any of us could pay tribute to your family's generosity and hospitality. I think the simple way is always to make sure the people inside and outside of our circle have a place to eat at Thanksgiving, whether they are family, friends, or the weird guy in Accounting. This is what you and Chris did, time and time again. Everyone was welcome in your home: Democrats, Republicans, gay, straight, staunch religious folks, non-churchgoers, and your skin color did not matter. The world can learn a lot from you. I thank God our paths crossed, and I am blessed to call you a close friend.

You might have cancer, but everyone knows it does not have you nor your wonderful heart. An oncologist or medical procedure cannot measure the true size of one's heart. I know without a doubt yours would be off the charts.

*Jane and I playing Duck Duck Goose
on an inflatable Twister mat.*

Angels, Cookies, and Windows

October 23, 2019 ☯

Last week I flew to Madison, Wisconsin, to spend some quality time with my dear friend Jane Bartine, who continues to fight kidney cancer courageously. However, she did not know I was coming because I wanted to surprise her.

During the weeks leading up to my trip, I was nervous because I was unsure what to expect when I saw her for the first time since last November. Before this decision, I told Chris I had decided I would not make a second trip because I wanted to remember her in my way. Late one night, Beth and I talked about my reasoning. Beth told me that any decisions about last visits should be about what Jane wants, not what I want. I realized my wife was right and that I had been selfish.

The other words that resonated in the back of my mind were from Jane herself. In July, she sent me a note saying, "Get your asses up here, one of you, four, five, all of you, I don't care." She wanted the Denver crew and friends to visit her. Now I understand why.

I arrived at Denver International Airport with my stomach already in knots. Then something odd happened. I met two strangers, and our conversations helped me in ways I could not have imagined. I was standing in line waiting to board when a gracious lady and her daughter asked me the inevitable question. I told her the reason for my trip, and she said she was from Longmont. I told her I had not set foot in Longmont in the twenty years I had lived in Colorado except for my sprint triathlon in September. I told her about how pretty the lake was, and she smiled and said she had completed the race too. Jane was working her magic already. What were the chances?

I could tell Jane's story moved her. It turns out she and her daughter were seated one row behind me. As I boarded the plane, I reached into my backpack and handed her two "Team Jane" bracelets. They immediately slid the bracelets on and said, "It is an honor to wear these." I did not catch her name, but if any of my friends see a mom wearing a Team Jane bracelet at the grocery store or the lake in Longmont, please hug her for me and thank her again.

It was time to buckle up and start writing something to distract me for the next hour and a half. The nice lady beside me cracked a joke that we could not switch seats even though we all paid the same price to select our seats in this section. She was the feisty grandmother type, and I shared a good chuckle with her and grabbed my pen. Then, something funny happened. She asked me a question and made another sarcastic, expletive-laden comment. There is something to be said for anyone who knows when and how to appropriately emphasize using a cuss word.

One joke led to another, and before I knew it, I had tucked my notebook and pen away because I was in stitches, and the conversation rolled from one topic to the next. She was Irish Catholic and was one of twelve children. We talked about our families, childhood, what I do for a living, and what makes us tick. It turns out her daughter works at a school where a good friend's wife has worked for years. Unreal! She spoke of her avid travel adventures, and it was all I needed to hear. Before I knew it, the dreaded hour-and-36-minute flight was over.

We hugged and made plans to keep in touch since she travels to Denver often. As I was walking away from Baggage Claim, the other mom, with heavy eyes, reached out her hand and said, "I hope your visit goes well," and "Go, Team Jane!" I thanked her and slowly walked out to the sidewalk to catch my ride. I told both ladies they helped me calm down and made what could have been a rough flight a good one. In my head, I kept thinking Jane sent me two angels to help me relax and genuinely enjoy our visit over the next few days.

As I walked into Jane's room, she had just woken up from a nap and was slightly groggy. It was close to 10:00 p.m., and Chris asked her if she wanted to say hi to someone. She sat up and blinked her eyes a few times and let out an expletive or two preceded by the word *holy*. We hugged each other for what felt like ten minutes, and she let out this deep belly laugh with a sniffle or two, and I did the same. Even when she is not feeling well, this girl knows how to put everyone at ease and make them feel welcome. It is a talent you cannot teach.

I took a seat by her bed, and we started talking, and the next thing I knew, it was 3:00 a.m. We caught up on her medical stories, good and bad; the Denver Crew; her wonderful neighbors; and other life stories. The stuff I had worried about went out of the window, and it was two old friends talking a mile a minute and genuinely excited to see one another.

It was such a relief to see my dear friend in her home, but I remained anxious on how to act. I reached out for advice, and one of my best buddies told me to soak it all in. If she needed her water cup refilled, I tried to help. If she needed a pain pill, I would ask Chris or Jean, Jane's mom, for the right bottle and proper dosage. I wanted to spend time with her and help however I could.

Jane was a nurse, as was her mom. Jean is a saint and is one of the strongest women I have ever met. I have known Jean over a decade and was aware of her cooking prowess, but nothing could prepare me for the cookie-baking frenzy on the horizon. We had peanut-butter chocolate chip cookies, molasses cookies, and sourdough roll-out sugar cookies. This lady made Martha Stewart look like a minor-league baker.

My new routine was to eat two cookies for breakfast, *each day*. These were not little cookies, either. They were monster-sized ones, and I could not stop. Every morning it was a new aroma coming from the kitchen, and the girls were helping Jean create a new option for all of us. I finally threw in the white towel and stopped counting after my fifth cookie.

This did not include the two trays of sweets already there. After this trip and the five pounds I probably gained, I am officially declaring the peanut-butter chocolate chip cookies Koski–Bartine Cookies. Monday arrived, and I was dreading saying goodbye to my buddy. Jane had mentioned earlier in the visit that maybe Jean could prepare some turkey and we could celebrate Thanksgiving early. I had agreed and said it would be neat and kind of fun. Later I remembered Chris bought some fresh turkey from the deli and told Jane we could keep it simple and eat turkey sandwiches. I prepared her plate of cold turkey and Triscuit crackers and grabbed a mozzarella cheese stick to put on my turkey sandwich.

As we were munching away, Jane looks at me and says, "Well, this is the most piss-poor Thanksgiving meal you've ever had at our house!" I said, "No, you are wrong, it is one of the most memorable ones, and I dodged having to watch you drop six sticks of butter in those famous cheesy mashed potatoes." It was a simple yet perfect meal and one I will cherish. After we finished, I left her to nap and binge-watch more of *Scandal*, the show I had told her about the night before.

Then it was time to play with the kiddos. I walked them to the park near their house for the second round of freeze tag. Chris joined me to ensure I was not the only old man scaling rock-climbing walls and dodging curvy slides and low-hanging monkey bars. By the way, the zip line they have is first class, and I might have tested it a few times, but my back and knees quickly reminded me of my age.

I walked outside and looked to the sky, longing for some tranquility, and snapped a photo because it felt like it spoke to me. The dark clouds symbolized our anger toward cancer, and the sunshine fighting to peek\through represented Jane's positive attitude, courage, and huge heart. The tree's color-changing leaves reminded me their daughters would weather this storm and bloom in the future.

It was time to leave and say goodbye to Jane. I reached out to my close buddies for advice yet again. They both shared the same sentiment, and I followed their advice. It was not a final goodbye; it was a "See you later, friend." I leaned over the bed and gave her a big Tosti hug and told her I loved her and that I was glad we had hung out for a few days, even if I had scared her with the unannounced visit.

Cancer takes things from a person—weight, hair, maybe appetite—but it cannot take the individual's personality and spirit. I can happily report that Jane's sarcasm and sense of humor are still intact.

Before I left, I tried to cope with this process and tried to find the words to frame the worry, the love, and the support this amazing woman has inspired in every soul she has met. As I stood on their front porch, staring at the sky, I thought about a single word: *window*.

Windows are built to let light in; sometimes, they get dirty. We open and close them for different reasons. Children often leave their mark on windows with their tiny fingerprints. When you think about it, all our windows are closing, but we do not know when. We must remember to live our lives to the fullest. A great friendship is like a good window. It protects us from the outside elements; it is resilient, it includes a few smudges, and, most importantly, it reminds us our light will always find a way to shine through.

A Recipe for a Life Well Lived

November 21, 2019 🌐

Our dear friend, Jane Bartine, passed away peacefully on October 30. Close to twenty friends from Denver flew to Madison, Wisconsin,to support Chris and Jane's family at her Celebration of Life ceremony. For the longest time, the Denver crew and I worried about Chris and their two daughters as they prepared for the next phase of their lives. Several of us flew back to spend time with her and the family, which also meant spending time getting to know their wonderful and hilarious neighbors.

Another close buddy, Suzanne Fischer, calmed some of our fears by telling us how great their neighborhood was, and what a wonderful support group the neighbors would be. One of the last things Jane and I talked about was the fantastic neighbors. I think she said it was like "the crew," but in their neighborhood. Those words provided such a sense of calmness for me, and I wish to thank every neighbor from one crew to another.

We all moved far from our families, and we spent countless hours working, playing, and celebrating Thanksgiving at the Bartine house. We grew up together and weathered life's storms, including marriage, miscarriages, children, divorce, loss of jobs, cancer, and death.

When Adam, Jane's little brother, was fighting for his life in a Lakewood hospital, their parents, Jean, and Jim arrived to see a waiting room full of the Denver friends at 2:30 in the afternoon. Jean looked at Jane and said, "What are all these people doing here? Don't they have jobs?" Jane smiled and said, "Mom, when you move this far away from home, your close friends become a second family, and this is our other family."

To Chris and his daughters: as you begin your journey down this path, I know deep in my heart that you will not walk alone. Two crews (Denver and the neighborhood) will pitch in and help with the big things, the little things, and everything in between. I promise you.

Thanksgiving is right around the corner, and for the first time I can honestly say I am not looking forward to the holiday. Right now, my heart and mind are both filled with a combination of rage and appreciation. I know it is part of the grieving process, and it might last a while. Jane would encourage all of us to remember the good times and try our best to make new memories. In my mind, Thanksgiving will never be the same, and that is a true testament to the impact Jane and Chris Bartine had on the many people they hosted for Thanksgiving over the years.

I say this on behalf of the entire Denver contingent. There will always be three open seats for Chris, Samantha, and Alexa at the Tosti family table, along with four plates. The fourth plate might be empty, but the rest of us know Jane's stories and memories will always ensure our glasses are half full, just like our hearts.

Wisconsin is famous for several products: beer, bratwursts, cheese, and accents. As with other states, there are always one or two cultural norms that define the state in ways words cannot. One of my college roommates was from Waukesha, so I was familiar with a few terms, but "towny bar" was not one of them.

The Celebration of Life was scheduled for Saturday afternoon. Friday night, we ventured to the local towny bar, Club 51 Bait and Tackle— or "Club 51" for short. We loaded up car after car, then made the five-minute drive from the house to the bar and parked in the back. As we approached the bar, we saw two entrance signs: one for the bait shop and the other for the bar area. We all chuckled and commented that this bar was exactly what we needed. Jane was bringing us together to hang out with one another one more time.

From the highway, the bar looks like a traditional two-story farmhouse, but one step inside and the tight quarters and dim lighting welcome you and immediately put you at ease. The walls were adorned with the typical neon beer décor, oversized metal Bucky the Badger signs, and Green Bay Packers images on every other open inch of space. However, the appetizer menu sign caught my attention for a different reason. It was one of those vintage types with the plastic letters and numbers someone manually adjusts when needed.

In perfectly centered bold letters at the bottom of the menu, it said, "Deep Fryer Menu Available." As if this was not enough home-cooking, the other appetizers listed on the bar menu included something by the name of Tater Keg. Imagine a gigantic tater tot the size of two jumbo marshmallows and the diameter of a State Fair piece of corn on the cob.

The owners welcomed us right away when they heard we were from out of town. As the night went on, we quickly became friends on a first-name basis. By closing time, someone had told the owner the meaning of our visit and made a special request to look out for our friend Chris. We mentioned we might return someday for a party or maybe to have a fundraiser for the girls. One of the owners smiled through her tears and said, "We're in; just let us know."

A bartender's job is multifaceted and not always as easy as it seems. They memorize mixed-drink ingredients and must remember how to make the drink taste right. One night their job might be to serve drinks and keep the party going, while other nights, the focus is on responsibly declining more drinks for someone who needs to slow down. Other times they serve a pitcher of cheer and a side of compassion the size of a tater keg.

The word *strong* is one word I have used to describe Jane. If you know the Koski family, you know where she gets it from. In a previous post, I used the term "country strong." I also reserve this term for her husband, Chris, who has been through it all with her from day one of her diagnosis. He never flinched and was there for her until the very end, which is how it should be.

For some silly reason, I told myself I had to be strong for her parents and two brothers, knowing well they were 25,000 times stronger than me and would most likely be calming me down at some point. As the Celebration of Life ceremony ended, I slowly made my way to the family table to say my last goodbyes and hug the family. I hugged everyone, and the last person was Grant, Jane's older brother, who runs the family farm and could easily pass for a WWE wrestler or an NFL linebacker based on his height and physique. I shook his bear-paw hands and hugged him for a second, but then something unexpected happened. Grant leaned over and told me how much my post about my last visit with Jane meant to him and the family and that it was much appreciated. Then the dam broke, and I lost it. He hugged me for a little longer, and I swear it felt like one of Jane's hugs. Thank you, Grant; I needed it more than you will ever know.

Sunday morning, we all made our way to the Bartine house to say our last goodbyes to the family, watch some football, and hug everyone who stuck around. As expected, there was no shortage of homemade desserts: containers of cookies (I stopped counting at four), two cases of cheesecake, and four dozen doughnuts. Of course, there were plenty of my favorite Koski–Bartine cookies. I wolfed one down and followed one with another. I ate two, and only two, for a reason: I know Jane would have told me it was okay to eat two. I decided I would eat one in her honor and one for her dear mom, Jean.

Jane always made every person she met feel welcome and never turned down the opportunity to make someone smile with a hearty laugh and the right amount of humor. The wonderful stories, photos, and memories will last a lifetime. There will also be a large group of friends, near and far, to play the role of Mother Hen, as Jane did for all of us.

To Chris and the girls, we know you will need space and time to figure things out, and we will all be here for anything you might need. Everyone will be ready with a hug, a cookie, or even a cocktail; heck, maybe all three. No doubt, our hearts are broken, but we must promise to continue to open them to others, as Jane did for family, her hospital patients, and friends for all those years.

Like most skilled chefs, she left us with a tough recipe to follow, and it was never written on paper. I believe Jane's recipe card for a good life and how to treat others would read something like this: A giant helping of an open heart, one open door at Thanksgiving, two bear hugs, 10 cups of laughter, and, most importantly, a pinch of sarcasm.

This is one of the wristbands I created for Jane. The Batman font was a reminder that not all heroes wear capes, the green text honored her Green Bay Packers, and the orange represented kidney cancer.

Chapter Five

The Big C

Sometimes, adversity strikes and adds some unplanned heavy construction on your path. You have a choice: You can pull off to the side of the road at a rest stop, or you can add some 4WD knobby tires and fight your way through it.

I documented my wife's breast cancer battle for a couple of reasons. One, I wanted to have something for her and our kids to look back on someday. Second, I was scared to death, and writing has always been my therapeutic way of dealing with life. Last, I wanted to share what it was like to go through this experience so others might be less scared if it happens to them.

The name "BRCA" is an abbreviation for "BReast CAncer gene." BRCA1 and BRCA2 are two different genes that impact a person's chances of developing breast cancer. Every human has both the BRCA1 and BRCA2 genes. Despite what their names might suggest, BRCA genes do not cause breast cancer. For years, Beth and I understood that because of a BRCA1 gene mutation, she was at a higher risk for breast cancer. Thanks to her aunt Mary Jo Kennelly, Beth took a proactive approach and monitored this closely for five years. I figured it would happen in her fifties or sixties, not in her thirties. Technology, Aunt Mary Jo's courage, and early detection saved Beth's life.

Family Update from Denver

July 2014 🌐

On July 8, Beth and I came home excited about our family's first camping trip only to be jolted back to one of life's harshest realities. Her doctor called to let her know they had diagnosed her with stage-1, grade-3 breast cancer. Stage 1 means it is only in one spot, and grade 3 means the cancer is aggressive and invasive. The good thing is they caught it extremely early, and the growth was under 1 cm.

Thanks to genetic coding research, technology, and the Rocky Mountain Cancer Center, Beth has been under careful watch for the past five years since we learned she has the BRCA 1 gene mutation. Simply put, upon that discovery, her known risk for breast cancer immediately increased from one in five to one in two. Cancer is the tremendous humbling equalizer, and we are prepared to fight it like other families and individuals. It is scary as hell, but you must stay positive and take things one day at a time.

On Friday, August 9, she will undergo a double mastectomy since her cancer has an eighty percent chance of spreading. She may or may not have to endure several rounds of chemotherapy, but we will not know until the day of her surgery.

It is incredible what a little perspective can do for a person. One minute, you are running around at a hundred miles an hour and stressed out about starting a new job; the next, this curveball stops you in your tracks instantly and makes you cry, laugh, and smile all in one breath. Perspective helps you realize the upcoming games, concerts, and events will go on with or without you, but your wife and best friend needs you a lot more. Suddenly, you smile and chuckle at the petty "stresses" we all face in our daily lives and are reminded of what matters most.

Beth and I always talk about how blessed we have been in our lives; this is no different. Some women cannot afford health insurance or fear mammograms and put it off until it is too late. By being proactive and addressing the issue early, Beth and her oncologists have been on top of things.

We both are incredibly positive-minded people, and we do not plan on changing. It will not be easy, and there will be rough and unpredictable days ahead, but we will face this challenge with love, faith, and help from all of you. Beth and I will need our family and friends for a multitude of reasons and will lean on many of you soon.

Our only request is that you not call her to ask questions about how she is feeling or anything related to the surgery. If you have questions, please contact me. We encourage you to call, text, or email her to say hi, make her smile, and offer words of encouragement.

To say we have been deeply touched and moved by the support we have received from our family and friends would be an understatement. One friend from home who has never met Beth offered to fly to Denver for a few days to help us with anything at all. Another friend in a band offered to host a benefit concert.

In closing, I wanted to share some advice from one of our dear friends, Peggy (Bowersox) Garcia. She told Beth lots of things, but one phrase stuck out for me. Peggy told Beth that, whatever happens, she should make sure to "Fight like hell!" We plan on it! We love all of you dearly and appreciate your support more than you will ever know.

Love,

Beth, Brandon, Kaden, and Emily

September 2014 ⊙

Cancer does a lot of things to a person's body and to their loved ones as well. It rocks you to your core and tests your faith, probably more than anything you have experienced in your life. Beth and I have never asked why, but rather, how we can beat this stupid disease. If you feel sorry for yourself, then the disease has scored a point on you. It is okay to let it get ahead of you for a day or two, but you cannot let it win the game.

There will always be someone else who has a more severe type of cancer or has been battling cancer for a more extended period. That is why we always respect other individuals when we talk about Beth's battle. We are not special, but we realize that it is okay to ask for a helping hand here and there. Our friends and family have supported us in countless ways, and we cannot say thank you enough.

I also need to thank my mother-in-law, Fay, who has been here with us for a long period of time. She has helped us in thirty different ways, and the kids will miss Pinky. I have been gone for long hours for work, and she has helped keep our house in order, and I am eternally grateful for that. Next, it is my mom's turn to spend a few weeks with us.

Cancer has also:

Humbled us, inspired us, motivated us to fight like hell, and brought us to tears of both fear and joy.

Stressed us out, brought us even closer as a family, reminded of what means the most in life,

Challenged us to figure out what we want to do with our lives, made us laugh, and made us tell our friends how much we love them often.

Helped us reconnect to friends from all stages of our lives.

On the day of her surgery, everyone was nervous, as anyone would be, but as we entered the Rocky Mountain Cancer Center's lobby, I saw my favorite sports movie playing on the TV. It was *Remember the Titans*. That movie always inspires me, and it is kind of special to me for a different reason. I have traveled a fair amount to large and small cities in my career, from Greenville, South Carolina, to Fargo, North Dakota. It was on a 3v3 soccer sales trip to Greenville where I met the real-life Ronnie Bass, the California quarterback featured in the movie. For the first time, I was calm and smiled because I knew everything would be okay.

As Beth approaches her first round of eight chemo treatments, we both are worried about the dreaded effects, but we have learned not to get ahead of ourselves.

It will be a long battle over the next sixteen weeks, but chemo provides her with the best chance for long-term success because of her aggressive type of cancer. There will be good days and bad days, but I know that she will make it through this rough patch. As we have both said before, we appreciate the cookies, flowers, gift cards, meals, greeting cards, and everything else that our friends and family have given us.

I want to thank everyone from the bottom of our hearts for their support. We promise to pay it forward, but in the meantime, we have a fight to tend to, and it is one we are going to *win!*

Chemo Round #1

September 26, 2013 ◐

Beth's first round of chemo was going to be a scary time; I knew she would be nervous, so I called in a favor. I wanted to make her and some other patients smile for a minute. Guess who came to visit Beth at the Rocky Mountain Cancer Center—Miles, the Denver Broncos mascot!

Chemo Round #2

October 9, 2013 ◐

No surprise appearances by professional mascots are on tap, but I will do my best to make Beth laugh and to take her mind off cancer for a few hours. Thanks for the continued cards, prayers, scarves, hats, and positive thoughts. Special shout out to one of the Pigskin Prognosticators, Jason Orange, because his church sent a card signed by multiple parishioners, and not even one of them has met Beth.

Chemo Round #3

October 23, 2013 ◐

Beth's third "rough" chemo treatment is in the books. Her sister, Stephanie, went with her. She has one more treatment like this one, and then she has four much milder chemo treatments. So far, she has avoided nausea and is blessed to have experienced one or two days of tiredness and one or two episodes of vertigo.

It takes a special individual to work in any cancer center. I tip my hat to the office staff, nurses, pharmacists, and doctors across this country who help cancer patients and their families as they battle this disease. Beth and I talked earlier about how we hate seeing patients sitting by themselves in the infusion center. I told her I want to run through the infusion center and hug them all and make them smile somehow, some way.

Beth has been rocking some new scarves from friends and family. Her strength continues to amaze me, and I just try to make her smile and laugh a bit. Keep on trucking, babe!

Chemo Round #4

November 7, 2013 🌐

The "rough" chemo is over, and Beth has four milder treatments on the horizon. I am thankful for Beth's good health and promising prognosis and for the support and love from family, friends, and strangers. I also appreciate the prayer lists, cards, texts, handmade scarves, and gift cards—not to mention the delicious meals and desserts friends have prepared for our family, and my coworkers who routinely ask how Beth is doing even though few of them have met her.

I am also grateful for a cancer patient who sits near Beth during chemo. He is a soccer-loving Brit, and he struggled to understand why everyone was so excited when Miles, the Broncos mascot, visited.

Perspective is a powerful thing. It makes me appreciate the advances in medical technology and the Rocky Mountain Cancer Center staff for their support, positive attitude, and kindness. Beth's story inspired a coworker's wife to get a mammogram after avoiding it for years. Her mom also had breast cancer.

Make today count, because we all know life has no guarantees. My advice is to do something you have always wanted to do but have been afraid or too busy with life to try. You might fail, or you might not even like the activity or project, but the fact is you took a chance and did it. What are you going to experience in life on this day, this week, or this year? Take a chance and see because I promise it will not disappoint you.

Chemo Round #5

November 27, 2013 🌐

Happy Thanksgiving! We are currently at Rose Emergency Room and Hospital. Beth started her second round of chemo last Friday. It was supposed to be milder, but it has generated more significant muscle aches, pains, and a consistently high fever. After a few days of monitoring and multiple calls to her oncologist, they admitted Beth to the hospital because of her high fever, extremely low blood cell counts, and low neutrophils. She has received multiple IVs and plenty of antibiotics. She is doing well and wants to get back on track. We are unsure if we will be here for one day or two, but we appreciate the offers to help watch the kids and help with the house. Pinky and Papaw Joe are both here and have it covered for now.

As we left the main lobby, a husband and wife who were probably in their fifties asked us for advice about chemo, since his wife was recently diagnosed. We both talked about our fears, side effects, and the reality of it all. We could tell they were nervous, as we were during our first appointment. I gave them a business card and told them to call or email us with questions because countless people have helped us on our journey.

Beth, you are my rock star. You are an inspiration to other people, and you continue to amaze me and others with your positive attitude and sheer toughness. I love you and want to remind you how many people are pulling for you. #stillfighting like hell!

Chemo Round #6

December 11, 2013 🌐

Beth's oncologist prescribed steroids and Benadryl to make this round a little smoother. Joe and Fay stayed with her for most of the session, and I was able to stop by and finish the day with her. I promised myself I would make all eight sessions, even if it were only for a few minutes. Thus far, I am 6 for 6. I feel it is important for her to know she is not alone in this battle.

This was the first session where she finally napped—thank you, Benadryl. We usually talk about life during her treatments, watch a little TV, and play with our phones due to nervous energy. We also look around and smile at the other patients because we all need a pick-me-up now and then.

Beth is gaining strength and is almost "back." I say this because she and I talked the other night and she dropped a hilarious sarcasm bomb on me. We both laughed out loud and almost woke up the kids. She is my fighter, my survivor, and my best friend. Two more treatments to go! January 9 will be a day of celebration in the Tosti house.

My Christmas Wish List

December 2014 🌐

Christmas has always been my favorite holiday for various reasons, but it means a little more this year. Beth and I play that husband-and-wife game where we say we're not buying each other a gift, then end up buying a few small gifts at the last minute and jokingly fight about not abiding by the rule. I have thought a lot about life and how breast cancer has changed our lives in various ways. Here is my Christmas wish list for Beth:

1. Four-leaf clover: I would choose this because Beth was lucky and fortunate to find cancer early thanks to genetic research, her dedicated oncologists, and multiple exams each over the past five years. I have said

it before, but technology and her Aunt Mary Jo saved her life. Grade 3 cancer is overly aggressive and could have grown to other parts of her body, but it did not!

2. Crucifix: The purpose of this gift is to remember our faith. We have friends from every religion praying for her. It sounds simple to tell someone that their family is in your prayers or that you added them to your prayer list at church, but it is powerful and much appreciated. We now make it a point to add someone to our church prayer list to pass on the positive thoughts.

3. Hope: This gift is not tangible, yet it is truly priceless, and it might be the most valuable one. Your positive attitude and calm demeanor from day one of your diagnosis has helped you and our family through every step of this journey. You have inspired people from across the country.

4. Pink ribbon: This gift is to remind you that you are never alone. You have friends, strangers, and family members who are survivors and will always be here for you.

5. A billboard in Times Square: This is to thank the family members, friends, and strangers who have prayed for us, sent tons of cards, brought us dinner, mailed cookies, played with our kids, called to check in, or walked in the Race for the Cure in Beth's honor.

6. A vacation to anywhere you want. We will figure out the details later. Pick a spot, and we are booking it, baby, because you deserve it!

We can never adequately thank all of you for the support we have experienced since July 8, but we will continue to try. We are blessed and will continue to fight this awful disease one day at a time.

Chemo Round #7

December 28, 2013 🌎

Beth finished her next-to-last chemo. Thankfully, it was uneventful, and everything went well. The combination of steroids and Benadryl made it increasingly difficult for her to sleep for a brief period of time. She was a trooper and fought through the fatigue every time. She powered through Christmas morning as the kids woke up at 5:00 a.m. I am continually amazed by her strength and resolve. Fay and I put together Emily's play kitchen, which did not require any decals. Kaden's toys were already assembled; we all lucked out there.

As we approach the final and eighth round of chemo, we are glad that the end is in sight and thankful for the support of our family and friends. Fay (Pinky) is a splendid cook, and luckily, I have not gained fifty pounds, but we appreciate her help with everything. Emily keeps waking up between 5:00 and 6:00 a.m. and asking me to carry her downstairs to sleep with her Pinky. I think Fay might sleep for several weeks when she returns home.

We cannot wait to celebrate with our friends when the chemo is over because whether it is a simple happy hour or a five-course group dinner, this hurdle will be behind us, and we will continue to look ahead and count our blessings. The experience has changed us in various ways, reaffirmed our faith, and brought us closer than we knew was possible.

. . .

Chemo Round #8

January 6, 2014 ⊗

Round #8 is in the books. She is done!

This day meant a little more to us than usual. Beth had her medical port removed. It was a good day and was the official end of chemo. No more needles, poking, or prodding for Beth! Below are some of my random thoughts on the last chemo treatment and our journey.

She did it! On Monday, January 6, Beth completed her eighth and final chemo treatment. Her brother, Jason, joined her, and I was fortunate enough to swing by for the last two hours. After the last infusion, one of the nurses came over to say goodbye and gave her a big hug. It sent chills down my spine and was one of the neatest things I have witnessed in my 39 years. The nurses gathered around her and said, "We want to see you again, just not for an infusion." It is bittersweet because those nurses and doctors become extended family members and offer kindness, support, and inspiration at every turn.

We also saw our friend Joe, who was also finishing his chemo infusion. However, he still has some radiation therapy left, and the tumor in his lung has decreased in size but is still there. I told him we should grab dinner sometime. He mentioned he had not been to Three Lions Pub yet, and he suggested maybe we could catch some soccer there. I am not a hardcore soccer fan, but I will gladly join him to watch some Euro soccer action whenever he calls.

I also encountered an older woman during the last infusion. She stopped me and said, "I can think of a few better places to be than this place right now." I smiled, and before I could even say anything, she replied, "I don't mean it, because this place is the lifesaving chamber." I smiled and told her to keep fighting.

During this journey, I have purposely tried to be respectful with my words even though I want to climb to the highest mountain in this beautiful state and scream, "Take that, cancer! [insert several expletives here] Leave her alone, and never come back!" Cancer has touched almost everyone in this world in some way, shape, or fashion. We currently have another friend in Denver battling breast cancer, and she is in a different stage, but she and Beth have helped each other and will continue to as they fight. Thoughts and prayers go out to Keary Sullivan. You go, girl! You have a *huge* support group, and we will be here for whatever you need.

One thing I noticed throughout this process is how people stare or look at cancer patients with a half-frown of sorts, kind of like, "Uh, I'm sorry, you poor thing." I am not a cancer expert, and I am not rude or negative concerning my thoughts, but the last thing cancer patients need is pity. They need a smile, a high-five or a hug—lots of hugs. I always tried to smile at patients I encountered at the Rocky Mountain Cancer Center because I felt like they wanted to be treated normally.

I cannot say what it feels like to lose your hair, eyelashes, and eyebrows, but I know how it affected Beth. It was not easy, but she dealt with it like a champ every step of the way. She was focused and determined to beat this disease regardless of what it did to her body or mind. It took away her flesh and hair, but it would not break her spirit. She is the strongest person I know, hands down, and that is one of the many reasons why I love her so much.

We are now two weeks past her last chemo treatment, and Beth is trying to gain some clarity. Chemo drugs are still coursing through her veins and will remain in her system for approximately twelve more weeks. However, the tired feeling will stay for a month or longer, according to her doctor. A restful night of sleep is still a challenge, but she can nap easier now, which is good.

We thought we would celebrate after the last chemo treatment (I think a lot of chemo patients have that expectation), but it will take a while longer for Beth to truly regain her strength emotionally and physically. Each day she regains more of her sarcasm and sense of humor. I know she is healing, slowly but surely. We always joke with each other, and it is good to see the genuine happiness return to her eyes and hear a good gut-busting laugh when it is least expected.

It is a tough transition to go from the chemo stage to the finish line. Since July 8, we have fought and thought about cancer every day because it is what you must do, but you do not think about the time it takes your body to heal. After the last treatment, you are exhausted, and you ask, what are we supposed to fight now? It is an odd letdown of sorts: We were going a hundred miles per hour, then suddenly it's as if we have hit the brakes and are inching along. We are thrilled to have this hurdle behind us, but we have learned that cancer is a series of stages, and the next one might be tougher than what you initially thought, but you will not know until you get there. You really must hit pause on life and tackle cancer one stage at a time, knowing it affects everyone differently. It has taught us a lot of essential life lessons.

I want to thank God that he did not need Beth yet because I honestly do not know what I would do without her by my side. In sports terms, she is our family's general manager, and I am the equipment manager.

Since July, the support we received has been nothing short of amazing, and we appreciate the thoughtful cards, inspirational gifts, and prayers. Beth even received gifts and cards regarding her last chemo treatment, which is a true testament to our family and friends.

I also need to thank our families for their support and the sacrifices they made since early August. They made sure we had someone at the house from August 6 through January 15. They helped clean the house, do laundry, cook meals, run the kids to daycare and preschool, and anything else in between. Fay (Pinky) spent three holidays with us: Halloween, Thanksgiving, and Christmas. Speaking of holidays and such, my Mom missed the Kentucky Apple Festival for the first time in thirty-eight years!

The circumstances were awful, but Beth got to spend time with her sister, brother, mom, and dad. Her sister, Stephanie, has three children, which meant she had to find help while visiting Beth for a few days. Jason lives in Bolivia, but fortunately he comes home for a month each year. It was not a simple task for any of them to visit, but I am thankful and glad they could be here for her. It meant the world to us, and I do not think we can ever truly repay them, but we will try.

Kaden and Emily adore Beth. She does countless things for our family; I want to make sure I help our family; however, I can as we move forward as she recovers over time. I am grateful the kids are young enough not to remember all of this, but I hope to explain someday how strongly their mom fought during this ordeal. We have been through hell, but we are stronger for it and grateful she is a survivor! Thank you all for your unbelievable support!

One Year Later: A Look Back at Beth's Battle and Our Perspective

What a crazy year it has been! I dropped off my parents at the airport, which was fitting because both families sacrificed almost a year of their lives to help our little family during this challenging time. Yes, both sets of parents are retired, but they still had to drop everything to fly to Denver and stay with us for long periods. Think about the number of days and months for a moment. It is incredible and a gift we can never repay fully.

Thank you, family, friends, and even strangers who listed Beth on a church prayer list. Beth received many greeting cards, gift cards, and other types of moral support. We are blessed in countless ways, but especially with the top-notch surgeons, oncologists, chemo nurses, and other medical personnel we encountered along the way.

When I told someone about Beth, people often would ask how it changed our outlook on life or comment that it must have provided a surreal reminder of what matters in life. This statement is the absolute truth.

Any medical challenge makes you question everything: your diet, time you spend with your family, hours spent at work, and what you want to do before you die.

It is often said that tomorrow is not guaranteed. We are trying to live life to the fullest and not get caught up in the little things that used to bother us. We take more last-minute mini-vacations. We sit back more often to watch our kids laugh and smile while merely running around the backyard.

Beth has been an inspiration to countless people, and I was lucky enough to have a front-row seat through the good, bad, and hellacious parts of the ride. Her diagnosis spurred friends to get mammograms and discuss plans with their mothers, daughters, and sisters. Beth is an amazing woman, and her strength is simply shocking. If you have women in your life you care about, please take the time to discuss this topic with them. It might save their life.

Our kids have been rock stars from day one, and they endured a bit of frustration from time to time. They are resilient and rolled with all the changes and stressful challenges. I can remember Emily telling our day-care person, "My mommy is sick," in her sweet little two-year-old voice. Kaden asked several good questions about her surgeries and would talk about breast cancer with us as only he could.

On this day, we celebrate the gift of life, and we will not look back nor live in fear of what might happen down the road. We have a long list of things in life we want to do rather than to sit and worry. Whether you were with us where we grew up, during the UK years, or over the past fourteen years in Denver, we thank you for everything.

Life waits for no one. Pick a goal, chase a dream, or climb a mountain to sit and take in the view. Life is not good; it is great!

I loved you with long, curly, and wavy hair.

I loved you when you had the Demi Moore G.I. Jane haircut.

I loved you when you were bald.

I loved you when you wore scarves.

I loved you when your hair slowly started growing back.

I love you with your pixie cut.

I love you now as your hair is getting a lot longer.

At the start of this journey, I told you we were going to fight, and I said that it would be okay, not knowing if it was true or not. I worried sick about losing you but never showed you the fear I felt or talked to you about it because I did not want you to worry about anything else. You already had enough on your plate. Somehow, you went through eight chemo treatments and one unexpected hospital stay and still worked part-time as a bridge engineer!

The cancer experience changed us, and I like to think for the better. Several of our friends know me as a coach because of basketball and baseball, but I enjoyed watching you coach and support other women as they fought their own battle. You are an inspiration to many people. In the past, you always asked me how fundraising worked, and you avoided it all costs. However, things change, and it is not the case anymore. In the past two years, you have established yourself as a remarkably successful fundraiser and an advocate for breast cancer patients and survivors. I am proud of you for all these accomplishments.

Your mind and body have been through hell the past two and a half years, and I know better than anyone the roller coaster of emotions, pain, and stress you have endured. On some level, the petty stuff does not matter because you made it through. As I sometimes tell you at night, I am glad you are still here.

The Power of Pink

It can happen to anyone, any age, straight, gay, religious, atheist, black, or white. Cancer is a gnarly, disgusting, and persistent disease that I hate more than anything. We are winning the battle with technology and research, but there is still plenty of work to be done. In the past year, I lost a friend to lung and brain cancer, but I also cheered for my best friend's dad as he fought and won his battle against cancer and for a dear high school friend who won his incredible fight.

It has been two years since I set foot in a chemo infusion room, yet I will always remember the sterile smell, the chill in the air, and the faces of those brave souls fighting for their lives. I can describe the room with my eyes closed. As you turn the corner, it takes your breath away because you prepare yourself mentally and emotionally for what you are about to see. There is a tall, see-through locker unit that holds the heated blankets for patients. Then you see the leather chairs, typically four to a row, evenly spaced from one another. As at most health-care offices, magazines and books are included at each station.

The last thing you see is the faces of the patients. Two or three are sleeping; some are alone, while others hold a loved one's hand. You do not want to stare, and you do not want to look sad because it is the last thing a cancer patient needs to see during a chemo round. All I wanted to do was high-five and bear-hug every damn one of them.

It is a room filled with men and women of all ages and body types fighting for their lives. The nurses and staff members are absolute saints and continue to exude kindness and a caring demeanor. They are some of the nicest people in the world. A handful of patients are lucky enough to know their visit is temporary, while others are there to receive some level of comfort before the inevitable result. I still think about the room when I am having a bad day because I know I am not in one of those oversized brown recliners, waiting patiently for the combination of anti-nausea drugs to cleanse my body before the chemo drip starts and runs for three or four hours. I hated the room more than anything, but I also appreciated it because it inspired me in ways I cannot explain. It taught me the true meaning of life and what it means to fight for your life.

As we approach October, there will be a spotlight on breast cancer and the color pink. A few people will complain that the pink-ribbon campaign has been over-hyped at the expense of other diseases? Maybe it is true, but, I believe there is an important lesson people are missing with that opinion. Instead of being upset, we should respect the color's power and what it has accomplished for breast cancer. Take a closer look and see what you can do for a cause close to your heart.

Cancer is cancer, and other types deserve as much attention as breast cancer. Become a champion and talk about other causes passionately with your friends, help raise money, or host a fundraiser with your neighbors.

When I see pink, I think of how it supports breast cancer survivors everywhere. Pink stands for survivors. Beautiful, bald women. It also provides hope and support from a sisterhood that you cannot comprehend until you are in the moment. The color means fighting like hell as a team to beat breast cancer.

Beth is one of the lucky ones. I am thankful that she is still here to put up with me and that we can continue to enjoy life together. I have tried to explain to people how cancer affects not just the patient but the entire family. I admit I sometimes struggle emotionally with daily life because once you fight cancer, it is difficult to look at life's trials as anything more than trivial details.

Here are a few things you can do during October to promote breast cancer awareness:

Send a card to a cancer survivor to let them know you are thinking about them, or bake a dessert for chemo nurses, patients, or their family members.

Talk about the importance of early detection with a friend or relative. Conduct a self-exam and schedule the mammogram you have been postponing for whatever reason.

I always tell people who are battling any cancer one important thing to remember. It is okay to have a bad day, but do not let yourself have an awful week. Stay positive, rest as much as possible, keep fighting with everything you have, and then fight some more.

To those who have lost their battle with cancer, we remember you. To those currently fighting, we stand by you as others did for our family. For those who will receive a life-altering diagnosis in the future, we will be here to support you, along with friends, family, and people you do not even know. I promise this much: Team Tosti will fight with you until there is a cure.

Cancerversary

July 8, 2019 🌐

It is often said that time heals all wounds. In the cancer community, this rings true for the lucky ones. The term *cancerversary* is a powerful and complicated word, but its meaning is filled with a tremendous amount of appreciation and gratefulness. There are no rules on when or how one should celebrate this life-changing date. Some mark the anniversary of the day they were diagnosed with the disease, while others focus on the surgery date when the cancer was removed from the body. Having a cancerversary is one of the most important goals for the individual battling the disease because it provides a sense of hope and a bit of relief. The five-year mark is a crucial day because that is the point when a doctor can claim that the patient is cancer-free.

We know it is not a guarantee. We cautiously acknowledged the one-year milestone with love, humility, and a touch of kick-ass attitude. Cancer can always rear its ugly head again, but we will take a day to appreciate life for now. I always joked we could not use the F word (free) until this day. I can also think of a few other choice F words I would like to use, but my mom and Fay might read this section. To be safe, I will keep it family-friendly.

Cancer changed our lives in a lot of ways. It brought us closer and drove us apart, reminded us to count our blessings while testing our faith. The journey reminded us to appreciate the little things in life and to be thankful for the brave women and men who walked this path before Beth did.

Cancer left behind physical scars and some emotional ones too, but it revealed multiple levels of courage we did not know we possessed. It changed the way we make decisions but also gave us the confidence to not live in fear. We no longer put off family vacations. It showed us the true meaning of family and friends and restored our faith in humanity. It also:

Reminded us why we were lucky to grow up where we did (special thanks to Beth's high school friends "The Pink Ladies" and to all my childhood friends from home).

Helped us to hug our friends for no reason and to tell them what they mean to us often.

Redefined what strength meant and looked like.

Ramped up an existing positive attitude.

Inspired us to pass good vibes along and send inspirational cards to anyone who is battling cancer, whether or not we know them.

The experience turned Beth into a rock-star fundraiser and cancer coach for other women. We learned that not all superheroes wear capes; some of them are Mary Jo Kennelly, Fay Obergfell, Linda Tosti, chemo nurses, and other survivors.

Emotionally, I covered all the bases. I cussed, cried, prayed, smiled, laughed, and punched the air a few times for good measure. I thought about those we have lost to this cowardly disease, those currently fighting, and those who will receive an ill-fated call someday.

Fortunately, Beth won her battle and fought cancer with pure guts and sheer determination. She somehow worked part-time through eight chemo treatments and exhibited grace and dignity with long curly hair, a pixie cut, a Demi Moore G.I. Jane hairdo, and the Mr. Clean bald look.

When Beth was diagnosed with cancer, the first few people who offered to fly to Denver to help our family were from my hometown, which says a lot. Think about it for a second. These friends, who I only see once in a decade, offered to spend their hard-earned money and vacation time to help us. As long as I live, I will never forget their generosity and goodwill. Thank you, Kristi Davis, Missy Osborne, Sabrina Rader, and Rob King.

Rob is from West Virginia and is an old friend from my Finish Line days. He has a heart of gold and might be one of the best salespeople I have ever worked with. We used to sell sneakers, and now he works for Mercedes-Benz and routinely wins sales competitions.

As Beth battled breast cancer, my mom and Beth's mom, Fay Obergfell, rotated every five to six weeks to ensure we were never alone, even though several friends repeatedly offered to fly out and help. Unfortunately, Fay missed her anniversary and spent the first Christmas away from Joe in probably forty-five or more years of marriage. Again, thank you from the bottom of my heart. It was a genuine display of unselfishness and unconditional love.

Fay, I also appreciate our Boggle battles because I think your vocabulary rivals John Bjorkquist's brainpower. My record against you is 2–100, but I still relish the challenge. To our moms; I promise there are not enough words in a dictionary or a bouquet large enough ever to properly thank the two of you.

The picture included above was one I took for our family to remember and reflect upon in another five years. The image was simple but powerful: four hands with five fingers interlocked with another, representing our family Team Tosti, (as our neighbor Mindy Alexander referred to us) and our journey the past five years. We fought as a family, and we promise to continue to fight like hell for Beth and anyone else who encounters this stupid-ass disease.

A Courageous Decision

Cancer is weak because it does not care if you are young, old, a teenager, successful, or famous. It can attack with reckless abandon and usually does. However, cancer also evokes powerful emotions and inspirational words such as *character* and *courage*. A few lucky individuals have the option to beat cancer before it can invade the body. Medical technology and decades of research are finally starting to pay dividends for a few brave women.

One of Beth's younger cousins opted to undergo a preventative bilateral mastectomy. She has the BRCA gene mutation, just like Beth, her Aunt Mary Jo, and Mary Jo's daughter. The BRCA1 gene mutation runs in the Obergfell side of the family. Thanks to one woman's courage and powerful decision, the emotional stress of having the gene mutation and a high probability of a cancer diagnosis can now be suppressed by fighting cancer before it even appears on an MRI or a medical chart.

I have tried to express my sincere and deep heartfelt appreciation for Aunt Mary Jo, but I feel as if I need to do it again because her courageous decision to pay for genetic testing saved many lives. Take a second and think about the power of the previous sentence. It's not every day that we play a part in saving another person's life. Mary Jo did it the day she scheduled her genetic testing appointment. Mary Jo Kennelly, you are and will always be an inspiration and a hero in my eyes.

Her choice continues to impact others' lives because it provides family members with knowledge and power. Our children and future generations who possess the gene mutation can now grow up with confidence and courage when discussing their options to stymie this disease from wreaking havoc on their bodies. This gives the women affected the option of preventative mastectomy, a courageous yet intensely personal and challenging decision. Now, women can stand up and fight cancer before it has a chance even to start. Advances in technology have allowed us the opportunity to beat some forms of cancer, including breast cancer, hopefully. This leg up is a game-changer for a variety of reasons for individuals who choose this option.

This powerful decision means no chemo ward visits, no hair loss, no weight loss, no nausea. Yes, the dizzying acronyms, medical statistics, and checkups will still be in play, but they become a positive thing to focus on and deal with after this proactive decision. It does not guarantee cancer will not strike or return, but it drastically reduces the chance of a breast cancer diagnosis from 80% to less than 8% in some cases. The numbers alone provide a sense of reassurance and help reduce the anxiety of when or where cancer will rear its ugly head.

This is my T-shirt that I wear at breast cancer events.

It takes a lot of courage to choose this option, but the most important by-product is what it provides for the individual and the family, which is *hope*.

This chapter is dedicated to my Aunt Betty Tosti, who ran out of time battling lung cancer. She was a nurse who enjoyed the beach and loved animals. We stayed with Aunt Betty and Uncle Louie when we drove to Las Vegas to see Garth Brooks (our favorite musician) play an acoustic concert at the Wynn Resort. They moved back to Kentucky a few years later, and we stopped by their farm a few times with our kiddos. She was one of the few individuals who could match my Uncle Louie's sarcasm, which is saying a lot.

Special Thanks to Friends

2015 🌐

Sabrina Rader

During Beth's battle, I had a boss who seemed to think work was more important than what Beth was going through. Let's just say there was some behavior that I felt was immature and disrespectful. But I could take that. I could take the chemo infusions, the doctor visits, and lab test update voicemails. I could even handle watching my best friend drop twenty-five pounds, lose her hair, and endure the other body changes cancer patients experience during treatment. What I could not handle was the twenty-minute commute to and from work. This was when I was most vulnerable and often broke down. Thankfully, I had a few friends I could call out of the blue and talk to during the drive to keep my sanity. These individuals included Adam Germek, Nate Baldwin, Missy Myers, and Sabrina Rader. They all knew why I was calling and were there to let me cry, vent, or simply stammer for a minute. Sabrina and I ended up talking almost daily, and she was her usual calm and reassuring self, but she always kept our talks real and did not mince words. I needed some support and a lot more.

MISSY MYERS

When Beth was diagnosed with breast cancer, Missy was one of the first two friends to call and offer to fly out to help with the kids and be here for us in whatever capacity we needed. It was such a generous offer and a heartfelt one. I appreciated her generosity and concern. We talked about dates and times but ultimately focused on consistency and stability of having the grandparents staying with us instead of a revolving door of people the kids did not know.

In some ways, I am glad Missy did not make the trip because it would have been hard to not collapse in her arms and cry like a baby. It was a stressful time, and understandably it would have been a businesslike visit with a close friend, not a fun one. We talked on the phone a lot, and she was there for me when I needed to battle my fears during my daily commute. When my little family needed moral support, Kristi Davis and Missy Myers were the original people from home to call with an offer to fly to Denver to support Beth and our family.

STEVE BELCHER

Steve and I chat often late at night on Facebook, and when Beth was diagnosed with breast cancer, he stepped up to check on her regularly, not just whenever it was convenient for him. He has seen cancer at its worst and knows the empty feeling when someone runs out of time battling the dreaded disease. A few weeks before Beth lost her hair, I asked a few buddies if they wanted to shave their heads to support her. A few of them did, and I am grateful for the support, but Steve went one step further. He posted a photo of himself getting his head shaved. It is a memorable cancer-related photo and for good reason. I often tell cancer patients the disease does not fight fair; you need modern technology, guts, determination, humor, tears, and every bit of positive energy you can muster.

The photo was simple yet powerful and packed a punch. Steve was not smiling in it. He was solemn, mad, and supporting a friend. He made a handmade sign for Beth and held it up, along with his middle finger.

Chapter Six

Xs and Os—The Power of Sports, Coaching, and Fitness

Coaches who share part of our path teach us the skills required, strategy, and the important reminder of what it means to compete every day. We do not realize it, but they are also instilling a love for the game that remains with us long after the days of orange slices, sunflower seeds, and Gatorade.

This chapter combines my personal experiences as a youth basketball and baseball coach as well as my journey to a healthier lifestyle focused on fitness. I coached for eleven years and documented the seasons when I coached our son and daughter. It was a simple way to share with out-of-state family members and reminded me to enjoy the lighter side of sports.

The section is filled with anecdotes, quips, and quick hitters from my experiences and stories from teams and kids that inspired the tales. It might read like a highlight reel or even appear a little fragmented in sections, but that is by design and how the material was initially written.

Sports have been a part of my life since I was a six-year-old kid playing T-ball. I was one of the fastest kids. I played pitcher's mound. It only took one errant throw into the creek for me to realize it was more comfortable, not to mention safer, to field grounders and chase down the batter before he reached first base. Basketball is still my favorite sport, and I was lucky enough to coach youth basketball for over 11 years. I have included a few stories and highlights from those years, including five years of coaching our son, Kaden.

I spent close to seventeen years of my life working in the sports industry from a career perspective. It was a roller coaster ride with more exhilarating hills than frightening loops, but with each corkscrew and stomach-dropping turn, I learned something new, and it all played a huge part in how I view a job and life in general.

Name That Team

November 2014 🌐

Any parent knows that kids are unpredictable, sometimes adorable, but always hilarious. Their little minds are filled with scattered thoughts and rapid-fire type questions. Puppy dogs or a new toy brings a smile to a child's face, but I would add one more item that elicits pure joy. That is the opportunity to name their basketball or baseball team. It provides the kids with a chance to be part of something bigger than themselves because each player expresses an opinion and have their voice heard. I think this is a simple and powerful lesson for every team I coach. I always let the players choose our team name, within reason. As you will see, it makes a difference on and off the court.

One common theme is to use the coach's last name as part of the team name. A unique name like Tosti lends itself to plenty of creative options. I lost count of the nicknames I had as a kid in elementary school and even high school. The most common one seemed to have a variety of Toast in it. Toasty or Toaster was probably the most common ones. When I agreed to coach a YMCA team of kindergarten kiddos, that nickname resurfaced, and I fully embraced it.

One of the parents called us the Toasters because of my last name, and the kids liked it, but they also like their Denver Nuggets. Our team name is now the "Nugget Toasters." Maybe we should play all our basketball games at 8:00 a.m. The kids made almost everything they threw at the basket this morning. Last week we attempted forty shots and scored ten points. The YMCA does not keep score, but the kids pay attention and let me know the score every time. It is a lot of fun coaching these little guys. I let them pick our team name, which might have been a mistake in retrospect.

The kids are having a blast and improving a little each week. You must appreciate the minds of five- and six-year-olds! The boys are 3–0 now and will be dangerous if they convert the elusive 3' to 4' put-back or jumper.

Final Game

December 2014

We concluded the Nugget Toasters' basketball season with a 7–1 record, and I am honored to coach these young men. We started slowly and found ourselves down 14–4, which remained until late in the second half. Every substitution break, and at halftime, I kept telling them we only needed to score a few quick baskets. These kids are smart and always tell me the score. In this case, they knew we were down a significant amount.

The next thing you know, we started playing great defense, and the shots started falling, including Kaden's jump shot from near the free-throw line! The smile on his face and the double fist-pump when he headed back down the court are etched in my memory. According to the kids, we won 18–17, but I told Kaden that I am still proud of them for not giving up and playing hard the entire game even if we lost.

These young kids are a special group. They started pre-K together and have since played soccer, T-ball, and basketball. The parents are great people, which makes my job as a coach that much easier. You do not realize how much energy ten kindergarteners have until you give each of them a basketball and ask them to listen to you. It has been fun to watch these kids improve in eight short weeks. Until next season . . .

Purple Sea Monsters T-Ball

August 2015 ◉

Another season of coaching T-ball is in the books. I love coaching this little guy, Kaden. The Purple Sea Monsters finished strong with everyone hitting well and fielding every grounder cleanly except the rocket line drive because it shot through the gap. Plus, we caught our first pop-up in the field. It was such a great way to end the season, not to mention the other team's coach and parents were first class. They cheered for our team, encouraged our boys on missed swings, and clapped for good hits.

I only played one year of Little League Baseball, but I have always had a knack for explaining sports fundamentals on a kid's level. Baseball is a little slower than other sports, and T-ball's pace can be snail-like. However, once a player hits one to the outfield, pure chaos breaks out as all nine players have this unrelenting urge to sprint to the outfield and retrieve the ball—even the first baseman, even though it was hit to deep left field.

In this scenario, I knew I had to simplify our strategy and the goal. Here is what I came up with, and you can use it if you help your son or daughter's T-ball team. If they hit the ball over a player's head, that player runs to the outfield to catch the first relay throw. Then, he or she can throw it to the infield. I called it our relay line, and it worked well. Plus, it prepares the kids for the importance of getting the baseball back as quickly as possible.

As the kids get older and the games become more serious, this type of positive coaching behavior will fade, but for now, it is merely a bunch of smiling kids learning the importance of teamwork and how to play a game the right way. I hope they never forget the lesson.

Pitch and Catch: A Story About Life, Leadership, and Parenting

May 2018 ❸

After a short hiatus, Kaden played baseball again. He joined a local team, the Raging Carrots. He has not played baseball in three years, but he still has a great arm. His coach asked him if he would try pitching because, at this age, it is challenging to find multiple kids who can throw straight, not to mention the safety rules created to track pitch counts for each player.

My close friends know baseball was never my sport. I had *zero* advice to offer Kaden about technique as he prepared for his pitching debut. The one piece of advice I gave him was to pitch like you play hoops: with no emotion. If you walk the first batter you face, show no emotion. If you strike someone out, show no emotion. If you hit a kid with a wild pitch, nod your head at him and apologize to ensure he knows it was an accident. Whatever you do, keep throwing the ball nice and easy over the plate and hustle to the dugout when the inning is over.

A few days before the game, I reached out to my mentor, Rick Hatcher, who pitched for Florida State University and played for the Durham Bulls minor league team for a few seasons. In 1982, he threw a perfect game with eighty-one pitches, and only two balls made it to the outfield. Impressive stats, and it was such a monumental accomplishment! Hatch, thanks again for always being there for me in both my personal life and my career.

I asked him for some pitching drills and general advice because he was an assistant coach for powerhouse NCAA baseball programs such as Georgia Tech, Tennessee, and Miami. He knows a few things about the position. Within a few hours, I received five or six pages of drills and advice for young pitchers.

Later, I went to tuck Kaden in and kiss him goodnight. He always reads a book before bedtime, but this night was different. The book was on the nightstand, and he had Rick's notes spread out across the bed, intently focused on each page, absorbing as much knowledge as he could.

Now back to the game, as the commentator might say. Kaden was the second pitcher to enter the contest. His teammate, who started the game, is nine years old, over five feet tall, and probably weighs 110 pounds. He struck out the side multiple times with ease, and immediately Beth and I started to worry because Kaden had to follow him.

Kaden started slowly with a few high balls over the plate but a bit out of the strike zone. He walked the first batter on four consecutive pitches. In my mind, I kept saying, *No emotion. Come on, K, don't worry about it.* He walked another batter, then struck out one. *Okay, we are in a suitable spot now.* Mom and Dad breathed a vast sigh of relief. K's team was up 14–1 at this point. There was no pressure regarding the score.

The next batter stepped up and drew a walk, followed by another and then another. I made sure not to cheer too loudly because I knew it would not help Kaden's nerves. As I was pacing back and forth, I quietly murmured my coach-speak: "You got this, keep throwing it over the middle, nice and easy."

Then something cool unexpectedly happened, and I am glad it did. Jacob, the catcher, called time, slid his mask over his fresh buzz cut, and jogged to the mound like a major leaguer. He was worried about Kaden and wanted to calm his nerves and reassure him. This is a Little League game, mind you. As the reader, you must know Jacob would weigh forty pounds soaking wet with a ten-pound weight around his neck, but the kid plays catcher with guts and intensity like a gritty veteran. He lives and breathes the position, and it shows. Someday Jacob is going to be an outstanding leader.

This simple yet common act had this dad and old hoops coach choked up and inspired at the same time. Jacob did not have to do it, but he reminded Kaden how to be a great teammate and how you show someone you have their back. It was one of those important life lessons I will remember for years, and I hope Kaden does too. Kaden stayed in the game, walked a few more batters, and struck out two more. I am happy for him for not showing any nerves, even though he was on an island by himself on the mound. I am grateful for Jacob's actions because he reminded Kaden, the Raging Carrots, and the parents of an important lesson. When life gets tough, you keep pitching, knowing someone always has your back.

Culture & Class: A Lesson or Two from the Hollers and Mountains of Eastern Kentucky

December 5, 2019 🌐

My hometown has two schools: a city one and a county one. The schools are heated rivals on and off the field, separated by a shallow creek. The Paintsville Tigers' colors are blue and white, and Johnson Central's colors are black and gold. As a young kid, you root for one or the other, period. Nothing changes until you graduate, and then you become best friends with your neighbors from across the creek you "hated" for years. You quickly realize your rival faced the same fears you did. They, too, dealt with bullies, bad cafeteria food, and kids with nicer clothes than you.

Even though I left the town twenty-five years ago, I try to follow the Tigers' academic and athletic news. The kids do not always hear or see our support from various cities across the country, but I hope they know their fan base stretches far and wide. We bleed blue, whether we are twenty-five years old or forty-five! Both schools excel in academics and athletics, which is impressive and should be acknowledged. PHS has had outstanding success with a few recent graduating classes where one hundred percent of the kids attended college, and JCHS has won countless academic championships over the past few years.

Both football teams were on the doorstep of making history after a string of multiple successful seasons. I know neither of the head coaches, but from what I have gathered and heard from family and friends, both men are not only great football minds but even better men off the field. To the coaches, I would like to say thank you for what you have done and continue to do for each school.

My beloved Tigers faced their rival Pikeville on Friday afternoon. The Panthers have been a powerhouse football program for what seems like a hundred years. My dad graduated from Pikeville High School and taught special education there for a couple of years. I have other relatives who were teachers and administrators at Pikeville High for decades. I was born in the town and spent the first five years of my life there; thus, the city has a special place in my heart. I still have relatives in Pikeville, and we never get enough time together when I am home, but we make the best of it.

In the late '80s and maybe early '90s, Pikeville routinely placed players on the All-State team. It seemed like they were always vying for a state title. Individual awards can be useful but also detrimental to a team's psyche. I remember my dad telling me the head coach would send an assistant coach to the hotel lobby to buy all the newspapers the morning of the championship game. They did this to prevent the players from learning who won what award, ensuring the team would remain focused on the title game. That story about the power of team dynamics has stuck with me.

One of my best friends from high school is the athletic director and head coach for girls' basketball at Pikeville High School. Kristy Orem knows a few things about building a program and instilling a positive, you-can-do-anything culture for young women. She did it for years at Fleming County and continues to work hard for the Panther family.

Kristy took her squad to the Sweet Sixteen last year, and I would bet the farm she does it again this year. She already knows I root for her Panthers every game unless they play our alma mater. Sure, she wins games, but she also prepares these young ladies for bright futures off the court. I hope the Panther fans know how lucky they are to have her pacing the sidelines in her trademark high heels.

Kristy's football coach has continued the winning ways of Panther football and is returning to the Kentucky Class A championship game for the second year in a row. The Pikeville Panthers won in a blowout, and I sent my buddy Kristy a note and was glad that both teams played hard and dodged any severe injuries.

A note about culture: Building a culture is one of the hardest things to do in this world. It is one of those things you cannot touch, but you feel it, and everyone on the outside sees it. A winning culture takes time, an unwavering positive attitude, old-fashioned discipline, and hard work. It also is one of the things I cherish and respect the most.

It starts before the first early-morning practice in the dog days of summer. The coach sets the tone and tries his or her best to establish the foundation of his program. Sometimes these principles and quotes end up on locker room walls, while other times they are shared and embraced by the student body, parents, and fans. Players buy in over time, and then the mental strength carries over to other areas, and success is expected and not surprising any longer.

The great coaches always receive well-deserved accolades and admiration from fans, but one of the essential life lessons they can instill in their players is what it means to exude class. Games are won and lost; refs make good and bad calls. How you carry yourself on and off the field means something. I stress the importance of winning and losing with class to my kids every chance I get, and I do the same when I coach youth sports.

I love my hometown Tigers, but I gladly cheered for the Golden Eagles to bring home the 4A hardware. A creek divides us, but the hills and hollers bring us together.

A Race to Tri

September 2019 🌐

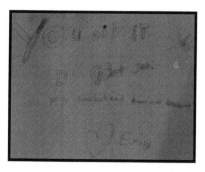 

Some people have bucket lists full of wild dreams and outrageous goals, and I am no different. Thanks to two years of Orangetheory Fitness classes, I decided that my body was in decent enough shape to train for a sprint triathlon, which has been an unmarked box on my checklist for twenty years. After I turned forty-six in April, I began researching training programs. I invested a lot of time, energy, and effort during the seven-week training program.

It was also a lot of alone time. I took photos along the way to document the different sides of the training process; some of them are included below. The orange highlighter is symbolic because Jane has been fighting kidney cancer like a damn boss with Chris by her side, along with both families and a wonderful neighborhood.

A triathlon comprises three segments: swimming, biking, and running. The distance of the race varies. The training schedule was straightforward and easy to follow. It looked like this:

Monday: Rest

Tuesday: Swim

Wednesday: Run

Thursday: Bike

Friday: Rest

Saturday: Swim

Sunday: Brick workout (bike, then immediately transition to a run)

Leg 1 of 3: Swim 750 meters (50 meters short of half a mile)

The swimming portion is typically the weakest leg for everyone, including yours truly. The first night I jumped in the pool and took off flailing like I was on fire. A few seconds later, as I was gasping for air, I looked for the end of the pool and realized I was not even halfway across!

A few things happened. I am sure I created a few new cuss words and thought Michael Phelps is not human. I slowed down and finished a few more practice laps before calling it a night. I left the pool shaking my head, wondering if I would ever swim half a mile when I was starting off barely able to swim half a lap. *What was I thinking? Have I lost my mind? I am forty-five years old; why am I trying this now?*

Soon after this experience, I reached out to some friends who swam in high school and college and currently work for US Swimming. I was eager to better understand the proper swimming technique and ensure I could get stronger and improve my swimming in six short weeks. A huge thanks to Eric Lazzari, Peggy (Bowersox) Garcia, and Tim Hinchey III for their advice and encouraging words! I also need to thank my friend Eli Madden, who helped train me for a few days and always encouraged me throughout my training. He and I have known each other for a decade. I still support him with career advice, but it was his turn to be the coach.

The other issue I encountered while swimming was that I would lose count of my laps. I brought a stack of quarters each night and move them a few inches from the left to the right side of the pool's concrete edge. This worked fine for a few weeks, but one night I did not want to swim at all, and I needed some extra motivation. On a piece of paper, I wrote the names of people who had asked me about my training and those of several people who inspire me for other reasons.

Next was good ol' Google. I spent hours reading about open water breathing, first-time triathlon experiences, and proper swim techniques. I watched what felt like thirty videos from around the world until I settled on a few I liked.

Finally, I knew I had to get at least two open water (lake) swims under my belt. The first piece of advice I heard about swimming in a wetsuit was to fill the suit with water. In my anxiousness to get going, I forgot to put water inside my wetsuit. I swam about sixty percent of the route and could not breathe. Imagine wearing a kid-sized Under Armour compression bodysuit with a fifty-pound kettlebell on your chest. My rookie mistake, combined with the enormous body of water, got the best of me. I calmly motioned to the lifeguard in her kayak and told her I was okay, and I could swim to her, but I needed to take a break.

I went home sad and dealt with a high level of anxiety for a week, but I knew I had to get back in the water. The following week, I told Beth I had to drive forty-five minutes north on a weeknight *again to* practice my lake swim.

The second time around went much better. I threw lots of water in my wetsuit for starters, which enabled me to breathe while I swam. I planned to swim one lap, which would be half the race's distance. I completed the first lap and was contemplating leaving the water since I had accomplished my mission, and, mentally, I felt a hundred times better. However, someone upstairs was looking out for me and placed someone in the water with me this night.

As I was getting dressed on the beach, I met an older gentleman who talked to me about triathlons, what to expect on race day, and how to maneuver in the water when there are 150 people around you.

Fred was his name. He was such a nice guy, and so supportive. After my first lap, he checked on me to see how I felt. I told him I was ready to go now. He told me to take another lap so I knew I could do it on race day. I took his advice, and he was right. The second lap was better than the first, and my confidence continued to rise.

As I was leaving, I thanked him multiple times and told him I would be sure to pay it forward and that I owed him a beer. I left the beach, ran to my car—still smiling about my practice swim—and left Fred a note and $5 for a beer.

Leg 2 of 3: Bike 13 Miles

The bike portion of the race was relatively flat and on paved roads. I started training on my mountain bike because it is what I had, and I figured it would not matter much because I would only be riding for thirty to seventy-five minutes. Plus, I could not spend $500+ on a new road bike.

Then one of my gracious neighbors asked me if I was training for a race, and I said, yes, a sprint triathlon. Little did I know, Michael Bohn had raced triathlons in the past and offered to let me borrow his road bike for training and the event itself. I knew road bikes were lighter and faster, but this was like going from my 1986 high school Buick Skyhawk to a 2019 Ferrari.

Michael went above and beyond: He took the bike in for a tune-up, telling me he wanted me to kick ass and fly on race day. Also, he shared pointers and race-day stories with me. Thank you again, Mike.

On the road bike, I felt as if I had hit every hyperspeed turbo arrow on Super Mario Kart. On my first few rides, I flew. My speed increased while my total ride time decreased. The difference amazed me; I knew it would be a game-changer. It took me back to my childhood days of bike riding everywhere I needed to go.

Leg 3 of 3: Run 5K/3.1 miles

I started running in eighth grade and fell in love with it. I ran cross-country and track for five years. I stopped running a decade ago, but I felt confident about this part of the race. However, running a road race differs from running a road race after swimming half a mile and biking thirteen miles.

The brick workout is designed to replicate and prepare your body to transition from the bike to the run. It is aptly named because your legs are numb and feel like bricks for the first half-mile or more of the run. Each Sunday, I practiced my brick workouts and gradually added distance and time to each portion.

After almost seven weeks of training and a strict diet, I was ready to race. I went to bed at 10:00 p.m. only to wake up at midnight. I was unable to fall back asleep until 2:30. I tossed, turned, and recounted my life's key experiences and some trivial ones, such as whether I still owed someone from fifth grade $2.

I set six alarms on my iPhone and had no problem jumping out of bed at 5:00 a.m. Race day had finally arrived! I felt comfortable pre-race, and hanging out in the water put me at ease. I was in the twelfth heat out of fourteen. We had to wait approximately thirty minutes to start, which was nerve-wracking, but I fared ok.

I started nice and slow with my swim, trying my best to relax and remember all the advice and techniques I had studied for hours. I stayed to the far right and let everyone go ahead of me. However, I still got off course and had to swim back to circle the buoy correctly. They call this *sighting*, and I swear to swim in a straight line toward a gigantic buoy in open water felt more like Lucy pulling the football away from Charlie Brown.

I used every swim stroke I remembered from Boy Scouts and flipped over on my back and swam like hell for most of the race because I could not get my heart rate to slow down. I rounded the last buoy and then knew I was going to make it.

I have always said the best feeling in the world is witnessing the birth of your children. I can now say the second-best feeling is the point during the swim portion of a triathlon when your feet can touch the bottom of the lake. I pumped my arms and slapped the water as I exited and headed to the transition area. I think I finally breathed and let my body slow down, because it took me eight minutes to change and get on the bike. I neither knew nor cared about my time because I was so relieved to be out of the water.

The bike ride was superb and my best part of the race. I passed several people and felt great. I am sure my caffeine-infused energy gel had something to do with it, though. The scenery was sunny countryside with the mountain range in the background. I wish I could have stopped to take a photo because it was genuinely breathtaking. My second transition was much smoother and faster than the first, and it took me only two or three minutes to park my bike and make my way to the run portion.

Then it was 3.1 miles to finish the race. I took off way too fast and reminded myself I still had thirty minutes of running ahead of me. I encouraged anyone who seemed to struggle because each one of them deserved to finish. I also took the advice of a business friend who has completed several triathlons: He told me to smile a lot and thank the volunteers along the course.

I turned the last corner and could hear the cheers. I saw my buddy Eli and my family encouraging me as I neared the finish line. To my family, I know I missed a few dinners and one gymnastics night, and I even made you go to the South Park pool with me when we went to the cabin for a Labor Day getaway, but I appreciated the support and patience more than you will ever know. I promise to make it up to you. Beth, thanks for letting me chase a dream while you held down the fort, and God knows what else. I appreciate your patience and support!

To Kaden and Emily, you each get to pick an activity to do with Dad. Thanks for making the homemade signs on race day because I needed the support! Thank you to some of our encouraging neighbors who asked me daily what was next on the training docket, picked me up when I doubted myself, and attempted to help me with bike parts. Thanks to the neighbors on "Sac 2" who enthusiastically yelled and clapped as I rode by during one of my brick workouts.

Maybe my story will help encourage someone to try something new; perhaps they will add a bucket list item or, better yet, cross one thing off.

Maybe it will provide a confidence boost to someone who wants to get in shape but has not tried to for whatever reason. Maybe an experience will open a door with a neighbor, and you will find that you have more in common than you thought.

To all my friends: I hope you chase a dream or do something that scares the hell out of you. Just know, without a doubt, your family and friends will have your back, including me. None of us knows when we will cross the proverbial finish line of life, which is why I jumped in a lake for a swim, rode like the wind, and ran down one of my dreams.

My swim lap counting sheet.

*Me finishing the swim portion with a
triumphant arm raised in the air.*

My triathlon coach and good friend, Eli Madden (left).

Time for the bike portion!

Me and Beth at the finish line.

Orangetheory Fitness: The Ultimate Game-Changer

July 2018 🌐

Per neighborhood tradition, we attended our school's fundraising event with a bunch of our crazy and wonderful neighbors. I was decked out in my Randy "Macho Man" Savage wrestling costume because it was an '80s-themed event. We covered our bases with Ferris Bueller characters, tons of neon, Flashdance, and a vintage MTV shirt with a perfect mullet wig. As with most fundraisers, there was a silent auction. I am a sucker for these and usually come home with something, even if it is insignificant.

Most of the time, I bid on items I want, but the money will help a great cause, making the prize irrelevant. One time I came home with a soccer jersey autographed by an English Premier League team I have never watched and probably never will. I could not name one player, let alone their mascot or what city they play in. Beth teased me and said, "You don't even like soccer." I responded, "It was for Tatum, and I wasn't walking out of his fundraiser empty-handed!" If you ever doubt my respect for our friendship, Tatum, look no further than the Tottenham Hotspur soccer jersey with many signatures and names we do not know.

This night was similar, except I won a thirty-day membership to Orangetheory Fitness. The certificate was valid for eight classes and valued at $100. I think I won the bid at $50. My thought was I would try a few classes to see what the hype was about because, as a marketing guy, I always appreciate a solid marketing campaign. Plus, several friends had routinely praised this fitness studio and how great a full-body workout it was for one hour.

As someone who struggles with ADD, it is no surprise I am continually moving or walking around at all hours of the day. It is part of my nature, and it always has been. I bought a Fitbit and loved the daily challenge of getting my steps in. I figured if I am not running or going to the gym, I need to walk 10,000 to 12,000 steps a day and watch what I eat. Thanks to the Fitbit, I now exercise daily to burn or walk off my ADD meds.

I went to my first Orangetheory Fitness (OTF) class with a combination of fear and a bit of excitement. We worked through a typical 60-minute workout, which felt like five hours of pure hell. We worked on muscles I did not know existed, and I took four ibuprofen tablets and hot baths for the following three days. On the treadmill portion, I wondered if I should update my will, call Beth to make sure she knows my passwords, and let Tatum know he can have the beer in our fridge and the goofy soccer jersey in case I keeled over in the studio. Thankfully, nothing happened, and I kept showing up, like thousands of members across the country.

Everyone told me the first few classes are the toughest, and it gets easier. It is only a one- hour workout; how hard can it be? *Yeah, right,* I thought to myself as I slumped over on the floor, trying to move my wobbly Jell-O legs. Picture Jim Carrey in the second Ace Ventura movie when he has spears in both legs. Now, add ten spears, two matches, and some gasoline.

Then something changed. I went to a fourth class, then a fifth. I started sleeping better, my arms were not as sore, and I could see an overall difference in my body. I renewed for two months, thinking I would tire of it after the initial excitement wore off and return to my normal lifestyle.

A funny thing happened, though. My body stopped hurting after every class. Well, it only hurt on certain power days, but my body started craving the workouts if I skipped five or six days. The workout is called high-intensity and heart-rate-based interval training for a reason. I also met some fantastic people, and the coaches treat you like family.

A certified coach leads each class, and he or she ensures everyone is safely progressing through the workout and positively pushing you. Yes, a few of them look like NFL linebackers, but others are like the rest of us. The upbeat music helps, and I feel as if I can run forever when Van Halen or AC/DC comes on, and they set the treadmill at some ungodly incline, and I have already burned 800 calories. In one class, the coach played some playlist with some great '90s tunes and one crappy Backstreet Boys song. I did not know if I should stop the treadmill and hit fast-forward on his iPhone or run faster in hopes the music would end soon.

The neat part for me is the fact that each member is burning calories for a different reason. Someone said they had dropped weight over time and can now fit their wedding dress. Another member wanted to improve their cardio fitness, while another was training for an adventure race. Initially, I thought it might be like a country-club environment, but it is quite the opposite. It is a genuinely inspirational culture intentionally designed to support everyone regardless of shape, size, or fitness ability. Besides, no one takes offense when a stranger running or rowing faster than you smiles at you and tells you to keep going even though your mind tells you differently. It is an outstanding class if you ask me, and I always leave exhausted yet renewed. It is only one hour, but it might be the best hour of my day.

I am now in my fifth month of membership, and I hope to continue burning calories one hour and one class at a time. I have burned 27,000 calories and am in the best shape of my life at forty-four years old. I say this not to brag but to inspire others. It is incredible what you can accomplish when you push yourself and others support you along the way. I must make it to January because a friend who is succeeding with his major health and lifestyle change told me his goal is to join me for one class. *What???* How cool! I am excited for him. He also asked me to show him how to lift weights safely and get started on his exercise path now that he has improved his nutrition choices.

There is no shortage of options to improve your fitness level, but you must take the first step and get moving in the right direction. Join a walking club, a group exercise class, or a running or cycling group, or try CrossFit. Find what works for you and get after it! I promise it will not disappoint you. A special thanks to a few of my fitness friends who continue to inspire me every day: Kristy Ward Orem, Tiff Baird, Angie Woodham, and Suzanne Fischer.

Kristy is an avid runner but is not afraid to mix up her fitness routine with a wide variety of fitness classes, such as Zumba. Tiff is a health and wellness coach. She has a blog at www.fitactivelife.com.

Angie is an old college friend from Gainesville and is one of my OTF friends. We cheer each other on from afar and typically discuss our workout summaries. Since she is two hours ahead of me, I sometimes sneak a peek at her comments about the workout to know what to expect for my workout or decide if I should stay home. Suzanne is on a different level and sometimes does two OTF classes in one day. Any class with *Boot Camp, Beast Mode, MAX,* or *Insanity* in the name is right up her alley, the tougher the workout the better.

One of the phrases you hear in almost every Orangetheory Fitness class is "Empty the tank." I always pride myself on being someone who respects the gift of life. When I die, I hope my tank is empty because it means I kept moving my body, and my heart will be full of experiences and memories from a life well lived, one hour at a time.

*Beth and I dressed as Miss Elizabeth and Randy
"Macho Man" Savage for the school's gala.*

Game Changer

July 18, 2020 🌐

"Game Changer" is what I named the group of fitness and health apps on my phone. Two years ago, I entered my local Orangetheory Fitness studio for the first time. I had no idea the impact it would have on my mind, my body, and, most importantly, my life.

I loved everything about the concept: the intensity and variation of workouts, the coaches, the catchy tunes, the positive environment, and the support from every level of the studio staff.

My last OTF workout was on March 10. A few days later the coronavirus (COVID-19) shut down all gyms. Like most of us, I figured that the studio would be closed for a month, maybe two, then we would resume workouts.

I wanted to stay in shape, so I wasted no time finding new ways to exercise. I ran in the neighborhood two or three times a week, and I bought a cheap rower on Amazon just to be safe. A month or so later, I walked down our stairs and my left knee gave out, not once but twice. I cussed under my breath because twenty years earlier, I felt the same pain and it resulted in a torn meniscus, knee surgery, and six weeks on crutches.

I stubbornly avoided booking a doctor appointment for a few weeks, then finally caved. The appointment was fine minus the referral to an orthopedic surgeon—again, more internal swearing, fear, and frustration. All I could think about was the pain that I had felt when I woke up from surgery, and those damn crutches.

A month passed, and I found myself in the same orthopedic practice that I visited twenty years ago. This time, luckily, it was a different outcome. The surgeon tweaked and pulled my knee in a few directions to test it. He also took several X-rays and released me with no surgery! He thought my knee was reacting to the abrupt change in running surfaces from the cushy OTF treadmills to unforgiving pavement. In his opinion, my symptoms were similar to an irritated nerve that extended throughout the joint.

He told me running was off the table for one month just to be safe. I could live with that, even though running is almost as therapeutic for me as writing.

Fast-forward to this morning. I finally jumped back to the OTF studio. I know it will be a long road to hit my past speed on the treadmill and other relevant numbers, but that will come with time. I mentally prepared myself that today will hurt two days from now and that I should not overdo it.

I jogged lightly and took it easy on the sprints. The rower was a different story as we hit 2,200 meters, but it was a slow and methodical pace. The floor section was similar: low weights and purposeful reps.

It felt great to be back under the orange lights and to see the trademark

OTF post-workout pyramid appear on my app. I was BACK in my happy place. Tomorrow I will rest, but Monday's game-changing class cannot come soon enough.

Raging Rhinos Basketball

December 2, 2016 🌐

I am coaching basketball with the Apex Youth League again this year, and our first game is in the books. It went well. My tradition of letting the kids decide the team name continued this year. Our squad will be known as the Raging Rhinos. The kids vary in skill level and athleticism. Two or three have never played organized basketball, and after the first practice, I was not sure if we could win a game. I told the kids not to worry about the scoreboard but to hustle, play hard, and have fun. We might go 0–8, and yes, it will be frustrating, but I am okay with it if these kids keep improving and dive after every loose ball, as they did during today's game.

A few weeks ago, we lost a scrimmage game 34–18. We played the same team today and lost 24–14. The kids played their hearts out and fought until the end. We missed several layups—that comes with the territory at this age—but we played lockdown defense on the opponent's two superstar shooters. Better yet, one of the Rhinos hit his first shot of the season. I think he grinned the rest of the quarter. It is truly one of the best feelings as a coach, and it never gets old.

On the proud Dad scale, this was one of Kaden's best games in three seasons. He scored eight points and had eight steals and a few rebounds. He said he should have made a few more short jumpers. I told him it would come with time.

He is the leading scorer on the team through three games, and I am excited for him. In case you are wondering, no, the offensive sets are not specifically designed for him.

Game 2

December 9, 2016 🌐

Like most teams this age, we missed fifteen or more five-foot jumpers but still shot the ball well. I tried to dance, wiggle, and bend the shots in, but none of it worked. I have coached long enough to know it usually takes four or five games to learn how to play together and understand the game. I always tell the parents to wait until the end of the season to see how much the kids have improved with practice and time. These kids came to play, and they have made great strides in a few weeks. I repeatedly told them how proud of them I was because a few of them have never played before.

The best part of the game was when the kid with the least talent scored his first basket. He smiled and ran down the court as if he had won the lottery. I even walked onto the court to high-five the little guy.

Kaden had a great game and scored 16 points. I was excited about the team, and I did not want to leave the gym. The reason is that we won 30–12 and notched our first win of the season.

Games 3 and 4

January 13, 2017 🌐

The Rhinos had the dreaded doubleheader this morning. The kids played well, and they held the second team scoreless for most of the first half. We won both games. Our record is now 3–1. We are second in the standings out of six teams.

I had two funny interactions with one ref during the game. The first was a proud-Papa moment. He complimented Kaden on his jumper because he knocked down several in the first game.

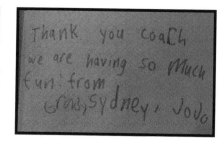

In the second game, he pulled me aside and chuckled with me about one of my players (our center) who would rebound the ball, dribble the entire length of the floor, and attempt a shot even if he had three or four open teammates. The ref laughed and said, "That kid is letting everyone know 'I'm getting mine today and I'm not worried about anyone else'!"

The truth is several players have improved their dribbling and do the same thing. I always remind them to pass to open teammates because they will get the ball back. I feel as if we could set up a pool of alligators, hot lava pits, and the Kool-Aid Man on the court, and they would still dribble the entire way. Excellent stuff!

Game 5

January 20, 2017 🌐

We were lucky enough to extend our winning streak to four games. The kids won 26–10. We are 4–1. K-Man scored 12, and he practiced his crossover earlier this week.

One kid—our center, who is built like a linebacker—made a great pass. After the game, I told him he looked like Magic Johnson. He gave me this serious look with absolutely no emotion and said, "Coach, I don't know who he is."

Games 6 and 7

January 27 and February 3, 2017 🌐

The team won the past two games, and we had a celebrity guest at the last one. I spotted Uncle Tatum in the stands. Kaden must have known because he played his best game yet and scored 14 of our 26 points. Lucky for me, Uncle Tatum kept his heckling to a minimum and left his "Fire Coach Tosti" T-shirt at home. I am not highly creative in artistic design, but I came up with a simple certificate for my baseball team and did the same for the Rhinos. Not every kid will move on with their athletic career, but I am a big believer in setting goals and building strong self-esteem for life. This year's version is a surprise for the players, and I hope it means something to them whether we win or lose our upcoming playoff games. We are 6–1 and the #2 seed.

Rhinos Playoffs

March 3, 2017 🌐

The kids won the semifinal game 33–26! It seemed like every shot went in, which scared me heading into the championship game. Kaden scored 19 points, but I had one of those coaching moments when you scream, "Nooooo!" followed by a resounding "Yes! Yes! Yes!" Kaden dribbled past half court and pulled up inside the 3-point line—I was thinking, *What he is doing?* A second later, the ball swished through the net; the fans all shook their heads in disbelief. I grinned and looked up in shock. He did not realize how far out he was when he shot it. The ref even gave him three points!

We played the #1 seed for the title, but the back-to-back games took their toll. We ran out of gas, but the opponent was undefeated for a reason. They were the better team. No excuses here.

As a coach, I preach the importance of hustling and trying to win because losing is part of sports and life. These kids came from different schools, and a few of them could barely dribble at our first practice. They improved a tremendous amount and finished second in the league with an 8–2 record, and our two losses were to the champion.

It was a hard loss, and I had several kids in tears as the clock wound down, but they did not quit and kept playing hard until the final buzzer. Kaden was upset with the loss, but the first thing he did when we got home was to shoot jumpers. As his dad and the coach, I am always careful not to praise him more than others, but as I look back, I realize how proud of him I truly am. He improved a lot this season. Even though scoring points is not always the most important factor, it is one metric to gauge progress. He finished with 133 points and made the only 3-point basket in the league, which includes third- and fourth-graders. After the game, the referee came up to him, put his arm around him, and told him he played well and that this loss would make him want to work even harder next year. As his coach and dad, I could not agree more.

After the first practice, I told Beth we might not win a game because we resembled the Bad News Bears. Boy, was I wrong. These kids came together as a team, and they worked hard to improve their dribbling, defense, and shooting. We played like a bunch of raging rhinos, and I would not have it any other way.

Running for Respect

October 2017 ◔

RIP, Coach Baldwin. He was our cross-country and track coach at PHS. He taught me a lot more than how to pass a baton during a relay race or how to attack a hill during a 5K cross-country meet.

He pushed us to be our best, and he was so much fun to be around. Like many other Paintsville students, I have so many great memories. One was how he would absolutely lose it and yell at us when someone dropped the baton during a transfer. I can still hear the aluminum baton bouncing and careening across the track—ding, ding, ping, pong—and then slowly rolling to a stop.

Me and Coach Baldwin with a team trophy.

The baton pass has two important steps, and clear communication is key. The first runner is responsible for yelling two code words. The first word is to let the recipient know to start running, and the second word is the notification that the baton is coming and to stick your hand out to receive it while you reach top sprinting speed. You couldn't say *Go*, because everyone would take off too soon. Our code words were *Bull* and *Stick*. Hitting a 90-mph curveball will always be one of the most difficult things to do in sports, but there is something beautiful to appreciate when the relay team and its four runners make clean passes with no hiccups and you cross the finish line first.

Our home track was not up to par, so we always ran at Central, Pikeville, or Raceland. Back then, the drive to Pikeville was close to an hour and it was dark by the time we were headed home. Coach Baldwin knew the games high school kids play, so he would randomly flip on the overhead bus light and yell, "Hand check! Is everyone behaving back there?"

I also jokingly blame him for one of the reasons I don't like soccer. After we ran three or four miles at practice, he would toss a soccer ball in the middle of the track and tell us to play soccer for extra conditioning. It was more like "kill the man with the ball"; we had no rules. Looking back, I don't know how we did not have any injuries.

Coach, thank you for everything you taught us, but most of all, thank you for teaching me what it means to dig deep and give it your all, even when you think you can't run another step.

Golden Demons Basketball

November 2017

I have started my tenth season of coaching youth basketball. I was unsure what outcome to expect at the first practice because we had two players out for tae kwon do testing and another because of a separated shoulder. One more player must have had some other activity because we unexpectedly ended up with five players.

This year's squad chose our team name. Drum roll, please . . . They voted for Golden Demons.

In past years I have coached Rhinos, Rams, and Nugget Toasters, and Tosti's Rockies once when the sport was T-ball. I think it is important to provide the kids with the opportunity to participate and have some ownership in the decision. I do not have a vote, but if they had suggested Blue Demons or Tar Heels, I would have exercised my veto power.

The first scrimmage game started sluggishly, as I expected. Both teams missed a lot of shots and were scrambling to find their man. After a while, we started playing great defense and went on a run. We won 28–12. I am proud of these young men for hustling and not quitting even though the opposing team had seven players. Here is to another exciting season! I look forward to watching each player improve and have fun along the way.

At our second scrimmage game, the other team had only five players. I left our smaller kids in for longer periods, to be fair. Kaden is wearing #24 this year. We won 31–20. After the game, the opposing coach spoke to me at half court, shook his head, and said, "24 is a baller. #24 is a hoss!" #proudpapa&coach #honoredbuthumble

Games 1 and 2

December 8 and 15, 2017 ◐

The Golden Demons are 1–0 after the season opener. We won 35–19. The smallest guy on the team had his first steal. Kaden finished with 27 points.

I received the second technical foul of my ten-year coaching career. After what I thought was an ordinary substitution and a minute of play, the opposing team scored a basket; the ref shook his head and chuckled. He asked me how many players I had on the floor. I looked on the court. Sure enough, we had six players. I laughed and apologized. I said at least the other team scored against us.

I felt awful and apologized to the other coach and his assistant coach. Thankfully, he laughed with me after the game. We moved to 2–0 and pulled away for a 29–22 win after a hard-fought back-and-forth game. We are a second-half team.

Game 3

January 12, 2018 ⊙

The Golden Demons could not buy a jumper anywhere near the basket, but they played great defense. We won 18–12. Kaden made a lucky 3-pointer at the buzzer as it banked in. As the saying goes, the banks in Arvada are open after 12 on Saturdays! 3-0 is our record. We play the #1 team (also undefeated) next on the schedule.

Games 6 and 7

February 2 and 9, 2018 ⊙

We finished the regular season with the dreaded doubleheader. We won the first game 16–12 and the second game 31–21. We finished 6–2 and will be the #2 seed in the tournament.

The best part of the game was watching one kid dribble back and forth for an extended period without picking up the ball or dribbling with both hands. We have diligently worked with him all season. It made me smile to watch it unfold.

We passed well. We missed another ten or twelve close shots, which is typical for this age, but I am happy for the kids and their overall development.

Special thanks to Uncle Tatum and our awesome neighbors for cheering us on and yelling at me to tell me that the clock had not been running for over a minute.

Playoffs

March 2, 2018 ⊙

The Golden Demons won our first playoff game and advanced to the championship game, where we lost by 10. We finished in second place again. Like last year, our only losses were to the #1 team in the league. Our final record was 7–3. I am glad that the kids played hard until the end, even though we knew the other team would win. I gave Kaden and another player the green light to shoot some threes because we were down by 11. Kaden made one of them, which was fun to watch as a dad and a coach.

We also had some surprise visitors. Aunt Suzanne Fischer and two of the girls who played on our team last year came to cheer us on. It is always neat to see former players.

I appreciate the team's parents for always helping me with practice drills, running the clock, and assisting with the scoreboard. I have always been lucky with supportive and helpful parents wherever I have coached.

This year I gave each player a basketball-themed card and a Hot Wheel. I closed with the following: "Remember to maintain a positive attitude, respect others, be a good sport, and always dream big!"

Super Team

July 2018

Thanks to the Colorado School of Mines for a couple of fun days of basketball camp. This was also the summer when the NBA superstars joined forces with their buddies to form "Super Teams." Kaden said he became friends with one or two players from the team that beat us in the championship this year. They told him he should join their team. Kaden responded, "It won't work because my Dad coaches our team." When does practice start?? #nosuperteamhere #proudDad

And the winning team name is...

November 2018

Typically, teams practice once or twice before the season's first scrimmage game. One of my traditions is to let the kids choose our team name. They were thrilled, and as the goofy ideas were flying around, I reminded the kids that whatever mascot they decided upon, I would have to coach ten games in a T-shirt with a picture of the animal on the front. Here is a list of proposed names that did not make the cut:

Golden Nuggets

Uninteresting Unicorns

Pink Hippos

Team Fortnite

Street Pigeons

And . . . the winning team name for what I think is my eleventh year of coaching youth basketball is . . . the Nasty Narwhals.

We have eleven players, four of whom are new to the team and have never played basketball before. Three of them have played football for a few years. Secretly, I hope our rebounding will be a strong suit.

I told the kids we will win some and lose some, but we will play hard and hustle until the clock hits :00, whether we are down 20 or up 20. I reminded them to respect our opponents, the opposing coach, and the referees. I told them not to argue with the referees, and I added that they should address the ref as *sir* or *ma'am* if they have a question about a call. I told them that I will discuss any terrible calls with the referees on their behalf.

Last, I told each player they will be better by the end of March and to write one skill they would focus on during the season. After our last game, I will hand each Nasty Narwhal a certificate with their goal and a note that says, "I did it!" Saturday morning's game cannot come soon enough!

Meatball Sub Drill

November 2018 ●

The kids were in rare form and full of energy tonight. It was eleven versus one (me). I took extra time to script each part of the practice to ensure we could move quickly throughout the hour. I knew it was time to introduce the famous Meatball Sub Drill.

So much of coaching kids lies in explaining things on their level to relate to the objective. In 2004, I was trying to teach the kids the importance of boxing out for a rebound, and I compared the basketball to their favorite toy. For whatever reason, this one quiet kid did not react to the toy piece. I quickly changed my strategy and told him to pretend the ball was his favorite sandwich. I asked him to tell the team what his choice was. He muttered under his breath two or three times, but I could not hear him. I encouraged him to yell it loud enough for someone in downtown Denver to hear him. And this kind soul belted out his version of a Viking battle cry at the top of his lungs: "Meatball sub, Coach!" To this day, it is what I call the drill.

As practice ended, two moms and a dad thanked me for my patience. One dad said, "I don't know if you drink beer or not, but you earned one tonight and should have one when you get home." Our second scrimmage is next on the schedule. I cannot wait to see how the kids play.

Nasty Narwhals First Scrimmage

November 30, 2018 🕙

The Nasty Narwhals played our first scrimmage against the defending champion, which was the only team that beat us last year. We jumped out to a quick lead, and both teams were nervous and sloppy with the ball as expected. The other coach and I shared more than a few chuckles and eye rolls at ill-advised shots and silly mistakes.

We were down two points for the longest time. During the final 25 seconds, we had three shots rim out. I told the kids how proud of them I was for playing through their nerves and anxiousness. I promised them we will improve this season. In two or three weeks, we will not miss easy layups or turn the ball over as quickly. We will probably still miss a few layups, but it is part of the process. I am excited about the potential of these kids and what the season may hold. It could be a glorious year.

Nasty Narwhals Game 1

December 7, 2018 🕙

The kids passed the ball as if they have been playing together for years. One kid who had never touched a basketball before November, made his first basket. He grinned for at least a minute, which is one reason I love coaching kids. We still need to work on rebounding, but our defense was solid. The Nasty Narwhals earned their first W of the season. The final score was 29–18. Kaden led the team with 10 points.

Nasty Narwhals Game 2

December 14, 2018 🌐

We played the defending champions, and we are 0–4 against them. I am not a perfect coach, but I always teach the importance of competing and playing hard—win or lose. We might lose this game, but we will learn from it and move onto the next game. At practice, I downplayed the revenge factor and said this was just another game. The kids were excited to face this team again because they all know each other, and some of them play football together.

We played smothering defense from the start and held an 8–0 lead heading into halftime. The kids played well, and we won 13–3. One dad, who stands close to 6' 6" and could easily pass for a professional wrestler, gave me a bear hug after the game and told me it felt good to get the monkey off our back. Yes, yes, it did, but it was only one game.

I told the kids our defense was superb, but it is also possible our opponent might have had a bad shooting day; now is not the time to get cocky. It is a long season, but I am excited about these kids and the W. Back to work!

Playoffs

March 2019 🌐

We started the semifinal game nervous and tight the entire first half. We were down 12–7 at the start of the third quarter, and then the kids turned up the defense and pulled away for the 17–14 win. Kaden went 4 for 4 from the free-throw line. The past two years, we played in the championship game against the #1 seed and came up short both years. This year the #4 seed upset the #1 seed, which meant we had only a few minutes before playing for the championship.

We jumped out to a small lead and were in control for most of the game. Kaden sunk three out of four free throws, which proved to be important down the stretch. The other team fought back. With one minute left,

we had a one-point lead. The clock seemed to take forever! The opponent had possession for the final 40 seconds. They had multiple shots roll around and out each time. Finally, we rebounded a miss as time expired—final score, Narwhals 14, opponent 13.

The Nasty Narwhals were the fourth-grade Champions! I ran around the court, trying to find Kaden, and he was doing the same looking for me. We hugged, smiled, and both yelled, "We did it!" I am proud of these kids and their hard work. It was an unbelievable feeling and a memory for these kids that will last a lifetime. #champs #NastyNarwhalsDefense

A True Balancing Act

February 2021 🌐

One common struggle that all parents encounter is the delicate balance of identifying the perfect sport for your child. Sometimes, he or she signs up for a team because their friend talks about it or because it was an enjoyable part of P.E. class or even a popular neighborhood game.

Most children start in a YMCA or recreational youth soccer league and then branch off from there. This was the case for both of our children. Emily is our second child, and as any parent with two children will tell you, birth order matters. Here is one reason why. The first-born is typically a rule follower and has a basic sense of safety, while a second-born is more likely to be a daredevil because they have to keep up with the older sibling and they mimic everything. Our daughter, Emily, had zero fear in regard to jumping into the deep end, even though she could not swim. Em is also a climber. She has always loved climbing tables and chairs since she was two years old. Looking back, I think Beth and I took that as a telltale sign of what sport we needed to enroll her in when the time came.

From the first jump in her gymnastics class, we knew Emily had found her favorite sport. She smiled every time she tumbled, spun, or lost her footing and fell on the mat.

Individual sports are more difficult than team sports in my mind because the athlete is on his or her own. The gymnast is alone in the spotlight from the opening steps of the floor routine to the final dismount. There is not a teammate to bail you out when you make a mistake or fall. Contrarily, I feel that this is a great confidence builder and development tool for young minds.

For parents watching their young gymnasts from the bleachers, the cringe factor is apparent and often difficult to hide. Mom and Dad spend most of the practice session leaning to one side, gritting their teeth, and exhaling loudly a few times. Think of a roller-coaster ride at an amusement park minus the smell of funnel cakes, burnt corn dogs, and soda-stained concrete.

It is fairly easy to internalize your fear when your child is pitching or taking a contested jump shot. It is different when your six-year-old runs full-speed and flips through the air hoping she lands safely, regardless of her form or the amount of soft foam cubes designed to break the fall. This explains the jubilant screams and enthusiastic clapping from me and Beth when Emily safely navigates her practice run.

She might be short for her age, but Emily has found her sport. More importantly, she has learned the importance of falling down, getting back up, and fighting through a rough patch—which I hope only helps her understand the significance of balance later in life.

Her Turn

January 26, 2021 ◉

For five years, Emily patiently watched me coach Kaden in basketball. She came to practically every game and sat on the sideline watching and waiting for her turn to play for Dad.

One day she asked me when I was going to coach her in basketball. At the time, she participated in two activities a week, and I had to explain that she already had a lot on her plate for a seven-year-old. Once she finished her Wednesday night Catholic prep classes, I told her, she could sign up for hoops and I would be happy to coach her. I could tell by the look in her eyes that this was important to her and she wanted to have the same experience that her big brother did.

Jump ahead to March 2020, when Emily was in third grade. After frantically searching for a league to play in, we landed with the local YMCA. Apparently there was not a lot of interest from this age group. The YMCA worked hard to combine kids from multiple suburbs to enable us to have a team of ten players. Emily and I were both excited to field a team and get started.

We arrived at practice, and Emily was filled with energy, excited that she was finally practicing basketball with her dad as the coach. I think she asked about setting screens multiple times because she and I had worked on them in the driveway for a week or two.

The process of selecting the team name came down to a few options, including the Green Tacos and Space Doughnuts. As previously mentioned, I had to utilize my veto on the Green Tacos idea.

Later that week, the COVID-19 pandemic hit full force and our season was cancelled so we were not able to vote on the team name. I was crushed and felt helpless as a father who just wanted to help his daughter see a wish come true.

The Good Sideline

February 5, 2021 🌐

A new year brings new opportunities, which means I am lucky enough to coach Emily this basketball season. Our first practice was strange for two reasons: One, we all wore masks, and two, no parents were allowed in the gym. I always enjoy meeting parents on the first night to get acquainted and explain my coaching style and my high energy level, but I couldn't do that this year. I did share the same philosophy with the kids by reminding them that we will win and lose games, but that I am more concerned about each player improving and having fun at this age.

I knew that the masks meant I would have to yell louder and ensure the players knew how thrilled I was to be back on the sideline instructing a team of new players. It took me only ten minutes to start clapping enthusiastically and running up and down the court with the players, even on a surgically repaired knee. On the ride home, Emily laughed and told me that I might have been just a tad too hyper.

I upheld my tradition of letting the players pick our team name. Our final options were Chaos, Red Hot Chili Peppers, Dynamite, and Peppy Tomatoes. The kids love this part because it allows them to be a part of something that they contributed to, and the smiles and laughs never disappoint. And this year's team name is . . . Chaos!

Game 1, February 6, 2021: Team Chaos! 🌐

The first game for kids in any sport is always a wild and unpredictable ride. Today, Team Chaos immediately jumped out to a big lead and played swarming defense for three quarters. I could not believe how well they played and the number of layup opportunities we had in the first quarter alone. We were in control of the game until the final 45 seconds, when we lost our four-point lead. One thing I have learned from coaching youth sports is that no lead is ever safe. As expected, we had several opportunities but came up short on too many layups. The opponent scored a basket and cut our lead to two. With 15 seconds left, I told our point guard to take her time getting the ball past half court, then quickly changed my mind and told her to go fast and dribble out the clock. She lost the ball just after she crossed half-court, and the other team stole the ball and drove down for one more shot. We played good defense and knocked a pass out of bounds. At this point we had two seconds left to secure our first win of the season.

The other team had to inbound the ball and make a shot, which they did. The league does not allow for overtimes; we settled for a tie, and it was completely my fault. My smallest guard could not see whom to guard, and the opponent had a wide-open passing lane and a two-foot uncontested shot to make. I should have called timeout, but I thought they still had to inbound the ball, catch it, and shoot it. I still left the gym smiling and told the girls I was proud of them and that we will get better starting at next week's practice. On to the next one!

Game 2, February 13, 2021: The Backboard Is Your Friend 🌐

For the first time in my coaching career, I have two strong, tall, and athletic point guards. It makes a difference because they can handle the ball, score at will, and rebound.

Emily played great defense and made her first steal. She has taken a few jump shots (she hasn't made one yet, but she will). As a parent, it is such a good feeling to watch her confidence grow with each game.

For eleven seasons, I have begged, pleaded, and reminded my teams that the backboard is your friend. I tell them to use it for layups and close-range jumpers. For whatever reason, it finally clicked today. Our team stole the ball, dribbled the length of the court, and made five consecutive short jumpers. I could not stop shaking my head. Underneath my mask, I flashed a devilish grin, nodded my head at my assistant coach, and kept pacing the sideline. I don't normally play Powerball, but I might buy a ticket tonight.

At last night's practice, one of the girls had this enormous smile on her face, and she told the team she was excited for a sleepover with her best friend. That same player came out on fire today. She was rebounding everything in sight and made our first four baskets. When she came to the bench, I joked with her about what she ate for breakfast. She smiled and said, "I guess staying up until 2:00 a.m. worked." I almost told her to ask her parents if she can stay with that friend every Friday night if she plays that well.

Game 3, February 20, 2021: A Few More Gray Hairs 🌐

Today's game did not disappoint. The girls came out on fire as usual and built a decent lead, but, as any coach and parent will tell you, no lead is safe at the third- and fourth-grade level.

Emily continued playing great defense and had to face a girl that was twice her size, yet she fought for a loose ball against her and dribbled right at her. I jokingly told the assistant coach that in her mind Emily probably said, "I've got a big brother. I am not scared of you."

The fourth quarter started with us up by seven points. I knew it was a matter of time before the other team got hot and closed the gap. Sure enough, they reeled off three consecutive baskets. With less than a minute to go, we were desperately trying to hold onto to our one-point lead.

The other team had multiple opportunities and kept missing close-range shots. A shot finally fell, and it happened with 9 seconds left. Down by one point, I immediately called a timeout and explained our play.

Knowing the defense could not guard us until we passed half-court, I instructed the passer to slowly roll the ball in bounds and told our point guard to pick it up a few feet before half-court, then take it to the rack after a teammate set a screen at the free-throw line. I told them we had one shot at this, so we needed to play fast and get to the rim for a high-percentage shot.

I looked over at the YMCA volunteer who was running the clock and let him know we were going to roll the ball in bounds because I didn't want him to start the clock too soon.

:09 seconds: The ball bounced into play and rolled slowly as planned. The point guard picked it up a little early and took off toward the basket.

:05 seconds: She turned on the jets, hit the screen, and gently laid it in off the backboard.

:02 seconds: The ball went through the net, and the bench erupted in jubilation. I yelled, "YEESSS!" at the top of my lungs and punched the air in celebration. I could not believe we pulled out the win—and on a layup of all shots.

I told the girls how proud I was of their effort and the fact that they didn't quit. We are two seconds away from being undefeated, but 2–0–1 is where we stand because I didn't call a timeout in our first game. In our postgame huddle, I reminded them that it was a team win, because all three players had to do their job for us to have a shot at the end.

Buzzer-beaters are great for fans but brutal for coaches at any level. In the first game, we had let the opponent take an easy shot to tie us, which was my fault. Today it was our turn. Sometimes in life, whether you win, lose, or tie, you must remember to just roll with it.

Game 4, February 27, 2021: Buckets All Day! 🌐

Today's game featured zero defense because both teams scored a lot of baskets. From the opening tip, it was a fun, competitive game between two great squads. We were lucky to hang on to the 29–26 win. Emily's defense is top-notch, and her confidence is improving with every game.

Game 5, March 6, 2021: Shoot, Rattle and Roll 🌐

Today's game was an odd one. We played a much smaller team and should have been able to score whenever we wanted to, but that was not the case. Shot after shot rolled and spun out. It felt and looked like a carnival game where the odds are stacked against you.

Two different players missed four consecutive layups, but overall it was a good reminder for the girls that some days you have to keep shooting even when it feels as if there is an invisible lid covering the rim.

Emily had multiple chances to score her first basket, but the ball bounced out every time. It was so close! On the next possession, she caught a pass, turned, dribbled to the baseline, took a jump shot, and . . . it went in! Emily raced down the court giggling and smiling the entire way. At the end of the quarter, she ran to the bench, smiling underneath her mask, exclaiming, "Daddy, I made my first shot!" I gave her a high-five and a quick hug and tried to cherish the special moment between a coach and a player—in this case, me and my daughter.

Chapter Seven

Giving Back

Sometimes on your path, you reach a fork in the road, but instead of taking the well-known route or the safe exit, you create a new road. Your heart and passion for doing the right thing serve as a compass guiding you in the right direction and ensuring that you do not get lost. As on a scenic highway, the beautiful parts catch your eye and steal your heart.

Rebuild. Rebound. Repeat.

Fall 2007 ⊙

On August 23, 2005, Hurricane Katrina made landfall with a devastating impact on New Orleans and other parts of the Gulf Region. The highest wind speed recorded was 174 miles per hour. The storm ransacked everything in its path. Lives were lost, homes were destroyed, and schools and businesses were demolished. Like most Americans, I watched the news coverage of the disaster unfold and shook my head in disbelief. I wanted to do something, anything, but I felt hopeless sitting on my couch in Denver. I figured the feeling would subside and life would move on to the next thing, but this time was different.

Two years later, I did something about my gut feeling. I read a *Sports Illustrated* article that focused on the devastating impact the storm had on the local schools. The graphic pictures provided a shocking reality of the state of school facilities. The vivid images revealed the appalling truth of the state of New Orleans schools and youth athletic facilities nearly two years after the storm. People wanted to help, but they did not know how or where to start. I realized that the sports industry had provided me the perfect mix of knowledge, experience, and contacts necessary to successfully execute a project of this magnitude. I had a plan; now, I needed a name for the nonprofit.

Sports for a Cause became a Denver, Colorado–based 501(c)(3) nonprofit organization in the fall of 2007. Its primary objectives were to restore playgrounds and youth athletic facilities that had been destroyed by Hurricane Katrina. To accomplish these goals, the organization would collect and distribute new and used sporting goods to schools and recreation departments. The nonprofit would change my life in ways that I could not fathom. On paper, it made little sense, and I told myself that, but my heart kept telling me to ignore the hurdles and focus on the more significant task at hand.

My goal was to unite employees of major-league sports teams, universities, athletic suppliers, sponsors, and other sports and entertainment industries to provide athletic opportunities for youth in New Orleans. We quickly expanded the charity's scope to include the less fortunate in the Denver area. In September 2008, over thirty Denver companies took part in an equipment drive to benefit inner-city sports programs on behalf of Denver Public Schools. Here are a few highlights of our efforts.

Donated 2,000 new Little League uniforms valued at $55,000 to the New Orleans Parks and Recreation Department.

Assisted in completing a new playground at the George Washington Carver School in New Orleans' Ninth Ward.

Distributed sporting goods to Denver Venture School and soccer jerseys for every member of Denver SCORES, an after-school soccer program for underprivileged elementary- and middle-school children.

Rehabilitated the infrastructure of Lower Ninth Ward Village, the first community recreation center to open in the neighborhood since Hurricane Katrina.

I could not have done it without several friends and Beth, who supported the idea from day one. A huge thanks to everyone who donated their time, energy, and money to help the cause. This wild idea quickly became a passion of mine, and the only regret I had was the fact that I had time for only two or three volunteer trips a year.

Together with friends and family, we donated over $150,000 in used and new sports equipment to schools in New Orleans and Denver. The experience changed my life in numerous ways, and I learned a lot about life, myself, humanity, and fundraising for a cause with all your heart.

To my friends in New Orleans, I love you dearly. Thank you for introducing me to key personnel, donating hotel rooms, preparing all those crawfish boils for us, and showing me what it truly means to rebuild something with your heart and hands.

Here are a few of my favorite memories:

On one of my seven plane rides to New Orleans, the gentleman sitting beside me asked me why I was headed to New Orleans. I told him my story, and he gave me a check on the spot. It was for $500.

We helped a small school's volleyball team on the eastern Colorado plains (Hi-Plains) by purchasing volleyballs and uniforms. The athletic director and head coach at that school, Kerry Sayles, reached out to me a few years later when Beth was battling breast cancer. Kerry is a phenomenal coach and athletic administrator with an enormous heart. Each year, her team raises money and sends a check to someone who is battling breast cancer. The girls selected Beth as their recipient. Kerry and I keep in touch, and one of these days, we will take the kids to visit her farm.

We rebuilt playgrounds, built a gazebo, painted, and did some landscaping, but my favorite project was a basketball court we painted and striped in the Lower Ninth Ward. The pastor at the church and youth center asked me about UK's mascot and jokingly said, "Isn't that the Blue Devils?" I told my good friend who works in the UK athletic department to tell Coach Cal about a Kentucky-blue-painted basketball court in New Orleans.

Our largest donation day was $10,000 at Denver North High School. We invited several pro mascots, dancers, and cheerleaders. I hope to eclipse the dollar amount someday.

Anything is possible, but you must believe first.

I toured a couple of schools. Water is a powerful thing. Some of the photos were gut-wrenching. It looked as if a bomb had exploded in some places.

Fundraising can be daunting, but always remember you are trying to establish a connection with an individual and match emotion with action.

I decided to put the program on hold after Emily was born and the fact that New Orleans had rebuilt all 130 playgrounds that were damaged by the storm. Eventually we were able to come back with a new focus on Colorado schools. The plan was to choose one school per year and help raise money to purchase sports equipment and provide volunteers for various school projects. For example, we worked with Jefferson High School from 2018–19 and donated $2,000 to their athletic program and P.E. department.

Thank you for your support, whether you have been on board since year one or are joining us for the first time in year ten! Visit www.sportsfora-cause.com for more information.

Items donated to Jefferson High.

Outdoor classroom in New Orleans.

Baseball Clinic with Ron Maestri

August 2009 ◉

Due to the level of damage across the city, there was always a volunteer opportunity to help a school, a team, or a neighborhood. One of my wonderful friends in New Orleans told me about a youth baseball clinic and mentioned that it would be great if I could be a part of it. This trip was a quick weekend excursion, but the flight was cheap, and it fit into my work schedule.

We had fun teaching kids in New Orleans how to throw a knuckleball. The baseball clinic was cut short by some nasty rain and lightning, but everyone still had a good time. Thanks to Ron Maestri for his time and for donating over twenty new Rawlings baseball gloves to the kids.

Ron Maestri is on the left.

Before my arrival, I was not familiar with Ron or his reputation in the city. He was the executive director and chief operating officer of the triple-A baseball team the New Orleans Zephyrs. Earlier in his career, he was the head baseball coach at the University of New Orleans and later served as the athletic director. After the clinic, he was gracious enough to treat me to lunch and took me on a driving tour of another area damaged during the storm, educating me on the unpredictable path of the storm.

Looking back, I remember his positive attitude, warm personality, and genuine care for others. He would have been a coach I would have loved to play for because of his extensive knowledge of the game and his drive to hold each player to a higher standard. You could tell he was a great coach but an even better person. I never looked up his record as a coach because it did not matter, but he earned a big W in my book that day.

Volunteer Trip

October 2009 🌐

I wanted to take some time and share some stories with anyone who might be interested in our volunteer trips. We had nine volunteers, which was our largest group yet. Volunteers came from California, Ohio, Colorado, and Tennessee. Below are some short stories and my thoughts about the trip.

We landscaped two significant areas at the Village utilizing materials Brian Tatum and Adam Germek found onsite, including an old barrel, a fireplace, and a door from a house in the Ninth Ward. We also spruced up the landscaping, planted trees in the back, and painted the library and the hallway.

We repaired and replaced a stairwell for a woman in the Ninth Ward who is working hard to restore her seamstress business. Her knowhow and skillset provided for her family. The storm ripped off a section of her roof. The steps and rafters were decayed, and the stairs had multiple holes as if they were made of cardboard. She shared two horror stories with our group regarding contractors who stole $80,000 and all her appliances. She has renovated her house by herself, and it looks terrific. She still has a smile on her face through all the despair and frustration, and I am amazed at what you can do when you are truly tested.

We distributed sports equipment to two schools: Miller McCoy Academy and Langston Hughes Elementary. Both athletic directors were ecstatic to receive a call from us because their budgets were frozen, and they desperately needed equipment for P.E.

The group also installed three sliding doors to help create a large storage area for Mack and the facility.

The October trip was my second one in three months. It was nice to see some familiar faces. In August, I noticed an older woman sitting on her front porch watching me as I talked to Mack about how we could help him and the Village. I smiled and walked over to introduce myself and gave her a new football. She was a genuinely kind woman and promised to cook for our group when we returned. I hugged her and told her I would return with ten of my friends in October. True to her word, she cooked a huge pot of red beans, rice, sausage, and pork. The pork was tender, and it fell off the bone. When I asked her if she needed any help carrying the food across the street to the Village, she said, "No, you and your friends can sit right here, and don't worry about taking your shoes off. You are welcome at my house." Southern hospitality is still alive, my friends.

I met another gentleman by chance. I was in the Village by myself because our volunteers went on an extensive tour of the Ninth Ward. A young man, probably fifteen years old, asked me a question about the event at the Village planned for the evening. We started talking about sports and his school; then I gave him one basketball we had on hand. Earlier in the day, President Obama had visited his school, and he told me he shook hands with him, and you could see the glow in his eyes. I also gave him some mini basketballs for his little brothers and T-shirts for his little sisters. It turns out he lived with his grandparents, and he asked me if I wanted to meet his grandfather.

We walked a few blocks in the Ninth Ward. I had only my backpack along with my ragged trail-running shoes, filthy shorts, and a grimy T-shirt. I truly felt like I a movie actor or a CNN reporter, living in the moment. It was surreal but inspiring to me.

His grandfather was a large man and soft-spoken. It turns out he and his wife are raising six grandchildren ranging from ages three to fifteen. The smallest children were very, very shy. I tried to talk to them a few different times, but they looked scared to death. I did not realize what was going on until later that night when a friend of mine who lives there explained it to me. It was one of the first times a person of a different color had been in their kitchen. I fought back tears and realized our society had made great strides in racial issues, but we still have some work to do. The grandfather thanked my friends and me for our effort and was glad people across this great country continued to help his city four years after the storm. He looked me in the eye and said the most amazing thing to him is that every volunteer could be doing a thousand different things, yet each one had taken time out of their schedule, paid for travel expenses, and spent a few vacation days helping the city however they can.

I met some amazing people and heard some inspiring but sad stories, which is part of the experience. Below are some of these stories. I will warn you that some details are graphic and disturbing; please proceed with caution.

Mack

Mack is the owner of the Village. He is a native of the Ninth Ward and grew up going to the Village, a recreation and cultural center. He is sixty years old but has the energy of a ten-year-old and always sees the positive in every situation.

He has not slept for over three hours at a time since the storm. He will wake up during the night, kill time for a few hours, then lie back down, but it is as if his internal clock prohibits him from getting a peaceful night's sleep. This morning, I returned to the Village to say goodbye to Mack, wrap things up, and start preparing for our 2010 trip. When he came in, he was smiling ear to ear. He looked at me and said, "Brandon, I slept for six hours last night. *Six hours!* Can you believe it?"

He thanked us for our energy because this will keep him going for another six months. It turned out I needed a ride to the airport. Mack ended up taking me, and of course he refused gas money, but I threw some cash down on his console while he was not looking. He gave each one of us a bear hug each morning and told me he appreciated everything and how much he loved us.

*Jim

Jim is unemployed and is a handyman who likes to help Mack even though he is not getting paid. He told me he left his house when the flood hit and swam down the block to a taller, historic three-story house, where he stayed for five days with no food or water. He said he slept and prayed he would make it out in one piece. He kept hearing someone screaming for help, but he could not see the person. Once the water subsided and he could leave, he saw the police removing a body from the house. He shook his head and said, "I could hear him, but I couldn't see him to save him, Brandon."

*Name changed

*George

Another individual was at the Superdome, even though his entire family had evacuated. He went without food for three days and said the restrooms were overflowing into the concourses and the stench was unbearable. He was standing next to a woman who received the tragic news that multiple family members had drowned in the storm. She screamed, then jumped to her death. They were on the sixth floor of the Superdome when this happened. Authorities evacuated George to Dallas, and he lost contact with his family until two weeks ago. He finally called his sister to let her know he wanted to come back home and stay with her. Unfortunately, their mother passed away before he made it home. He and his sister both swear it was his mother's way of taking care of him and reuniting the family.

*Name changed

Things are slowly starting to improve, but the destruction is still widespread, and we will have plenty of projects to keep us busy for years to come. I promise you the experience will change your life, and you will appreciate your own home and belongings more than ever before.

NOLA Volunteer Trip: Thoughts and Reflections

October 2011 ⦿

Most of my friends understand *what* drives me; however, some do not understand *why*. I respect the small number of friends who do not understand why I volunteer my time for a city thousand miles away, but I also have issued them the same challenge I tell everyone I meet. Allocate $500 and four days for a volunteer trip with me, and if you return home and your life has not changed, then I will gladly refund your money and write a personal check to cover your expenses. To date, I have led nineteen people on this adventure, and I have yet to write a check.

This past trip, my family and in-laws joined me. Fay, Beth's mom, graciously watched Kaden both days while Beth, Harold Jackson, Jason (Beth's brother), and Joe (Dad) helped us complete our projects. Harold is a UK graduate and was good friends with Jon Andrews. This was Harold's second trip. We painted a basketball court and installed two rims for a church's gymnasium in the Gentilly area. We also donated two volleyball nets, two volleyballs, knee pads, and dumbbells to a local high school.

The head volleyball coach at that high school is successful on and off the court. She has won over 500 games and multiple state championships. However, when she first started at the school, the principal handed her one ball. Coach asked, "Is this for practice or games?" The principal responded, "This is your one ball."

The players soon became a little creative and collected leftover volleyballs from some of the more affluent schools as they played in various tournaments. Since the balls were worn down, the coach told the players to paint them with school colors, cartoon characters, jersey numbers, or even wisdom words. Many years have passed since those days; however, Coach now buys each girl a brand-new volleyball out of her own money when a player makes the varsity team. The player can paint the ball, and most of them do. She continues this tradition to remind the girls of where the program came from, including Hurricane Katrina, since they lost everything.

Shortly after thanking the organization for the donation, she ran down to her office and gave me the coolest gift. Coach handed me one of the colored volleyballs one girl had left behind. It is yellow and has *Livestrong* written across it. I thanked her and said, "Now I have a talking piece for when I speak to classes and other groups in Denver." So, if you are in the audience at a future speaking engagement, you can touch and see the ball. I think it is important for people to grasp a sliver of what these kids experienced after Katrina. I also plan on emailing a friend to see if he will let me have the basketball net that survived Katrina but was replaced by the new nets. The net is a lot like me: a little older, rough around the edges.

There is an MTV show titled *The Buried Life*, and it is one that I watch regularly. It is about a group of four college buddies who drive across the country in a Greyhound bus, marking items off their bucket lists—their lists of things they want to do before they die. The twist is that for every item they complete, they find a stranger and help that individual mark off an item on his or her bucket list also.

As some of you know, I have had a list like this for over twenty years, and as I started watching the second season, I kept asking myself which item I would choose to check off my list if I met the guys. I have an assortment of items and I could not place my finger on just one and struggled with it for quite some time. In the end, I added one more item to my list. I know what I would tell the *Buried Life* guys I want to do before I die: I want to help Mack McClendon (see Chapter Three) move back into his home.

Harold, Beth, Joe, and the author painting the new court.

That's a wrap!

Special Thanks to Two Dear Friends

MARTY PRESTON

When I started my charity, Sports for a Cause, I wrote personal checks for a few things to get it started but reached a point where I needed additional funding. Marty was my first call, and his generosity covered the IRS application fee on my behalf. I am not sure how you truly repay a close friend who helped start a nonprofit that impacted hundreds of lives in New Orleans and Denver, but I will figure something out. I asked him repeatedly what I could do to return the favor. He said I could help him navigate the rules and procedures of establishing a nonprofit because he started a charity for adopted children. Consider it done, my friend. I promise I will be donor no. 1, just as you were for me.

MATT BURCHETT

Matt, like Marty, also a generous person who does not like to talk about it. I was raising money for a local underprivileged middle school to buy basketball uniforms. Over dinner and drinks, Matt asked for an update on Sports for a Cause. I asked him if he would donate a small amount, maybe $50 or $100. He asked me what the total amount needed was, and I told him. The next week he mailed me a check for more than double that amount. I still have the handwritten note in which he told me to keep up the excellent work and how it was good to catch up. As I previously mentioned, he and Marty Preston were two of the top three largest donors in over seven years of the time I ran the nonprofit.

Thoughts on Hurricane Katrina: Five Years later

August 2010 ◉

As the fifth anniversary of Katrina approaches, the media will unleash its typical flurry of emotional stories, filled with reports of progress or lack thereof and mind-boggling photos. The good thing is Katrina will stay fresh in society's mind for another week or two until a young Hollywood celeb does something silly to regain the spotlight. However, I could not forget about the people in New Orleans since the fateful day I read Alexander Wolff's *Sports Illustrated* article in the fall of 2007. I still cannot explain why I felt compelled to help the rebuilding efforts because I do not have any ties to New Orleans.

I spent a fair amount of time working on the foundation, building it from the ground up. However, I did not accomplish any of it by myself. My loving wife has supported me from day one, along with my Board of Directors and countless other friends. I want to thank everyone for their time, energy, and dedication. It has been frustrating, fulfilling, inspiring, and stressful, but worth every minute.

An important fact that is not publicized nearly enough is that the residents of the Ninth Ward had one of the higher homeownership rates in the city, if not the highest. True, many of the houses might have been small, dirty, or neglected for financial reasons, but the occupants still owned them. Often those houses had been passed down through generations. Try as I might, I cannot imagine walking into our home and seeing walls covered in mold and everything we own doused in mud or torn to shreds.

This is what residents experienced after they returned home from Hurricane Katrina, if not much worse. I have shared some gut-wrenching stories in the past—it seems as if I hear two or three more every trip I make—and it truly breaks my heart. It does not seem possible what they endured.

One of my faults is that I wear my heart on my sleeve, but you will always know where I stand on an issue or what I believe in. My dad taught me that lesson: Always stand up for what you believe in, even when others do not agree with your position or support you. I am glad he instilled in me the courage to sometimes stand alone.

I understand one can gain a similar feeling by traveling to a third-world country or an economically depressed area and performing some volunteer work. I am not advocating one or the other, just that you volunteer, regardless of which organization you support. I understand and respect others' opinions if they choose not to support anything related to New Orleans. All I ask is that you not assume everyone in the area devastated by Katrina is lazy and waiting on FEMA to rebuild their house or send them a check. If you do nothing else after reading this note, go volunteer for a nonprofit you like. I promise it will not disappoint you.

Too many times in life, we sit back and talk about what it would be like if we could [Insert a far-fetched goal or dream here]." Then we forget about it and move on with our lives. I decided moving on was not the best option for me regarding New Orleans. I could not sit back and hope that, some way, somehow, the problem would fix itself. My advice to anyone who reads this is to take a chance in life, follow your dreams, and step out of your comfort zone occasionally. You never know what you might accomplish or whose life you might touch. The funny thing is that I started this organization to change others' lives, yet, in the end, the people of New Orleans changed my life.

Since I lived 1,300 miles and four states away from New Orleans, the distance presented some logistical hurdles, but a few individuals helped me overcome most of the issues I encountered.

Jay Cicero was my field guide, and he always went above and beyond what I needed or expected. Jay is the President/CEO of the Greater New Orleans Sports Foundation and was a friend and peer of my mentor, Rick Hatcher. I called Rick to ask him if he would call Jay on my behalf or vouch for me, whichever option he preferred. Jay was nothing but professional and beyond helpful from the initial call. The nonprofit 501(c)(4) organization's mission is to attract and manage sporting events that have a positive economic impact on the state of Louisiana and the Greater New Orleans area.

Jay knew the major players in the city and helped guide me whenever I had a question. If I wanted to talk to the New Orleans Hornets (now Pelicans), he knew who to call. If I wanted to set up a media interview, he called the sports editor for me. He was well connected throughout the city, and if he did not know who to call, he knew the person's best friend, which was just as good.

Horacio Ruiz worked for the New Orleans Hornets and was responsible for introducing me to Mack and the Village. He and I became good friends. Horacio was instrumental in the logistical and planning process. He would run around the city talking to teams and schools, and he helped us in numerous other ways, whether it was housing, meal plans, or securing tool rentals for the next volunteer trip.

I stayed with Horacio on one trip, and he made sure I had a ride to the airport and anywhere in between. His generosity and unconditional support were invaluable. I am grateful for his friendship and belief in what we were trying to accomplish.

This note is dedicated to all the wonderful people I met during my multiple volunteer trips to this historic city. I cannot possibly list them because I do not want to leave someone out. I love you all dearly and pray good things will follow you for the rest of your lives. God bless you for your unbreakable spirit, endless hospitality, and, most of all, the ability to smile, even after your world has been changed forever.

Mack in front of his house.

An Honor for Mack

September 6, 2015 🌐

I want to repeat my thanks to the Paintsville High School Alumni Association for inducting me as a Distinguished Alumni last night. It is a humbling award and one that I will cherish for a long time. It meant a lot to my family and me. I am never at a loss for words and have always felt comfortable speaking in front of people, but I choked up last night during my speech. I graciously accepted my award in honor of my friend, Mack McClendon, who passed in February.

Thank you to all the amazing teachers, counselors, and administrators for caring about every student and pushing us to go to college. That 100% of the last few graduating classes attended college is an extraordinary achievement, and it should not be taken lightly. Small schools sometimes must fight for funding to get new equipment for academics and athletics, but size has never stopped Paintsville schools from being competitive in both the region and the state.

To the current students at PHS, enjoy your time and days walking the halls and cheering on the Tigers. Someday you will miss it and realize how lucky you were to be a Paintsville Tiger.

Chapter Eight

The Positive Post Project

At some point on our path, we need to stop, recharge our batteries, and fill our tank with positive vibes, wonderful memories, and inspirational stories. I am hard-wired with a positive attitude and always searching for the elusive sliver of hope in the darkest moments.

I created this series during the early fall of 2016. The presidential election was heating up, and it seemed that the country was divided. I wrote positive stories related to current events. My goal was to make people smile and provide relief from the constant news cycle and what felt like a steady stream of negative social media posts.

Brian Tatum

September 2016 ◉

Life is a beautiful gift. It can inspire you and take away your breath in an instant. The subject and purpose of the first post is easy. It is not every day a best friend spends ten days in two emergency rooms, the ICU, the CCU, and the hospital's rehab ward. The terms CAT scan, MRI, and arteriovenous fistula (AVF) became common terms for the Tatum family and the Denver crew last week.

It was an emotional roller coaster filled with lots of prayers, positive thoughts, lit candles in churches across the country, gasps, fear, determination, and tears of stress and joy. I cannot forget the mass amount of frantic texting, emails, and calls. This week has provided some clarity and relief, but we are still taking things one day at a time.

Brian underwent successful brain surgery on Sunday morning to repair an AVF (arteriovenous fistula) located deep in his brain, along with two blood clots. The neurosurgeon used a scope and glue to fix the tangled artery and vein. It took a day for the irony of that to sink in. Of course the neurosurgeon used this type of material on the friend whom we often referred to as "the glue guy" in our crazy and wonderful group of friends.

I saw Brian briefly this morning in his hospital room and jokingly said the next time he wants to hang out, he can just call me and we can skip the extended hospital stay. We shared a few deep and hearty laughs. I also told him repeatedly it was great to see him in a much better state of health. He is doing well on his path to recovery. It is utterly amazing how his brain bounced back in a short amount of time and how his body has rebounded. The healing process will take weeks or possibly months, but he is in expert hands and on the right path.

I want to share my new favorite positive-thinking quote from Brian's mom, Nena. Late Monday evening, we were breaking camp after another long day, and we talked about how life throws us curve balls. Nena flashed a gritty grin and, without hesitation, proudly proclaimed, "Yes, but we have big bats." I am stealing this one, Nena, and will give you all the credit.

Tatum, none of us knows what lies ahead for you, but we know you are prepared to kick some butt and will come out stronger on the other side. You will experience a wide range of emotions, including love, gratitude, adversity, support, and other types of challenges and rewards. There are two things I want you to remember:

1. Call or email your friends with whatever help you need, because no favor is too big.

2. *You will not walk this path alone.* We love you, brother!

The Power of a Bike

August 8, 2016 ●

As anyone who enjoys writing will tell you, you wonder what story will be next, but sometimes the story finds you. Recently our daughter, Emily, learned how to ride her bike. It was one of those memorable parent moments you never forget. Kaden learned how to ride his bike in the alleys of Cory-Merrill, our old neighborhood, and I remember it like it was yesterday. Both kids thought Beth and I were still holding on when they started riding. Then they realized they were pedaling without us, and those memorable and gigantic smiles last forever.

The same weekend Emily learned to ride, I took Kaden on a three-mile bike ride near the cabin at an elevation above 9,500 feet. He rode the entire distance on a one-speed bike without complaining at all, which impressed me. It was fulfilling to spend time with him outdoors.

Teaching a child how to ride a bike presents a fine line between trust and guts. The child wants you to hold on to their bike seat as long as possible, but you know that if they are to flourish, you must let them pedal and build their confidence.

The experience made me think about my bikes—as in every bike I have ever owned. I remember my first bike was a Huffy. It had black, green, and white text and a number on the front. My next bike was a red and blue Huffy, complete with a banana seat. Then I moved up to a black and silver BMX bike. When I left for college, my uncle Peter gave me his old mountain bike, a blue Pacific one. Finally, I broke down and bought an entry-level Specialized mountain bike in 2015.

A bike builds confidence and is a kid's first form of transportation. My neighborhood in Paintsville was built for bikes. We rode them all day long. Saturday mornings started early with one or two cartoons; then it was out the door to meet your neighbor and add to our pack. I have mentioned the grass paths in posts before. They stretched for six or seven blocks. To this day, we do not know who mowed them for us, but I want to say thank you thirty-six years later.

I recently received an invitation from a childhood friend, Beau Spurlock, to join a Facebook group about a biking group based in Prestonsburg. I accepted the invitation and checked out a few photos, and I was impressed with what I saw. Beau and several other individuals—including Charles Lusk, another high school friend—have volunteered time and energy building mountain bike trails in the area. Their work has included group rides, maintenance, construction, and promoting the newly developed trails. Next is the development of maps, trail signs, trail markers, directional signage, and kiosks. This group has done some amazing work, and the local government agencies are pulling their weight, which is a great thing.

Beau and I exchanged a few quick messages early in the day and then resumed talking on Facebook after dinner. Beau has some great ideas. (Author's note: I am bragging on him because he was not interested in taking credit for the group's effort.) With this group and a little bit of money, they can add a full-fledged mountain bike trail system in the heart of eastern Kentucky. This is something that makes sense on multiple levels. The hills and abundant trees in the area are picturesque. We all can benefit from a little more exercise in our lives. Plus, if they can develop a significant trail system, bike enthusiasts will start making the trek to discover what makes this area unique. These tourists will need hotels, restaurants, and other outdoor leisure activities to pass their time, and the longer the trail, the longer tourists will stay in the local towns, which equates to an economic boost.

Beau and I talked for over an hour, and I sent him notes and ideas as fast as possible. He and the Prestonsburg city officials have grand visions. I hope they can garner some financial support from local businesses, including other influential individuals. This could be a real game-changer and the start of something bigger than a few mountain bikers slinging mud and sweat on an abandoned railroad track.

I will sign off with a few nods to cycling lingo. The leader in the Tour de France wears the yellow jersey. This is a team effort, and Beau may or may not be wearing the yellow jersey, but I know he and the other volunteers need a large support team. I encourage family and friends from Salyersville to Pikeville to make a difference in the community.

When mountain biking on an uphill climb, you downshift to granny gear, which is the slow and steady grind that propels you. On the downhill section, you lean back, brace yourself for the unexpected bumps, and speed down the trail, your heart racing as you take in the scenic views. I can jump on one of the hundred-plus trails in Denver, but the next time I go home, I will let my legs and lungs burn some calories close to the city that built me. Here is hoping the lower altitude helps me ride a little faster than I do now. Thank you to all the individuals who have donated time, sweat equity, and equipment to make this biking trail concept a reality. I truly hope our paths cross on the trail someday. Keep up the fantastic work and dream big!

Music to My Ears

September 2016 ⊗

I have ZERO musical talent, but I love music. I grew up listening to all types, but country music is probably my favorite. I can remember riding in the car with Mom and Dad and listening to 8-tracks of ABBA, Crystal Gayle, and other groups. After 8-tracks, we moved onto cassette tapes and eventually CDs. My iTunes library is a diverse collection that includes Motown, Trombone Shorty, country, Van Halen, and Disney songs for the kids.

I learned a lot about the music business from my dad's involvement with booking the country acts for the Kentucky Apple Festival. The booking side of the music "biz" has always interested me. Dad's annual challenge was to identify an affordable rising star, then book them in March for an October date. The goal was to secure them at a fair price, then keep our fingers crossed that the artist would have another hit by October or, better yet, win an award or two. This took on a new meaning this past year as our family watched Chris Stapleton win award after award. All I kept thinking was if his asking price was $40,000 before the CMA Awards, then it probably rose to $300,000 or more shortly after the post-party. Dad and I spoke soon after the show. We both said, "Good for him!" (Author's note: These numbers are hypothetical.)

For those of you who know my dad, you understand his sarcasm and sense of humor. Here is a story to illustrate my Dad's reputation as a practical joker. Singer Trace Adkins came to Apple Day one year. During his set, he joked about how he had walked through downtown and could not find any apples to buy. He referenced the festival's name and thought it was odd that visitors could buy everything from apple butter to apple pies, but not a simple apple.

That gave Trace's wife an idea for a prank. She pulled Dad aside and told him he should tell Trace that one of the festival board members was upset about his earlier joke and that they had left the concert early because of it. After the show, Dad approached Trace and said all of it with a straight face. Trace looked my dad in the eye, reached out his hand, and said, "Ray, I am sincerely sorry. Please call any board member who left early and have them come back over to the gym. I will stay here and gladly take pictures with each of them and sign autographs." His wife snickered, and Dad started grinning too. His wife playfully punched Trace and told him the joke was her idea. Well, Trace was shaking hands with my dad, and instead of letting go, he smiled and clamped down with a little extra force. Keep in mind, Trace is one tough dude. He is a former football player, 6' 6", and survived a gunshot wound through his heart and both lungs. Thankfully, that handshake didn't break any bones. Later, Dad told me it hurt a little but it was worth it.

Music and songs serve different purposes in life. A good song makes you think of an old flame, a memorable event, or a group of great friends. A song's lyrics can serve as motivation for a workout, a rallying point for a team, or a battle cry when someone you love or a dear friend is fighting for their life. Take a minute to think about the power of music and what it can do for people:

Religion: Different churches have different beliefs, but certain hymns cross those lines in a positive manner and for all the right reasons.

Sports: The Paintsville High School Band had some exceptionally talented musicians. As I look back, I can see that our band was ahead of its time. Where most bands might play the school fight song and a simple melody or two, our band played Van Halen's "Jump" and the Guns N' Roses song "Welcome to the Jungle." The group featured electric guitars, electric bass, and a drum set. My good friends Darren Patrick, V Grino, Scott Bradley, and Beau Spurlock were the ones responsible for the electric guitar riffs that pumped up our cracker-box gym. We might not have had a huge gym or new bleachers like a big-city school, but the Tiger Den was our home, and those guys rocked the house every time. These guys formed a garage band called Innovation and they played several weddings and special events.

Weddings: I have told my buddy V if *The Voice* or *American Idol* had been around in the '80s, he would have won one of those contests. He and his brother James sang at our wedding. My only regret is that we did not record James singing "Ave Maria." It was terrific, and his voice is incredible.

National anthems: The Olympics provide a global platform for the world's greatest athletes to showcase their talent. It is a powerful moment each time the gold medal is handed to an athlete and the winning country's national anthem is played. It is a moving moment for the athlete and his or her country. Beth and I went to the 2002 Winter Olympics in Salt Lake City, and the medal ceremony was such a neat experience. If you ever get a chance to go to the Olympics, do it, because you will not regret it.

Mixtapes: Kids today will never know the pure joy of composing a mixtape. First you had to write the list of songs. Then you had to put them in order because the songs' order was important. Next, you had to buy the six-pack of blank see-through Memorex cassette tapes from K-Mart. Then came the agonizing process of recording the actual tape. Do not forget, you had to have a dual cassette player to dub or copy a song. You started with the original tape in one deck, then you put the blank tape in the other deck and shut the doors. Next up was the crucial timing: You had to hit the red RECORD button at precisely the right time; otherwise there would be an awkward silence on your new mixtape. Oh, I can hear the plastic buttons and the doors closing in my head like it was yesterday.

The mixtape has now evolved into a playlist. Kaden loves music and sings along with every word. I must be careful with my country selections because he remembers lyrics. Thank God we have never gotten a call from the school asking why our son was singing about beer, heartbreak, or why someone's dog died. Emily is choosing her favorites. She is the animated one, and she sings at one volume, which is extremely loud. I always get them to join me as my drummer and air guitar player when we are driving long distances. They smile, and it is the one thing they can share and not fight about.

When I get the urge to write a column, it is the one time I can be at peace and focus on a project. I sit down and open my 2016 version of the mixtape: my iTunes library. Sometimes the words flow smoothly; other times, it might take me an hour or two to finish my thoughts. When it happens, I do not fret because it means I get to listen to some great tunes and play some air guitar for a little longer.

The Olympics

September 2016 ◑

I am a certified sports nut and can and will watch almost any sporting event. I love college football and college basketball like a kid loves candy. Before we had kids, I could sit on the couch from 10:00 a.m. to 10:00 p.m. watching college pigskin. However, as much as I enjoy talking smack about college teams and watching my beloved Wildcats cut down the nets during March Madness, the Olympics will always have a special place in my heart. I consider myself a lucky man when it pertains to the Olympics and what I have experienced firsthand. Here is a quick overview of my time spent with the Olympic movement:

1. Atlanta, 1996: My good buddy Mike Guelcher and I had a bright idea to drive to Atlanta because it was only six hours away—plus we had a free place to stay at Emily Neer's apartment. Guelch was and continues to be one of my close college friends. We are both wired in similar ways; yes, we had a few disagreements as good buddies do, but we never let it affect our friendship. I think it brought us closer because of the amount of respect we had for one another.

We both are true competitors at heart, but he is the better athlete by far. He lived in Blanding 3, and our halls split two of the popular intramural league championships. We won the softball title; they won the basketball one. If I am ever in a close game of hoops and Guelch is on my team, I know I am throwing it inside to the big fella to seal the win. Mike was the UK student who sunk a half-court shot at a UK women's basketball game and won tuition for the next semester. The best part was when he turned to the TV camera, pointed with both fingers, and did his version of ESPN SportsCenter jingle: da da da da da da.

Okay, time to get back to the trip. We saw Australia play the United States in baseball at Atlanta–Fulton County Stadium, across from the Olympic Stadium. As an event guy, seeing both stadiums empty out simultaneously was an amazing sight to witness. I think the baseball stadium held 45,000. The Olympic Stadium held close to 80,000. It was chaos! Fans lined the area from one side of the eight-lane expressway to the other.

2. Salt Lake City, 2002: My second Olympic trip was much smoother, and Beth and I made the eight-hour trek to Utah for a long weekend. We saw ski jumping and a hockey game. Unfortunately, the women's downhill was postponed because of wind—we were bummed to miss that event. We attended a medal ceremony, which was truly incredible in every sense of the word. We were lucky enough to witness an athlete from the USA accept a gold medal, which made it even sweeter.

The hockey game was cool because the avid fans were cheering, "Go Swiss, go Swiss!" It sounded more like "Sweeeesss." Late in the game, two players got tangled up, and one of them popped the puck from the ice. It was not a slap shot, but more like a short pop fly in baseball. The puck was approaching our section, but it was in slow motion. I did what any red-blooded sports fan would do: I threw my ski coat on top of Beth, jumped up, and caught the puck. My hand was slightly red, everyone around me started screaming, and the group exchanged high-fives.

3. Athens, Greece, and Denver, Colorado, 2004: No, I did not get to make the trip, but I met and played hoops with the USA women's Olympic basketball team here in Denver. I was working for the Metro Denver Sports Commission at the time and served as their team liaison for a few days as they played their final scrimmage games before leaving for Athens. Yes, all 5' 11" and 186 pounds of my scrawny body ran full court with Lisa Leslie, Sue Bird, Sheryl Swoopes, Diana Taurasi, and Tamika Catchings.

I remember how my heart raced as I checked the ball and passed it to Sue Bird. I vividly remember seeing those big and bold USA letters on her jersey, and my knees started shaking. Somehow, I managed a smile because this lucky kid was getting ready to defend Sue Bird. I cannot imagine how other Olympic basketball teams feel when they take the court against the USA women, but I have a feeling it is some combination of admiration, respect, and sheer terror.

I also caught a moving pick from Taurasi and thought I would be in rehab for a week. I called her out for it, and she flashed her million-dollar grin and then calmly sunk a jumper after her nasty pick.

I kept in touch with Tamika, and she was nice enough to send me a Christmas card. To this day, I try to read about her special events and commitment to the community in Indianapolis. She treated me as if I were one of the USA team's full-time staffers, and I have never forgotten her caring attitude towards everyone, but especially this former Wildcat. Yes, we joked about the UK and University of Tennessee basketball teams, but I did not have much to say other than that I worked as a manager with the UK team.

Another great story was when Lisa Leslie blocked my shot and sent it about 50 feet down the court. All I had to do was pull up for an open 3-pointer and drain a shot from the corner. No, I decided I would try to dribble in a little closer and take a baseline jumper. After Lisa swatted my shot, she smacked me on the back and said, "Brandon, sorry about the block, but you are not the first guy I've done that to." I laughed and said, "Lisa, are you kidding me? I will tell my great-grandkids you blocked my shot. It was my honor, believe me." The team gave our office a team-autographed basketball, and my boss let me have it. It is a limited-edition gift and one I will pass onto Kaden when the time is right.

In 2012, I worked for Ihigh.com and was asked to fly to Omaha to assist with live streaming and production for the USA Olympic swimming trials. I arrived and helped with some logistical issues and other marketing items, as I had for other large-scale events we had done in the past. Suddenly, a coworker hands me a microphone and says, "Tosti, you need to get ready because we are going to interview the mother of Michael Phelps in a few minutes." Wait, time out . . . I was talking to a random swim club from Austin, Texas, and now I am going to play Jim Nantz? With *zero* broadcasting experience? Did I mention this was live with no tape delay? The only thing I had going for me was that I generally can talk to anyone anytime about anything.

I frantically thought of the worst sideline reporters and told myself that whatever I said, I did not want to sound clueless or come across as a fan. The Phelps interview did not come to fruition, but I wanted to be prepared so I made a quick mental list of questions, and shortly after that, I interviewed Amanda Beard, Pablo Morales, and another medalist from Beijing. I was disappointed because Dara Torres and Natalie Coughlin did not stop by, but it was still a blast. I also interviewed one of the world's top Paralympic swimmers. At the time, she held thirty-four American records, fifteen world records, and two Paralympic medals.

I will always consider the Olympics a powerful competition for the world to see and to behold. It is woven with underdogs, triumph, disappointment, sportsmanship, and sheer determination. The athletes sacrifice their personal lives during the off years. Their hard work and training come down to one shot, one lap, or one hundredth of a second. I appreciate and enjoy it all, one event and one race at a time.

Once a Scout, Always a Scout

September 2016 🌐

I love it when a close friend from home visits Denver. I get to catch up with an old friend and show them the city. One of my favorite people in the world was passing through Denver earlier this month. Don "Doc" Bryson was my Scoutmaster, but he was much more than a Scout leader.

He and I went to dinner at the oldest steakhouse in Denver, the Buckhorn Exchange, because it was on his bucket list. To see the glimmer in his eyes meant the world to me. I think we all need to share more bucket-list experiences than negative stuff in our lives. We shared the rattlesnake appetizer, and I ordered the elk and quail combo plate. My good friends Brian Tatum, Kieran Cain, and Jeff Mathews are doubtless shaking their heads in disbelief at this point in the column because of my normally "vanilla" cuisine tendencies.

We had a grand old time swapping stories, and he relished the opportunity to tell some tall tales about me to Beth, Kaden, and Emily. True story: One time, I poured a bottle of hot sauce on Doc's spaghetti during a cooking lesson. He knew I was up to something, and he sat across from me and wolfed down the entire sample without a wince or a whimper. He was not about to let me have my moment, but he admitted to me this week that he guzzled a gallon of cold water shortly after that, making sure not to let me see him suffer.

Doc did so much for me, and I have thanked him privately and believe it is only right to publicly thank him. He was one of those adults who positively impacted my life, and we both share a zest for living life to the fullest. He was one of those friends who routinely asked about Beth during her battle against breast cancer.

Doc was my Scoutmaster, a great leader, and a phenomenal coach. He knew how to motivate me without pushing me too hard, and it is a particular skill that not all coaches have in their motivational repertoire. He inspired not with fear, but with respect and a positive attitude. He believed in me long before I did and made sure I faced my fears and moved on in life with confidence to make things better and always dream big.

I received my Eagle Scout badge on my mom's birthday, which was only fitting. The Scout receives only one badge, but I passionately believe duplicates of that tiny piece of embroidered cloth should also go to my parents and to Doc Bryson. Without their positive reinforcement, unconditional love, and support, I might not have made it to that level.

I was 14, and I remember my old friend Keith Tackett was there for my ceremony because he knew what the award meant to me. Auger (that was Keith's nickname in high school), I want to let you know I have not forgotten your gesture.

Now let us get back to the old Scoutmaster. Dr. Bryson taught me invaluable lessons along the way, and below are some of the most important ones:

How to build a campfire four different ways, safely handle a knife and an ax, and swim using four or five different strokes.

How to tie twenty-five different knots—especially the bowline, which is used in rappelling—and how to whip the end strand of a frayed rope.

How to use a compass (Beth might question this one).

How to combine six logs and a rope to create any number of useful camp gadgets.

How to cook in the outdoors.

How to show pride in my little town, home state, and this great country.

How to compete and always demonstrate good sportsmanship, especially when we lost a contest to our highly respected friends from the Prestonsburg troop.

How to save someone who is drowning—I earned this one! Doc was the meanest drowning victim in the world, but it was an important lesson that I shared with Kaden and Emily.

He taught me to chase my dreams with unapologetic passion and tenacity. The closest sports personality I can compare him to would be Jim Harbaugh. My favorite quote he always recited was, "Success is biting off more than you can chew and chewing on it."

How to splint a broken bone, save a person's life, survive in the wilderness for an extended period, and be prepared . . . *for anything!*

Fundraising for a Friend: A Little Sand and a lot of Hustle

September 2016 🌐

Recently, one of the good guys in this world experienced one of life's major speed bumps. Brian Tatum suffered a stroke and spent a few weeks in the CCU, ICU, and rehab unit between two hospitals, Good Samaritan and Swedish. He had brain surgery to repair an AVF (arteriovenous fistula) and has continued to make great strides in his recovery. His body was healthy enough to leave the hospital a week earlier than expected. He continues to amaze all of us and is getting stronger every day.

A week or two ago, he even asked me if I would join him for a test drive in an empty parking lot. I told him I would agree on two conditions: (1) I wanted to call my State Farm agent and increase my life insurance policy, and (2) I wanted to contact NASA and get a space helmet to protect my head from any crashes.

All joking aside, a bunch of us decided we needed to come together and support Tatum with a fundraiser. I lost track of the number of friends from near and far who called, texted, and asked what they could do to help. This trend has continued as an old friend asked me yesterday about his health status.

This event was a little different because the purpose was to help everyone's best friend with some extra money during his time of need. We did not have a 501(c)(3) letter, which limited our fundraising options and silent auction donations, but this large group of amazing people pressed on anyway.

Tatum is the friend who *always* made sure everyone, guy, or girl, made it home safe and sound. Maybe he called a cab or an Uber for one of us. Maybe he walked one or three of us to our cars and made sure a sober person was driving, or, better yet, agreed to stay until the end of the night to ensure every single friend made it home in one piece. It would be difficult to find a person who cares more about everyone else than Brian Tatum.

On the day of the fundraiser, a gentleman none of us knew walked in the door and dropped a hundred-dollar bill in the bucket. Someone brought it to my attention and asked me who it was, and I was not sure, but I will find out. I walked up to him and introduced myself and asked how he knew Brian. He said he had been a Colorado Rapids season ticket holder for twenty-one years, and as soon as he saw the Facebook post, he told his girlfriend his goal was to walk in the door and donate $100. A minute into the conversation, he mentioned to me that he pulled money out of his pension and his budget each week to make sure he had set aside enough money for the donation. I honestly did not know if I should hug this stranger, give him a high-five, or run outside and cry. This man's generosity was such a positive light in this sometimes dark world.

We planned this event in less than thirty days! None of us knew how much money we would raise or what the attendance would look like, but we pushed ahead and made our plans. Will Stevens handled the event location, which was a giant sand volleyball complex and bar. Keary Sullivan managed the silent auction and kept everything in check, including the cash collection and fulfillment. Everyone else did their part by inviting friends, generously donating at the door, and bidding on silent auction items. Somehow, yours truly came home with a team-signed soccer jersey from some London team—and I do not like soccer. For those soccer fans, it was a Tottenham Hotspurs jersey.

We thanked everyone for their donations of time, money, expertise, and creative silent auction items. Family and friends collected over thirty unique items for the silent auction. It alone raised over $3,000 for Tatum. The best part was we all knew who we were bidding against, which provided an opportunity for funny notes and trash talk scribbled on the bidding sheets.

Tatum is an event guy, and I am glad he could make it to the fundraiser and stay the entire duration. It was great to see such a good guy and great friend hug, smile, and welcome his family and friends. We all left with a little sand in our shoes and gratitude in our hearts, glad to have provided a bit of financial relief for one of those special friends everyone hopes they have in their lifetime.

Bidder's Name	Bid Amount	Bidder's Email Address
Ean Kelly	$40	
Tosti	$45	
Cam	$50	
Morgan	$55	
Cam	$60	Tosti told me to Cam. beat it Tosti!

"Tosti told me to, Cam."
Cam's response: "Beat it, Tosti."

Bonnie Brae Ice Cream—the Best in the World!

September 2016 ⬤

I am not a world traveler by any means. I have only visited four countries, but two of those were Australia and New Zealand, which is cool because those are both on the other side of the globe. I have a soft spot for sweets and am always up for sampling a new variety on a trip. Australia had Red Bull–flavored gelato, and I tried it. It was not bad. I passionately believe the best ice cream in the world can be found at the corner of University Boulevard and Ohio Avenue in Denver. They make the ice cream and waffle cones on site, and I *refuse* to buy a waffle cone anywhere else. The cones have the right balance of sweetness and crunch that hits the spot every time.

We were in our old neighborhood for a birthday party and had to make a stop for our favorite ice cream at Bonnie Brae. Triple Death Chocolate and a homemade waffle cone for me, please. Beth went with her favorite, Cappuccino Crunch. We drove the kids by the old house and stopped by to see an old neighbor, Lexie. It was good to see her, and as expected, our other neighbor was out on hands and knees, manicuring his lawn and part of our old yard. The little things in life mean the most. We all smiled a lot and enjoyed the quick trip. To the owners, if you ever expand to Arvada, please call me.

I love the old-school sign. Do not miss a drop!

Fighting Cancer Like a Superhero

October 2016 🌐

We all know someone battling some form of cancer. We also know this stupid disease does not discriminate against gender, race, or age. Joey McDonough-O'Neil was three years old last year when a repetitive fever did not seem right to his mom. So, Stephanie took him to the hospital. After myriad tests, the doctors told her the news no one ever wants to hear: Her loved one—in this case, her baby boy, Joey—had cancer.

Stephanie and I worked together at the 3v3 soccer and basketball company in Denver. She is the most positive-minded person I know and is fearless with *any* job-related challenge. I enjoyed working with her, and we became friends and kept in touch after she moved back to the East Coast years ago.

The bad news dealt her family a nasty sucker punch. Little Joey had a massive tumor in his abdomen and another near his spine; it was stage 4 neuroblastoma. Stephanie said within minutes of the news, sixteen doctors rushed in to discuss a plan of attack.

For the past year and a half, Joey has endured more pricks, pokes, and prods than most people will in their lifetime. He had to undergo multiple stem cell transplants, was kept at home for a hundred days straight under a strict isolation mandate, and made countless trips to the local children's hospital.

As a parent, I cannot imagine what Stephanie has dealt with as she watched her son go through this process. She is a tough cookie, and we have prayed for her and Joey often. We sent him a few care packages because we wanted to make him smile, at least for a little while. We picked out a large Superman figurine, some Hot Wheels, crayons, and a coloring book.

Later we sent him another small box of Hot Wheels. Stephanie mentioned Joey would have to take a daily shot for the next six months to bolster his white blood cells. She said she let Joey pick a Hot Wheel or other item out of the box as a reward after the shot. My gut reaction was this: Joey will need 180 Hot Wheels, so let's send him cars from across the country! I quickly realized it might not be the best idea. I figured we could send him cards with smiley faces or positive messages on Facebook instead—maybe a few cars if we checked with Stephanie first.

Through it all, this little guy has fought cancer and is on a much better path now. He made it to preschool last week, and a few more scans are on the horizon for additional monitoring, but the doctors seem positive at this point.

I have not met the little tyke, but I hope to soon. Joey, you have inspired our family and me in different ways. I do not know which superhero is your favorite, but I can tell you one thing for sure: You are mine. I hope you continue to receive positive news, and I look forward to more photos with your thumbs up and a big smile. If you ever come to Colorado, you can pick out a toy racetrack or a giant bucket of Hot Wheels to take back with you, along with your favorite superhero. Hug your mom from all her Colorado friends!

A Friendship of Convenience and Crossing Paths

September 2016 ⊗

If you have taken the time to read one of my posts or columns in the past few years, you know I often refer to the fact that I have some of the best friends in the world. Some are saints, some are class clowns, one or two could be models, and a few have been extremely successful in business ventures. It is a collection of well-rounded people to be associated with. I count these crazy kids among my blessings and thank God they put up with me all these years.

My high school friends know my UK friends, and my Denver friends are familiar with both groups. There is one friend I have not mentioned to either group yet, but after hearing some fantastic news from him, I could not wait to write this post.

Jon is outgoing, friendly, and says hi to nearly every person who crosses his path. It does not matter if you are male, female, black, white, tall, short, skinny, well dressed, or in blue jeans; he acknowledges you with a hearty hello and a warm smile. I am guessing he says, "Have a great day, sir!" a hundred times a day. He is a sales guy, and it is probably part of his DNA. He and I have known each other for half a year.

I work in downtown Denver, as does Jon. We cross paths often, sometimes two or three times a week. Sometimes we simply wave and say hi to one another, while other times we chat for a few minutes. We sometimes joke like Statler and Waldorf, the two old geezers on *The Muppets*. If I am on my phone, Jon will wave, and I will wave back. We talk about the weather, politics, and life. I usually see him in the morning on my way to Starbucks and sometimes in the afternoon.

The main reason none of my Denver friends have met Jon yet is because he is homeless. He mostly stays at a shelter, and he rides the bus from a northern suburb to downtown Denver each day to sell copies of *The Denver Voice*, a general-interest newspaper with a socially-minded slant. The paper is sold by people who are currently or formerly homeless, unemployed, or trying to get back on their feet. The paper is $2, and the vendors keep $1.50 from each paper sold.

Today as I walked to get an afternoon coffee, I stopped and chatted with Jon because we have not talked lately. I remembered he said he was on the waitlist for temporary housing. I cautiously asked him the first question. He eagerly replied with a gigantic smile, "Oh, yeah, I got a place. It is an efficiency studio unit, and one of the homeless nonprofit organizations helps pay the rent. I have to pay a small portion, but I can stay as long as needed or until they sell the building." I grinned and said, "That is awesome, Jon. You made my week! Congrats!" It is close to midnight, yet I am still smiling for him.

Jon told me he makes between $10 and $13 a day selling the papers. That is not a typo or a misprint. He usually works from around 10 a.m. to 4:30 p.m., give or take. I asked if I could help gather anything for his apartment, and he said no, he had most of the basics. He had asked one of his friends, a local businesswoman, if she could find him a used Crock-Pot. Sure enough, the next day, she brought him a brand new one. He said he needed a can opener, but a used one would suffice. I asked about plates and utensils, and he said someone gave him a four-piece dining set even though he lives alone. I am always impressed because he never asks for anything new.

He said the transition from being homeless to having a permanent residence had been a struggle, but his caseworkers told him it would happen. It is a feeling he is slowly but happily getting acclimated to with time.

Next, we discussed a laundry list of what he might need. I started with a list of toiletries, necessary utensils, and types of food. He laughed and said, "You know, I have to admit it's getting old eating peanut butter in the morning and tuna at night, but it is all I can afford."

I asked again if there was anything I could help with, and I could sense that he was uneasy, that something was not right. I went down the toiletry list again, and we reached that most basic of essential household supplies: toilet paper. He has plenty because individual establishments will give him a few rolls at a time, but he said it embarrassed him to ask me for this item.

We talked about the efficiency studio and how he has nothing to sit on. He and I joked about a bean bag or a simple chair. For whatever reason, he liked the bean bag idea.

I told him we needed to grab lunch one day at Sam's #3 since it was close to the office and one of my preferred restaurants. He said he really liked the restaurant and that the manager would sometimes buy him a meal. I have always enjoyed Sam's, and our kids love it too, but now I like it even more.

Life is good; life is really good. We all need to slow down sometimes, smile, and say hi to people on occasion. You never know what might happen or what will come of it. I know I am glad I have gained a new friend by walking the same area and crossing paths with a kind soul. He now has a roof over his head, just like the rest of us.

Raise a Glass and Cheer for Holidaily Brewing Company!

October 2016 🌐

Tomorrow is the start of the Great American Beer Festival in Denver, Colorado. The three-day event includes 700+ breweries, and my good friend Karen Hertz and her team from Holidaily Brewing Company have five entries in this year's festival! I am excited for her because winning a medal can only help Holidaily boost brand equity, PR efforts, and, most importantly, revenue.

Karen is someone I respect for multiple reasons. Her can do attitude is contagious; she is a two-time cancer survivor, yet she has maintained a positive outlook on life. She is also an intelligent businesswoman who will continue to be successful as the brewery expands and adds new beer options. Her creativity and zest for life lifts up family, friends and her employees.

She is a dreamer, but she is also a doer. This past year, she fulfilled a dream of brewing a tasty gluten-free beer and turned it into reality. She has always enjoyed craft beer, but doctors instructed her to eliminate gluten from her diet to be safe after her cancer diagnosis. At the time, a good-tasting gluten-free beer was not an option, but that is no longer the case.

Good luck to My Favorite Blonde, which is the name of the brewery's first beer. Karen's grandfather's nickname inspired it for her. Best of luck! I hope you bring home a medal or five!

A Cup of Joe and a Grocery Store Trip I Will Never Forget

November 2016 🌐

Last week, I bought my friend Jon a cup of coffee at Starbucks. We had to discuss our upcoming grocery store trip. This was due to the generosity of people who read my previous posts. I received $270 in donations from friends. As usual, my awesome hometown stepped up to the challenge and was responsible for $250 of it! The support from this tiny town never ceases to amaze me. Thank you from the bottom of my heart, and Jon thanks everyone as well.

Jon and I arrived at the store, and I told him we had $240 to spend on food and cleaning supplies. Earlier in the day, I bought him a 10-pass for Denver's public transportation system. This would provide a safe and dependable ride on snowy days. It was $23, and I gave him the remaining $7.

Jon headed straight to the meat section and grabbed a family pack of Polish sausage, two large hamburger trays, and bologna. I told him he could buy some ham, turkey, or chicken if he wanted it, but he passed. Jon might walk slow on the street, but we were booking it down the aisles. It appeared he was on a mission. He would stop and if ask me his choice in the aisle was okay, and I said, "Yes, anything but alcohol and cigarettes." It amazed me that he bought almost all generic-brand items. I told him it was okay if he wanted Sara Lee bread because it is the good stuff. He kindly declined and threw in the 88-cent loaf instead. It was utterly amazing to see how gracious he was because he repeatedly asked me for a dollar-amount update. He also bought a few clothes hangers, cleaning supplies, Clorox wipes, and a broom because he wanted to keep his apartment clean and wash the walls.

I offered to pick up some Ziploc bags for him, but he said no because he uses Target's plastic bags to wrap his food when needed. Again, I offered to buy him some cheap Rubbermaid containers, but he kindly said no thanks. He uses the black plastic Jimmy Dean breakfast bowls and washes them to reduce waste.

We made it to the checkout stand, and the cashier made small talk as usual. I told her we were celebrating Jon's new apartment and his story. I mentioned my friends had sent money for him to buy groceries. She smiled and said, "I transferred here from one of our other stores that generates $1.5M per week. This store is much different, as you know, and we see a wide range of individuals. I see something good every day; today, you two are the good."

I laid out the stack of twenty-dollar bills, and suddenly the cash register went from $264 to $244 with a store coupon of $20. I sheepishly grinned and said, "You must be a manager." Jon stepped away to load the grocery bags. She smiled and said, "Yes, I am. Please tell your friend my name; in case he comes in, I can tell him about any special discounts we occasionally have on gift cards."

Later that afternoon, a good friend of mine stopped by my office with three pairs of Nike tennis shoes, a pair of dress shoes, an extra pair of socks, and several ties for Jon. I gave them to Jon, and he was in disbelief and kept shaking his head.

When our country is questioning what seems like everything, I think it is important to remember that sometimes we must find the good, even when it's in simple things such as a cupboard filled with food, a closet with shoes, and, most of all, love.

The cart was full!

Donated items from my friend.

Jon's cupboard.

You Might Leave a Small Town, but the Spirit Never Leaves You

November 2016 🔘

In the fall of 1993, I packed my little Buick Skyhawk and headed down the Mountain Parkway to attend the University of Kentucky. I was eager to leave and ready to spread my wings. At college, you meet people from all walks of life, and it does not take long for you to appreciate your childhood, your family, and the friends and town that built you.

One story resonates with me to this day. A friend who lived in our residence hall grew up in the streets of Queens, New York. Chris called me Brandon Walsh, after the *Beverly Hills 90210* TV character, except it sounded like *Waaallsh* when he said it with his New York accent. He was tough as nails and told us his parents chose UK to slow him down, change his pace of life. Chris was a gentle soul but molded by the streets and feared nothing except algebra. When he was thirteen, he was standing beside his best friend when a bullet took his friend's life. I quickly realized how lucky I was to have grown up in a rural community. There were positives and negatives, as with any town, but it was a special place in the

'80s and early '90s for this young lad. It was safe, the schools were strong academically, and the people were and continue to be some of the nicest people in this messed-up world.

It was safe to ride bikes all day long and play baseball with your friends until dark, without a parent in sight. We left those bikes in the front yard because people respected others' property. Times change; I cannot imagine letting our kids run outside for eight hours unsupervised in present-day society.

As they say, with age comes wisdom. I came to realize why people stay in Paintsville or return to the area after college. The pride of the area is unmatched and often overlooked by outsiders and critics. The land's natural beauty provides ample growth opportunities, but it will take a concerted effort and requires old and new money to join forces. Things seem to be on the right track, and I hope they continue to stay the course.

This little town also hosts the Kentucky Apple Festival every fall. This event is close to my family's heart because my dad has voluntarily served as its executive director for more than thirty years. It is a homecoming weekend for college kids, and I always looked forward to bringing college buddies and girlfriends back home for Apple Day. We always had a good time, and my mom relished the opportunity to cook for an army of my crazy friends.

This past week, my dad sent my friend Jon not one but four Kentucky Apple Festival sweatshirts. I do not usually see Jon every day, but this week I ran into him several times, and each day he was wearing a different sweatshirt. Dad, he wanted me to tell you thanks because he loves them. He said they are comfortable and warm. I told him my hometown was a small one. Jon said he would look it up on the Internet. You can always count on Google to provide quality photos and factual statistics, but what it cannot quantify is the heart of our little town.

Another thing our town is known for is the athletic talent it produces. It is safe to say most of its star athletes were basketball players, but there was always a variety of other sports. In the past few years, football has taken over some of the spotlight.

Tonight, the Paintsville Tigers will begin the five-game march to the state championship. You might think the start of the high school football playoffs is standard. What is the big deal? We are a Class A squad. When I was there, we had a little over 200 kids in grades seven through twelve. We are not giants, and we do not always have cornfed linemen like some southern states, but we do have speed, an immense amount of pride, and team unity.

When I was in high school, we always came up short against our rival, Pikeville, and I lost $10 to my dad five or six years in a row. Last year, I was home for a week, and we hosted the Panthers. It was a great matchup and Kaden's first high school football game. We stood on the railing and watched the winning TD catch fall into the receiver's hands. I did not ask dad for $10 because he knew by my smile that I had finally won our bet. I was happy, but more like relieved.

Pikeville beat us in the semifinals and concluded their season by winning the state title. I have several friends and relatives who attended Pikeville High School or currently work there, and I will always respect their program and school. Plus, my dad taught special education at Pikeville High School for a few years in the early 1970s.

I hope this is the year for the Tigers. It will not be easy, and the big-city schools might taunt you because you talk funny. My advice is to let them say and think whatever they want, but be sure to ignore them and outwork them on the field. I have always tried to do the same. Money can buy shiny cleats and new uniforms, but it cannot purchase sheer determination and hustle. Let the chip on your shoulder be motivation, not a crutch. To this day, people still ask if I am from Alabama or Texas.

Brandon (left) and Jon chatting on the corner.

I can say the same for our cross-creek rival, Johnson Central. JCHS is a big school (4A, if I recall correctly) and has been a tough opponent to defeat the past few years. They not only compete with the big city schools, but they also have consistently won a lot of games. To my Golden Eagle friends, I hope you earn a big win for your school and for the county. Good luck, JCHS!

As for the boys in blue, always remember your hometown has your back, and you have a cheering section that spans the country. Bring home the hardware! #Onceatigeralwaysatiger #smalltownKYboy

For the Love of the Game

November 2016 ⊗

I love coaching youth basketball, and I try to cherish Kaden's time because I know I can coach him for only a few more years before he will be playing for a school team. Some of my best childhood memories were playing Buddy Basketball in the Johnson County league. It was a great opportunity for kids and included teams from the county, the city, and our Catholic school, Our Lady of the Mountains. I vividly remember my team names: Richland Supply my first year, then the Knicks after the league began to name teams after NBA organizations instead of local sponsors. We wore Chuck Taylors one year with knee-high tube socks, and then we moved up to the Kentucky Dunks or Skywalkers, which were like Air Force Ones. To this day, those basketball shoes are some of my favorite sneakers of all time.

We had a talented squad. Marty Preston was at point guard, and Brian Bailey was shooting long-range 3s as a ten-year-old. We even won the championship one year. One of our coaches, Ron Smith, was a local radio personality, and he invited us to the radio station for a tour and the chance to play DJ. Each player selected a song to play on the air. I chose "Jacob's Ladder" by Huey Lewis and the News. David Wright was our other coach. These two men taught me what it meant to be an excellent coach to kids.

I had the chance to coach the Catholic school kids (where I attended from first through seventh grades) for two years, and it was eye-opening but a lot of fun. Paraag Maddiwar and I shared coaching duties during our senior year. It was also the only time I received a technical in my ten years of coaching. There was a "no full-court press" rule if you were up by 10 points. I taught all my teams the importance of defense. Besides, it was our only way of scoring baskets because, at their age, jump shots do not seem to fall as easily as one might think.

Late in the game, I remember we were up ten, and my kids kept pressing because it was our first 10-point lead of the season. I received a warning and a technical because of it. I was screaming and wailing my arms like a madman trying to tell our kids to start at half court, but to no avail. The ref smiled and told me I had to leave the bench. I listened to the final few minutes of the game from the locker room. It was at the old Oil Springs gym, which I swear was one of the coldest gyms in the country, and I am still not convinced they did not store meat in a closet somewhere. We *always* started the 8:00 a.m. Saturday games in sweatpants.

My first basketball practice with our new team is a few days from now. I am fired up! According to my roster, we have a few sets of twins, and it is also a coed squad, which will be fun. The best part is that Kaden likes to practice. I do not have to push him or ask him to shoot hoops with me. This time last year, he was six years old and would ask me to run shooting drills with him in the driveway. He even beat me twice while playing Around the World, and one of those times I did not get to shoot at all.

He might not play competitively when he gets older, and I am 100% okay with that. I want him to find a sport he enjoys and pick a game he can play with his friends for years to come. I cannot control his future, but I teach him a few things: the importance of playing hard, shaking hands with his opponent, and cheering for the University of Kentucky Wildcats!

ADD and the Power of a Diagnosis

November 2016 ●

I have not discussed this with more than a close friend or two, but I thought it might help someone else down the road if I share my experience. For over thirty years, I have made it through life with Attention Deficit Disorder (ADD). The first time it hit me was when I was in a class, and the instructor gave us a sheet of paper with numbers from 1 to 50 randomly placed on the sheet. The objective was to connect the dots; naturally, we started with the number one. The instructor told us to begin. I drew my line from one to two; then she started talking slowly. I tried to find the elusive number three, but I could not do it. Finally, after three excruciating and painfully frustrating minutes, I gave up. I think I connected three, maybe four numbers. My mind and fingers were temporarily paralyzed, and I could not move the pencil. The more I tried to concentrate, the louder her voice became, and I wanted her to quit talking and shut the hell up. I was beyond frustrated and could not understand why. The exercise's point was to remind individuals how easy it is to become distracted while driving a vehicle.

Fast-forward to last fall. Kaden was trying to tell me a story, and I could not pay attention to the end. He got mad at me and asked why I was not listening to him. A similar incident occurred with Beth, and I thought I must be selfish and not a wonderful dad or husband. Bless Beth's heart, because she has always been incredibly supportive. She and I have had a lot of discussions about the condition, and she has discovered her coping mechanisms. I have tried to explain to her that the joke about my mind being like a man channel-surfing on TV is the most straightforward analogy.

I finally broke down and asked for professional help. I signed up for the comprehensive testing and paid $1,500 out of pocket to complete the process. After two appointments and four hours of testing, I received the official diagnosis that I indeed suffered from ADHD. I was tired of running from it. I am glad I finally faced my fear.

I am a highly creative person, but it scared me to try any medication due to the side effects, primarily that it might stifle creativity (which, it turns out, is a myth). The funny part was that the doctor said my competency scores were high, which meant I was highly functional even with the condition. Beth chuckled heartily when she heard the line and joked that she would like to have a word with my doctor.

At the end of the testing, I received a comprehensive packet for official documentation. The doctor mentioned I qualified for extra time allotments for tests, tutoring help for note-taking, and other accommodations. I smiled and said, "Where in the hell were you when I was at UK?"

People with the condition tend to share specific personality characteristics such as risk-taking, adventurousness, deep passion for activities or hobbies, and experiencing everything in life as part of the plan. Many people fear failure and the unknown, but a person with ADD thrives on them. The ADD mind operates differently because the emotions and the experience itself make life such a beautiful gift. Even when some new endeavor does not work out, the anticipation and emotional rush of experiencing new things is part of living your life. This explains a lot about how I live my life.

The doctor asked me if I was hyper-focused—if there was something I was passionate about or believed in with all my heart. I told her about my charity, and the fact that if I had been twenty-four years old and single, there is *no doubt* in my mind that I would have moved to New Orleans for two or three years to help rebuild the city.

Another example that comes to mind is from my time in graduate school at UK. I had good grades in high school but struggled in college and could not understand why. I am passionate about legal matters and have always been an avid reader for as long as I can remember. It would kill me to read 20 pages for an elective class in undergrad, but reading 275 pages of my Sports Law book in graduate school was easy and enjoyable.

After undergoing myriad tests, the one that stood out the most as my a-ha moment was simple. They asked me to repeat a string of numbers. Sounds simple, right? Keep in mind, it was just the doctor and me, with no external stimuli. The room was peaceful and eerily quiet. We started with this list: 2, 7, 14, 26, 40, 56, 100. The first three numbers were easy, but soon I could not recite or remember the fourth number, no matter how hard I tried or how intently I listened. The moment was surreal. It felt as if something or someone had waved a white wall in front of me. I physically could not hear or concentrate on the number. I already knew the outcome and the official diagnosis. I have ADD. It is okay, because I am doing something about it.

When I started my Positive Post Project, I knew I wanted to write a column about this topic, but I did not know when or how to share it. I did not write this column for pity or support. I wrote it for my kick-ass wife, Beth, our rock-star children Kaden and Emily, and my family and friends who have been impacted or hurt over time. I also wrote it for anyone struggling with something in their life, because sometimes we all need a little help.

Getting treatment for ADD has been a truly life-changing experience. I told Beth the effect of the medication sometimes feels like an out-of-body experience because it's a bit of a shock to realize that this is how ordinary people live. I now remember things on my task list—they naturally surface in my mind, like Outlook appointment reminders. In the past, I would space on a task and remember it a day or two later or not at all. The challenge is that the medication makes it difficult to fall asleep. At

2:00 a.m. I am wide awake, but not in a hypersensitive way; it is more like a steady level of energy. I do not feel tired at all. I am still tinkering with the right mix of medication. It is not something I need every day, but it slows things down for my mind.

I would be remiss if I did not thank a former coworker who suffers from the same condition. This person also chose medication and was the one who supported and encouraged me to get tested. Out of respect for your privacy, I won't mention your name, but you know who you are, and I want to say thank you, because I owe you one.

To all my wonderful family members and crazy friends, I apologize for interrupting you in the past or not being able to look you in the eye for a five-minute conversation. I promise I am trying to do better, even though some things will always be out of my control.

For anyone struggling with this condition or wondering if they should reach out to a specialist, please know you are not alone. Sometimes a diagnosis can lead to positive things. I promise I will be your biggest cheerleader, as I am for the kids I coach.

A Soldier, the Gentleman's Game, and a Dream

December 2016 🌐

Once again, I was fortunate to teach another Sports Marketing class at Johnson & Wales University. I began the lecture with an overview of my background, failures, successes, and how the sports industry has changed. I also discussed the importance of believing in yourself and getting involved to make the world a better place. I closed with a piece on the nonprofit organization I established in 2007. I told the students the idea had made little sense on multiple levels, but with a bit of money and tremendous support from friends and family, we made a difference for schools and other recreation centers. After seven volunteer trips, my life changed forever, and New Orleans will always have a special place in my heart. I tell all my students that when someone tells you that you cannot do something, try it anyway. Tell them you know a particular person who has a different opinion.

When class ends, it is common for a few students to approach me to shake my hand and introduce themselves. When the last student approached me, I was not expecting what happened next. The young man started by referencing my statement regarding pursuing something even when the signs of life seem to be telling you not to because it would require too much work or be impractical.

This student, JJ, was an Army veteran and had a therapy dog for his PTSD. I knew not to approach the dog since she was working. I asked this student a few questions about his dog and his Afghanistan experience. Delphi (DELL-fye) was extremely friendly and jumped in my lap, and she started pawing at me as soon as he gave the all-clear sign.

When JJ was nineteen, he was patrolling an area when his interpreter stepped on a landmine. JJ was less than two feet from the explosion, and it knocked him unconscious for a moment as twenty-four pieces of shrapnel struck his body. His interpreter survived the explosion but, unfortunately, lost his foot and part of his leg. JJ's description was eerily like Hollywood portrayals of war-related incidents: the bright flash of light, the loud explosion, and then a confusing combination of silence and darkness. One of his fellow paratroopers appeared from the cloud of dust, seemingly in slow motion. He started to drag JJ to safety, but JJ started shaking his hands because they felt as if they were on fire, but luckily that was not the case. The military-issue gloves had two heavy-duty Velcro closures, yet the explosion had shredded the closures. When he shook his hands, both gloves dropped to the ground.

JJ suffered a traumatic brain injury and a ruptured eardrum in his left ear, and he received a medical discharge from the military. He considers himself one of the lucky ones and still smiles a lot for someone who has been through hell.

In 2013, he started working at a golf course in the grounds department and started playing golf regularly, which provided some comfort, but PTSD made it difficult to enjoy life, including golf.

A year later, JJ and his wife moved to Denver for a new start. He resumed playing golf and paid for some golf lessons. Over time, his average scores dropped from 100+ to the low 80s and often dipped into the mid-70s. The next step was to take part in golf tournaments. He played events on the Golf Channel Amateur Tour, on the Veteran Golf Association Tour, and at his local Men's Club. He notched multiple wins and finished in the top ten most of the time.

JJ's focus now is to finish his degree in February, then move to North Carolina to pursue his dream of being a professional golfer. Few golfers ever qualify for the PGA Tour, and it is an expensive dream to pursue. Expenses include green fees, golf clubs, apparel, lessons, and range balls. Then come tournament fees, meals, and travel expenses. JJ asked me how he could sell sponsorships for himself. I told him it would be an uphill climb because he is starting from scratch, but that I would gladly support him however I can. He responded by saying, "When I make it, I will remember any company that sponsors me."

My mind kicked into high gear. We started formulating a laundry list of what his next steps should be, and I immediately rattled off a few critical things. First, he needed to tell his story with a blog and set up a GoFundMe page. Second, he needed to build his brand, design a logo, and create a strategic donor/sponsor plan. I explained what people look for when deciding whether to support a cause and other compelling reasons people donate to causes. I told him he needed to be transparent with all funds, send handwritten thank-you notes, and offer various support levels. For example, a bucket of range balls costs $10; he should list that as an option. I told him that including both short- and long-term donation options would broaden his donor base.

I also stressed the importance of researching and identifying which companies sponsor veteran programs. I advised him to build his network, because contacts can lead him to individuals who possess an affinity for golf and are well-known philanthropists. I summarized our discussion with this advice: You have a story to tell. You need to let the world know that you intend to chase your dream, but you need a little help along the way.

I realize the odds are stacked against JJ. He might not make the PGA Tour, but that does not mean I will not support his dream. Out of curiosity, I looked up some PGA-related stats. The following is what I found. Out of the 80 million golf players in the world, 245 play the Tour. That means JJ has a 1 in 326,000 chance of seeing his name on a Tour leaderboard, or about 0.0003 percent.

I told JJ I would help him develop his sponsorship plan and introduce him to a brand agency that I trust, to graphic designers, and to some of my marketing and PR agency friends. Life is full of second chances. In golf, a second chance is called a mulligan. I think we can all agree that JJ is making his mulligan count.

Junior Bookworm

September 8, 2020 ⦿

Today was the first in-person school day for Emily. Beth always laughs and says that Emily is definitely my kid. She is a people person, wears her heart on her sleeve, and always offers to comfort her friends when someone is having a bad day.

Another characteristic that Emily and I share is the fact that neither of us is a morning person. However, this particular morning was different. She woke up an hour early but did not make a sound or say anything to us. Instead, she sat in bed and read her new book for 20 minutes by the dim light of her alarm clock. (Like most parents, Beth and I let some rules slide and make mistakes every week, but the one thing we stress with both kids is the power of reading books.)

After that, she sprang out of bed, packed her lunch, and prepared her backpack. She was ready to go at least thirty minutes earlier than usual. We relished the moment because she was excited to see her teacher and classmates. It was a gentle reminder for us to slow down and smile as our baby girl anxiously turns the page of a new school year.

Granny Is Always Paying Attention!

September 16, 2020 ⦿

Last week, I was working at one of the drive-in films at Red Rocks. We have two lanes available for cars to enter the parking lot, but guests typically use one lane because they see one of us first.

We wave or motion vehicles so they can use both lanes. I kindly waved at this large van to let the driver know that I could help them, but she didn't see me for a few seconds. Then she waved at me and safely pulled into my lane. She apologized for not seeing me sooner, and I told her that it was not a big deal.

Then a voice from the back screams, "Marsha, I don't know how you missed him—he's only 6' 5"!" I started chuckling as I was reciting the rules and protocols for the event. I gathered myself and looked at the grandmother tucked in the back and said, "Ma'am, I am only 5' 11", but I appreciate your comment." She responded, "Honey, I'm barely 4' 8", so anyone over 5' is automatically 6' in my book." After they drove off, I laughed so hard and told my teammate about the grandma who made my year with that comment. #littlethings

A Few Words

September 17, 2020 🌎

Earlier this week, Mark Harrison, a business friend of mine, released his first book, titled *What Sponsors Want: An Inspirational Guide For Event Marketers*. Mark is the founder and owner of the T1 Agency, based in Toronto, Ontario. The company focuses on marketing and sponsorship activation, sales, and consulting.

Mark and I met in Nashville a few years ago at his company's Sponsorship X conference. I was impressed with him right away. I have very little patience for cocky people, but I have an immense amount of respect for successful people who remain humble and down-to-earth.

Mark falls into the latter category. At the conference, he easily transitioned from hosting a Q & A with the CMO of Pepsi and the National Marketing Director of Pizza Hut to learning about my job and what motivates me while we shared a bus ride to the next activity.

I had the opportunity to read the manuscript for his book, and it was everything that a sponsorship book should be and then some. I am a sucker for a good business book. To my amazement, Mark asked me to submit a few words to be included in the Endorsements section in the front of the book. I still shake my head in disbelief that this unique opportunity came my way.

This is a humbling honor that I did not take lightly. Thankfully, my word count was capped, but I spoke from the heart. I hope that I can return the favor if I am lucky enough to write a second book someday.

To my bosses, coworkers, and interns, past and present: I encourage you to purchase Mark's book. It is a powerful combination of case studies, interviews with sports and entertainment executives, and true stories from a wide variety of sports. Mark's thought-provoking approach is one we can all learn from.

The sponsorship industry is a multi-billion dollar one that is driven by data, impressions, sales, and creative activations that leave a lasting impression on fans. A successful sponsor activation generates more than just a temporary media buzz—it creates a story that lasts, kind of like a great book.

Sweet and Sarcastic Sixteen

September 25, 2020 🌐

Today, Beth and I celebrate sixteen years of marriage and twenty-two years together. We started our day with some caffeine and a cinnamon roll—Beth's favorite breakfast treat—at a mom-and-pop coffee shop called Red Silo Coffee Roasters. Shortly thereafter, the thoughts and stories trickled into my mind. I didn't make it to sixteen, but I wanted to share a few fun tidbits and my thoughts about marriage that everyone can relate to.

1. Sleep patterns. Beth lies completely still for ten hours and does not move an inch. I toss, turn, flip, and wake up looking like an extra on the jungle set of *Jumanji*.

2. Dishwasher-loading templates. First, there are two mindsets in the world, and these two kinds of people *always* marry one another. Beth, who is an engineer by trade, follows rules and rigid procedures: $x + y = z$, always. Her mindset is useful for obvious reasons; designing safe, sturdy bridges is kind of important in life. I, on the other hand, am a marketing and sponsorship guy. I am a DJ, a firefighter, a diplomatic negotiator, and an event planner. My job is to fix things and ensure that everyone is happy.

Not surprisingly, Beth and I have different views of loading the dishwasher. For Beth, every dish, utensil, and plate has a specific landing spot, and every square inch must be methodically inspected and approved before the door is closed. I have ADD, so I focus on efficiency. I stuff, cram, and push the eleven bowls and all the awkwardly sized coffee mugs into the tiny space. I enjoy slamming the door and seeing if it closes on the first try—if it does, I win the prize.

To draw an analogy to children's games: Beth loads the dishwasher like Perfection, and I do it like Hungry Hungry Hippos.

3. Passionate Foodie vs. Plain Jane. Beth appreciates the spice and flavor of the world's simplest and most extreme delicacies. She will sometimes order a new dish, as one normally should. She is a good cook and is never afraid to bake something new. I eat a ham or turkey sandwich with lettuce, cheese, and tomato, no sauce or condiments required. My stomach somersaults when I just look at spicy food, although I do enjoy some mild Cajun seasoning every now and then. I order the same thing at every restaurant, and the rare times I stray, I am usually disappointed in my choice.

4. Project-management pro. Beth is intelligent and is fascinated by how things work. She has saved us thousands of dollars over the years when it comes to home projects. I (jokingly) aggravate her about having to submit blueprints to her before I start a project, but she knows my weakness. She knows how much time a project will take in reality, not in my space-cadet's mind. She has taught me a lot about the importance of planning and preparation.

5. Shared passion. It is important to maintain your respective hobbies when you get married. It is equally important to share one or two passions. For us, that equates to travel and hiking. We love to do both and have the stories to prove it, including helping a Swedish couple reach safety in New Zealand on Christmas Day (the wife had suffered a broken ankle) and me screaming like a small tyke when I almost stepped on a rattlesnake in the Badlands.

If we ever win the lottery, I guarantee you will find us on a cruise or one of those around-the-world excursions.

6. Sarcasm and silliness. Marriage is not always rainbows and unicorns. Life can be stressful. Some days you disagree and argue about serious issues or even simple ones. Other days, you lose focus on what brought you together in the first place. It happens, and it is scary when it does, but it is part of the deal. If you doubt it, ask a couple who have been married for forty years. This is why it is important to have fun and not take things too seriously. We both appreciate a gut-busting comedy or a good one-liner. We often use sarcasm to break up the stress and remind ourselves that it is important to laugh.

Laughter makes life more fun. Beth and I may or may not be guilty of repeating the same movie lines. This is perfectly normal until you hear your nine-year-old daughter say, "Craig, every time I'm in the kitchen, you are in the kitchen!" One of our neighbors is named Craig, so our kids have heard me say that line a few times. Dear Emily's teachers: Just for the record, she has not seen the movie *Friday*.

As I take a moment to reflect on the past sixteen years, my heart and mind are a mixed bag of emotions. We have lived in four houses, had two kiddos, fought cancer, lost some dear friends way too soon, and landed on a wonderful cul-de-sac that supports our little family with fitness, wine, sarcastic humor, and, most of all, love.

Chapter Nine

A True Appreciation of Time

It is important to pause on your path and take some time to appreciate the ride, the detours, and the express lanes. Life is short, and there is never a wrong time to reflect and reminisce. Do not forget to take time to look ahead and plan your next adventure, whether it is a weekend with college buddies or a road trip of a lifetime. Minutes and moments are the true currency of life.

Six Strings, Seven Seasons

February 6, 2020 🌐

For most of the 20+ years of my career, my work life has revolved around a season. Whether it was a 65-city national 3v3 soccer tour, a ten-game high school football schedule, collegiate sports, pro sports, or the 160+ shows of a Red Rocks concert slate, I lived and died with the downtime and, alternately, the hair-on-fire uptime of my work season. I am sure someone in the sports and entertainment industry coined the term "the grind" a long time ago, but employees commonly use it, and has a deep and real meaning for myself and many of my peers.

I recently completed my sixth season with Denver Arts & Venues. My job is to manage corporate partnerships and activations at Red Rocks Amphitheatre and other city-owned venues. Before each season, I take a moment and a deep breath, and I think about all the little things that come together to make each season a success. I appreciate the time invested by the various groups, from bands and promoters to vendors, police, fire, and paramedics, as well as the corporate sponsors whose accounts I manage. I value all the crucial relationships. Most importantly, I treasure the memories from specific shows.

Maybe it is the Eagle Scout in me, or maybe it's because I have experienced every kind of weather imaginable during my time at Red Rocks. Either way, if you set foot in my SUV from April to November, you will probably see a winter coat, a hoodie, rain pants, a bag of beef jerky, and several Clif Bars. I know a quick drop-in to check on a sponsor activation does not always end with a smile and simple handshake. Mother Nature can bless or curse your evening. I try my best to be prepared for anything.

One perk of my job is the opportunity to discover new bands. I enjoy going to a show with low expectations and walking away a fan of some new artist or band. Last year, I discovered the Icelandic blues/rock band Kaleo and found a new favorite song. My good friend Kristen Kelly and I also realized we might have a future hosting a talk show from a Red Rocks parking lot. We laughed until we cried as we covered important topics such as our favorite tailgating food options, poor shoe decisions, and questionable wardrobe choices.

Sometimes music provides healing when you need it the most. Last fall, one of my childhood buddies lost his father. I could not offer much solace, but I thought he could use a night out as a temporary distraction. We went to Red Rocks and saw Trombone Shorty, one of our favorite musicians. While we waited for the headliner to take the stage, my buddy and I shared our memories of his dad. He had been our Little League coach and our all-time QB whenever we played football in the front yard. He was one hell of an athlete and always encouraged us to play any activity outside.

We both walked away even bigger fans of Trombone Shorty after his high-energy dance party of a show. From the opener to the encore, he did not disappoint. This summer, my friend and I went to another Trombone Shorty show in Boulder at the historic Chautauqua Auditorium. Once again, the band brought its trademark high energy and jammed for almost two hours.

The 2019 season was another successful year for Red Rocks in terms of the number of shows. Also, history was made, which is always fun to witness in person: Stevie Wonder made his first appearance at the amphitheater. He mesmerized the crowd and had a lot of energy, cracked jokes, and brought out a surprise guest, Usher, for a few songs.

Diana Ross also made her second appearance, the last time being fifty years ago. Fans relished the opportunity to see a Motown legend live in Colorado, and they commented on her multiple wardrobe changes and her powerful, crystal-clear voice.

Sometimes music provides a new level of appreciation for reasons other than just entertainment. Beth and I always try to go to a country concert each season. This year was no different. We saw two of country music's rising stars: Luke Combs and Tyler Childers. We had the pleasure of sitting with Luke's dad, and we could see the happiness and pride in his eyes as his son sang his heart out for over 9,000 fans. It was a combination of a heart bursting at the seams and pure bliss. He was friendly and down to earth.

Tyler Childers was born and raised in Lawrence County, Kentucky, which is about thirty minutes from my hometown, but he graduated a Tiger. One of his songs references a boy from eastern Kentucky, and I yelled a little louder than most during that part of the song. I still must pinch myself when I think about the two famous Kentucky boys who have taken the stage at Red Rocks. Beth told me I should have brought the poster she made for me when we saw Chris Stapleton at the Bluebird Theater with 400 people. She drew it on the way to the show. It had the state of Kentucky with a flag and the words *I'm from Paintsville*.

This season also included plenty of Yoga on the Rocks and our new winter sports conditioning program, SnowShape. My teammate has been working on SnowShape for two years, and it was fun to see the vision and his hard work finally come to fruition. We partnered with Stefan Olander and Eric Waller, the owners of Fitness in the City. They and their entire team brought a positive attitude, a tremendous amount of energy, and a lot of strength and cardio knowhow to our participants for all four sessions. They varied the workouts enough to challenge all fitness levels, not to mention our door prizes were not too shabby either. Our partner Red Bull even provided some of their professional athletes for a special appearance, which was cool and a fun surprise for the participants.

I have always said I love working with good people, and Stefan and Eric at Fitness in the City are first-class at what they do. Also, they do some great things from a civic standpoint in our city. If you are looking for a new workout option, I encourage you to check out http://www.fitcdenver.com. Be prepared to sweat!

As the curtain closed on the 2019 season, I enjoyed a little downtime, then shifted my focus and energy to the 2020 season, which will be my seventh season. My job often reminds me that regardless of job title or rank, we all need the ability to work with one another to get the job done. So, to conclude this column, I have jotted down seven takeaways from my job.

1. Every season, you will probably see or hear something that shocks you and catches you off guard.

2. Someday I will write a book about what I have seen and dealt with during my career. It probably will not make any bestseller lists, but the colleagues I have spent time with at soccer fields, football stadiums, and iconic music venues will enjoy a good laugh or two.

3. My job has prepared me to handle a wide range of situations and taught me how to read people. I might have a second career as a detective, FBI profiler, or negotiator.

4. As with most things in life, you see a person's true colors when a sponsor activation goes awry.

5. Remember that mistakes will happen. Sometimes it is your fault, and sometimes it is not. Understand the difference. Own it when it is your fault, but do not take mishaps personally and waste precious time and energy dwelling on them. Solve the problem and move on together.

6. The successful sponsorship employees are the ones with the most creative minds. They present innovative concepts that benefit more than their own brand. I always thank one of my accounts because she pushes me positively to "elevate my game" and be a better sponsorship activation manager.

7. Sponsorship starts with an investment and a contract, but it still comes down to relationship-building and working with people to accomplish the brand's goals.

X Marks the Spot: My Thoughts on the Sponsorship X Conference

May 2, 2019 🌐

I am far enough along in my career to have been to several conferences. Some were bad, some were good, and a few were spectacular. Sponsorship X undoubtedly fell into the last category. The T1 Agency is based in Toronto, but its first U.S. conference was held in Nashville, Tennessee.

When I started researching potential sponsorship conferences to attend, I found options in Las Vegas, Malibu, and a new one in Nashville. Sponsorship X appealed to me for a variety of reasons. I reached out to Simon Nassar at the agency. Since it was less than a month until the conference, I had several questions for him. I sent Simon a few emails, and each time he responded quickly with answers and additional information. He even followed up a week later to make sure I had everything I needed.

I have always been a people person at heart, and I relish the opportunity to network and establish new relationships. I had the chance to talk to the agency's owner, Mark Harrison, on multiple occasions. I appreciated his down-to-earth personality and how he was constantly interacting with attendees. I know he probably had more important things to do with his time, but successful people like him always impress me because they have not forgotten what has the most significant impact on life and business: people.

The panelists were a well-rounded group of fantastic talent, and the topics included sports, entertainment, music, marketing, e-sports, and millennials. For me, the best part was how most panelists stuck around to shake hands and talk shop for a few minutes with the attendees.

From a business perspective, my favorite presentation dealt with the challenge of integrating sponsors with the Grammys because the sponsor branding needs to be subtle and not outshine the stage. The presenters talked about several eye-catching and creative activation opportunities they had implemented for the Grammys. This resonated with me because we face a similar challenge with Red Rocks Amphitheater.

Another powerful panel took place at the nearby offices of the Country Music Association (CMA). We heard from the executive director of the CMA Foundation and learned more about the popular multi-day CMA Fest event, which is the Super Bowl of country music festivals. The panel concluded with a Songwriter Series featuring three aspiring country artists, which was fun.

The after-hours activities were first class. On night one they treated us to a traditional Southern dinner and an intimate performance with a great Canadian country group, The James Barker Band. Being a long-time country music fan, I was happy to discover a new group to listen to and tell my Denver friends about when I returned home. The members were full of energy and played their set with a passion usually reserved for an arena show. After the performance, they stayed and took photos with everyone.

Another unique activity at Sponsorship X was the opportunity to exercise and play flag football at Vanderbilt's stadium. Our team's performance was nothing to write home about, and I do not think Vandy's head football coach had any interest in anyone on the field. The best part for me was that Simon neglected to tell me he had played professionally in Europe for a season or two. I should have known something was up after the first time we rushed him, and he calmly threw a perfect strike for a 40-yard touchdown.

The conference concluded with an NFL Draft watch party. As a proud University of Kentucky alum, I must admit the once-in-a-lifetime opportunity to see a Wildcat football player go in the first round was an unforgettable memory. I also appreciated that we could take in the festivities on a rooftop because the streets were jam-packed.

As you know by now, I was raised in a small mountain town in eastern Kentucky. I feel as if I know what Southern hospitality truly means. After spending a few days in Nashville with the team from T1 Agency and Sponsorship X, I must say our wonderful neighbors to the north know a thing or two about it as well.

Simon and I remain good friends and have kept in touch. He told me he has used my column several times when speaking to potential attendees who were on the fence about whether to attend the next Sponsorship X. I look forward to seeing my friend again. Hopefully, Simon's touchdown total will be one less.

Me and Simon after the football tournament.

Rooftop view of the crowd on NFL Draft Night.

The Big Four-Oh! Thoughts, Musings, and Life Lessons Learned Along the Way

April 2014 🌐

I created this list as I was approaching my fortieth birthday. I am glad to add another number to my age. I have been blessed in a hundred different ways and honestly cannot complain about anything. I tasted success and endured failure, but I have learned from both and keep on smiling because it is all part of the journey. Life is the greatest gift. Take time to enjoy the ride because we only go around once. Make it count.

1. I have been called a lot of things in my life, but "Daddy" is my favorite by far.

2. Marriage is one of the best things that can happen to a person.

3. Having kids is the best thing that can happen to a person.

4. I am lucky I married my best friend, and I do not think anyone else could put up with me as she does. She is the strongest person I know, and she is my cancer survivor. God bless her!

5. I was blessed with some of the best youth sports coaches and Boy Scout leaders a kid could ask for. Thank you, Don Bryson, Johnnie Ross, Jerry Adams, Ron Smith, Robert Baldwin, and Bob Daniels.

6. I enjoy almost any sport, but you will never convince me that tie scores make sense.

7. My childhood neighborhood was one of a kind, and as I get older, I realize more and more how much I cherish those times and those friends. We had our own "Red Monster" baseball fence, along with Wrigley Field ivy (or shrubs in our case) and endless bike paths. We would meet on Saturday mornings after cartoons and plan our day.

8. I have learned a lot from both poor people and rich people.

9. Cancer sucks, but it brings out the absolute best in people.

10. Sometimes the chase—whether for a girl, a dream job, or anything else—is just that, a chase, and not what you thought it was when you started the journey.

11. I have said this before, but if there were a way to bottle and contain the emotion you feel when you hold your newborn child for the first time, then we might have a decent shot at world peace.

12. A person can take away a job, but they can never take away your dignity, drive, or positive attitude. Chalk it up to experience, and go kick ass somewhere else. Karma usually finds its way to those who treat people like crap.

13. I have some of the best friends a guy could ever ask for, and I am thankful for the trials, tribulations, and funny stories along the way.

14. I have been fortunate to travel to a few foreign countries and close to forty states. We can find some of the nicest people in the world in eastern Kentucky and in New Zealand.

15. I have an extremely low tolerance for pessimistic people. The game is not over until the clock hits :00.

16. Money is valuable, and it is important, but a friend in my life who had millions always told me he would trade it all to have a family. I have never forgotten those words.

17. You are never too old for a home-cooked meal by Mom.

18. You are never too old to call Dad for advice.

19. If you grow up in a town where your dad knows everyone, it is best to tell the truth when you wreck your car on Homecoming. The reason is that he will see the truth before you get home. The grounding will be brutal until your best friend's dad convinces him it is acceptable to end the punishment. *P.S. This was the only time I ever lied to my parents.*

20. You can discuss religion and politics with a true friend.

21. I love people and hearing their stories. I would like to have a talk show, not for fame but to meet everyday people and learn about their lives. Even though I had zero broadcasting experience, I thoroughly enjoyed interviewing Olympic swimmers for Ihigh.com. Mom says I can talk to anybody about anything, and I think she is right.

22. Road trips are the best way to travel. The stories and memories go on forever, and the tall tales will continue to grow with age and a drink or two.

23. I think it would be neat to run for public office, but I know the political system would drive me insane.

24. I genuinely believe you can accomplish almost anything with the right people, a little money, and a passion for making something better. Special thanks to my childhood friend, Marty Preston, for giving me the $750 IRS application fee to start Sports for a Cause.

25. Ego is a tricky thing, kind of like using salt when you cook. If you use too much, the meal leaves a nasty taste in your mouth. It is best to let your personality and passion be the extra spice. There are plenty of egomaniacs in the world; do not add yourself to the list.

26. Two things in this world are impossible to master: (1) golf and (2) managing people.

27. Do more than write a check to your favorite charity. Volunteer to serve on a committee or help promote the annual fundraising campaign. Your friends and contacts are more likely to donate if they know you are passionate about something.

28. Good grades are important, but networking is paramount. The kid from Harvard will come in second place if the kid from a small college has a better connection to the hiring manager.

29. My favorite job in my career paid the least amount of money.

30. Networking is the most crucial career skill. Master it, and you will never be out of a job for long.

31. One cannot truly fathom the concept of free time until one has a child. Then you are always wondering what in the world you did with the infinite amount of free time you had in a former life.

32. I would love to write a book, but my ADD means it would be a bunch of short stories or maybe a lot of funny rants and unfinished storylines. Perhaps I should write one of those choose-your-own-adventure books. Whatever happened to those?

33. Some of life's most important lessons come from failure, not a textbook.

34. You will never regret calling an old friend to say hi, even if it is only for five minutes.

35. I love to travel. It always reinvigorates me to see a new state or country. If I ever win the lottery, my goal will be to visit every country in the world.

36. I have never claimed to be the best manager, but I always treat my employees with respect and try to prepare them to land their next job, even if it means more work for myself and the rest of the team.

37. Sometimes you start a charity because you want to help others, then realize your life is the one that has changed. The determination, resilience, and gratitude the people of New Orleans demonstrated while battling through a historic catastrophe are still unfathomable even years after the fact. This is for my friends in New Orleans who opened your doors during our seven volunteer trips. I appreciate you guys and wish the world could know you as I do. You will always have room to stay at the Tosti house.

38. I have the utmost respect for any single parent.

39. I like teaching and coaching people. I have been a substitute teacher at the high-school level, and I have taught college courses in sports marketing and management. I often think I might have missed my calling as a high school P.E. teacher and coach. When I was five-plus years into my undergrad at UK, I could not fathom spending another year and a half to earn my teaching certificate. I bypassed the teaching option and finished my degree. Life usually steers you down the right path some way, somehow.

40. It is not the size of the town you grew up in that matters, but rather the size of your heart and your ability to dream big.

Here is to another forty-plus years!

2020 Addition

April 2020 🌐

41. A development company invests money to build a block of homes on empty plots of land. Then the families in each house make investments of time—by working out together, drinking a beer or a glass of wine in a sunny driveway, sharing laughs at special holiday parties, or sharing tears at times of sadness. Those investments of time are what make a neighborhood great. It takes time, energy and effort, but it is always worth it. Trust me.

42. I appreciate the power of music and different genres on a different level than ever before. A song can inspire you, make you savor a moment in time spent with a close buddy, or help you power through a run when you do not know if you can keep going or not. Crank up the volume a notch or two, and I promise your legs will follow.

43. A good neighbor might ask how your son's first attempt at pitching is going, but a *great* neighbor takes time out of his day to catch for him or show him how to properly warm up. Better yet, he advises Kaden on his form and delivery. The same neighbor and his amazing wife also came to watch Kaden pitch. Randy and Julie, you two rock!

For my childhood friends, now I understand on a deeper level why Mom and Dad appreciated and loved Ken and Maggie Meade and Christine and Ottis (Ott) Blankenship like family.

44. Over the past few years, I have started living a richer life, and it has absolutely nothing to do with material possessions or the money in my bank account.

45. I think a lot about what gifts I want to leave behind for Kaden and Emily. I don't mean money or sports memorabilia.

46. When writing your first book and after sending out over ninety-nine release forms, you realize why one of your favorite authors, John Grisham, writes fiction titles.

47. Sitting and talking to a best friend on a front porch is my favorite form of therapy. The porch and the friend might change, but the soothing feeling of being able to talk about anything and the level of comfort it provides the soul never gets old.

Time Part 1

2019 ❸

Time is a funny thing. We all have the same number of hours in the day despite our differences. How we spend those days often defines our lives. Do you work out multiple days a week to stay healthy? Maybe you work ten to twelve hours a day to support your family or to create the next big thing. Perhaps your job requires you to be behind the wheel for ten hours a day, chasing down bad guys and keeping our community safe. Maybe you dedicate time to your church each week and not only Sundays. Maybe you stay home with your kids and hustle to keep everything in order.

Time is the one thing we can control to a certain extent, but how we use it defines, separates, and brings us closer to the things we love. As 2019 ends, I took the time to reflect on how I spent my time this past year and what I want to do differently in 2020. I put together a list of my thoughts regarding time. I hope it makes you take a moment to smile, celebrate your successes, call an old buddy you have not talked to in ten years, or accomplish something you have been putting off for way too long.

Take time for yourself.

Take time to read. I love reading, but my ADD gets the best of me. I have at least five books in the house with bookmarks saving the spots where I left off. I also happened to ask for another five books for Christmas. Knowledge is power, and I enjoy learning how someone else made a difference in this world.

Take time to call your loved ones for no reason at all. I sometimes call my mom and dad on my way to work in the morning, and Mom will always ask what is wrong since it is early in the day. I call because I still can.

Take time to talk about good and bad things in life with your kids because they need to understand their blessings. Unfortunately, there are some terrible things and people in this world. Perspective is a powerful tool.

Take time to coach your kids in a sport. I was blessed to coach Kaden's basketball team since he was five years old.

Take time to cheer and support your kids in their favorite activities. Emily loves gymnastics more than I love chocolate chip cookies. Beth and I wave and smile enthusiastically at her during practice and advise her how to improve on the balance beam or her cartwheel technique.

Take time to exercise. Your body and mind will thank you later. No one ever goes for a run or returns from the gym and regrets it.

Take time to train for a race. The distance or type of event is irrelevant. What matters is proving to yourself that you can make a commitment and finish the damn race.

Take time to call an old friend. The longer you have known him or her, the better.

Take time to spend with a dying friend. This one will initially frighten you, but your heart and mind will appreciate it. You will not regret it, and your friend will bless you in their special way.

Take time to heal from old wounds, let go of your demons and write down your dreams.

Take time to listen to good music, laugh, vent, and gripe with your neighbors.

Take time to tell a special friend what their friendship means to you. Eulogies have a place in life, but a heartfelt message at a funeral is good for everyone except the person who needs to hear it the most.

Take time to chase a dream with everything you have.

Take time to do one thing that scares the hell out of you.

Take time off from social media.

Take time for your faith.

Take time to travel. The experience lasts forever, and the stories from the road are usually funny. Plus, you always meet some interesting people along the way.

Take time to play board games with your kids. Remind them how to win and lose with class.

Take time to eat lunch with a coworker. Matt and I eat together every

Friday. Our standing tradition is to buy a cookie and a lottery ticket. We have not cashed a lot of tickets, but the cookies always hit the spot.

Take time to share your passion with others.

Take time to learn a new skill. We stop growing only when we stop trying to learn new things.

Take time to pick someone else up when life throws a curveball their way and listen to others when they need to talk.

Take time to return a favor to a friend or neighbor.

Take time to volunteer for a local charity.

Take time to sit on a front porch and talk to a good friend about nothing and everything in the same breath.

Take time to write. I have two book-related projects on deck for 2021 and beyond.

Take time to enjoy this wonderful, messy, beautiful thing called life.

Time Part 2: the Great Equalizer in Life

2020 🌐

Some people in this world have good looks, while others possess great wealth, or great strength that enabled them to climb and scratch their way out of an unpleasant situation. Society sometimes pushes us to judge others by the size of their home, the car they drive, or the brand of clothes they wear. However, the one thing everyone shares is the time in a day. How you use the hours in the day can make a tremendous difference in your life and the lives of others. Here are some of my thoughts on how to maximize the world's greatest equalizer.

Take time to . . .

SHARE

Share your passion or hobby with your kids, but do not push too hard. Beth and I encourage our children to try different sports and after-school activities to figure out what they like to do, and we let them make those choices. The only rule is they must finish the season and honor their commitment. Our son played soccer for a few seasons, then decided he did not want to continue with it because he did not like getting kicked all the time. I sat down with him and said, "I agree with you because I don't like to get kicked either. Good job finishing the season, and you can try a new sport now."

TEACH

Coach a youth sports team. Do not get caught up in your ability or lack thereof. Remember it is not about you; it is about spending time with your child or providing a positive experience for kids in the neighborhood. I coach both of our kids because I know this opportunity is limited, and it is something I will cherish for the rest of my life. I have coached basketball, soccer, and baseball with kids ranging in age from 3½ to 12. I always identify the kid with the least amount of athletic talent and cheer them on the loudest because even though they might not be the fastest player or the most coordinated, they showed up and are trying their best. Whatever you do, make sure it is fun for the entire team.

I have several favorite basketball coaching stories from the eleven years I spent on the sideline. One of the funniest ones pertained to being a supportive teammate. For whatever reason, my teams would always struggle with making layups, and one player continuously forgot which side of the court was ours. The poor kid would stop the referee before a jump ball and ask one or two times to be sure. One game, he stole the ball and, you guessed it, started dribbling the wrong way. Of course he was wide open, and he made the layup. The entire bench started laughing in unison. I looked at them and said, "Hey, guys, stop laughing because none of you has made a layup yet. He might have made it for the wrong team, but at least he made one."

My goals in coaching youth sports are to teach the importance of competing in life and instill a lifelong love for the game. Long after a child hangs up the cleats or the jersey, he or she will still be a fan of the game and can pass it on to their kids.

REFLECT

It is okay to stop for a moment and think about how your life experiences have shaped your thoughts, emotions, and mindset as you age. Sometimes we all need a break from reality and the dizzying pace of the world. Slow down occasionally and be thankful for what you have. Reminisce. Remember not only the good times you shared with family and friends, but also the tough times because those moments help you appreciate the good ones. Plan life goals and create a list of things you would like to do before you die.

UNDERSTAND

Take time to learn why someone else holds beliefs different from yours. You will learn tolerance and patience, but more importantly, you will learn how life impacts people differently, whether the issue is politics, religion, or some other controversial topic.

EXERCISE

This is an essential part of a balanced life. You do not have to train for a Tough Mudder race or a century bike ride. Simply walk around your neighborhood three times a week or ride a bike for a few miles. Just move! Your heart and mind will both be grateful but for different reasons.

HELP A FRIEND

This can come in various forms. Help a friend move to a new house. Proofread their résumé, play an important role in their wedding, introduce them to a contact for a job lead, or be brutally honest when they need it the most. Be there for whatever the reason is and whenever the time comes when life comes crashing down, because your friends will always return the favor.

SEND A CARD OR A HANDWRITTEN NOTE

Send a note with a few lines to let a long-lost friend know you are thinking about him or her. Yes, you can do the same thing with a text or an email, but ask yourself which one would mean more to you.

When my wife was battling breast cancer, we received a ton of notes and cards from friends, family, and even strangers. The messages, thoughts, and support came in different forms, but they all helped us cope during the most challenging time of our lives. The support meant the world to us, and now we always try to send a positive card to other people fighting any type of cancer.

In closing, life's clock is ticking for all of us. My advice is to decide what you want to do differently and take time to prioritize what is important to you. Then, go like hell and act as if the 24-second shot clock is getting ready to hit :00.

A Note from the Author

I hope you enjoyed the book. I hope you laughed a lot, but I also hope you shed a few tears because it is good for the soul. I encourage you to reminisce about your childhood and relive some of your best moments spent with family and friends. Most of all, I hope this process helps you appreciate the precious gift of life.

I also have one straightforward request, and that is to **make the call.** If you do nothing else after reading this book, call one person who has impacted your life and let them know how you feel. It might be a long-lost friend, a high school teacher, a coach, or a family member you disagreed with years ago.

When you make the call, I encourage you to tell me about it. You can reach me at www.brandontostiauthor.com; click on the Connect link. I plan on creating a list and including it on my website as inspiration for others. Use the prompts on the next page to get started.

Thank you for purchasing my first book and for helping make one of my dreams come true.

Make the Call

Childhood friend: _____

Long-lost relative:_____

College buddy: _____

Co-worker: _____

Neighbor: _____

Teacher: _____

Coach: _____

Mentor or boss: _____

Acknowledgments

MOM AND DAD

Thanks for the unconditional love and support from day one. You taught me it was always okay to dream big and that giving back to the community is a way of life, not a seasonal thing. I hope these stories bring back some good memories of all the wonderful people I have met along the way. Brittany and I are lucky to call you our parents. None of this would be possible without you. I love you both!

BRITTANY TOSTI PRUITT

Thanks for being a great little sister and for putting up with me all these years, especially since you did not have a choice. I am glad that we still aggravate each other with sarcasm and jokes regardless of the situation. I hope you enjoy the book since you know most of the people and the associated stories. Similar to birthday gifts and holiday checks that I send late, this project took longer than expected to arrive. Ha ha ha. Love you, BMT.

SARA BLAIR

I hope you know how much I appreciate your support and how much it has meant to me from early on. You have always been in my corner, and for that I thank you. Yes, you taught me a lot about writing, but you also taught me a lot about life, and I am forever grateful.

CHAD RANDALL

Where do I start? We have had some good times and were lucky to escape with just a bruise or two. I could write a second book about the years we lived together and our shenanigans. Let's face it: This book would not have been possible without your encouragement and suggestion. Thanks a million, brother. I hope you like the book, and I am so grateful for your support, then and now.

AMY CLAY

Thanks to a close friend who helped me with some promotional materials for the book. Amy always offered encouragement when the process felt like it hit a wall. She is a talented writer and speaks from the heart. I hope she writes a book someday.

DAVE BLANKENSHIP

Thanks to my high school buddy who said my writing style is like a fireside chat on Facebook. Most importantly, Dave told me to write a damn book! I did not write a Focus on Friends Lent column about him because our best stories are not suitable for the public. His dry sense of humor has always been a gift, and he helped with several legal facets of this book. Thank you also for helping me name the book!

ANGELA BAILEY

To an old high school friend who encouraged me to write a book in the early days of my columns.

ANGELIKA STOCKWELL

To a good friend from our Denver Impact leadership class who pushed me to keep going when the days were long and always knew what to say to keep my emotions in check.

COURTNEY (DANIELS) GROSSL

To an old childhood friend from Paintsville. I nicknamed her "Bookworm" in middle school because she is such a fast reader. Court, do me a favor: Take your time and let this one soak in for a bit. By the way, you need to call the family that bought your grandmother's house and let them know that you and I need to sit on their front porch so we can catch up the next time we are home.

Dr. Jason "Pudge" Glenn

Thanks to a close high school friend who generously contributed financial resources to help offset some of the publishing costs.

Jon Andrews

Thanks to a good friend who often told me I should write a book many years ago. I am beyond grateful for his creative mindset and artistic ability. Twenty years later, I am still jealous of his Super Mario Kart skills. Jon is responsible for the book's fantastic cover artwork. Please consider using his company for any graphic design needs. http://brainfirecreative.com

Lawrence Matthews, Justin Manna and Mike Arthur

Thanks to these three friends for helping me reveal the book title with pure comedy and plenty of sarcasm.

Paintsville High English Teachers

A special thank you to these teachers who influenced my writing style in their own special way. Words are powerful tools that we all use to accomplish different things in life. Choose them wisely.

Eighth grade: Mrs. Suzy Preston taught me kindness and compassion. I think she might be related to Katie Couric because of her outgoing personality and warm heart. Her cheerleaders might disagree because she was a tough yet fair coach.

Ninth grade: Mrs. Deanna Gillespie taught me discipline. She might have been short in stature, but you did not sass or backtalk to her. Some kids made that mistake and earned the opportunity to run laps around the building. Something tells me that would not fly in today's world, but maybe it should be allowed in some cases.

Tenth- and twelfth-grade Journalism: To Mr. Clyde Pack, thank you for inspiring so many students in our little town and pushing us all to be better writers. You made journalism fun, but I must admit I struggled with one or two classic novels. Your encouragement and support meant the world to me.

Eleventh grade: Mrs. Anna Scott showed me that teachers had the ability to use sarcasm when necessary, and she was not afraid to hold her ground when someone tried to be cute. She was quick with her words and always knew how to make us laugh.

Twelfth grade: Mrs. Dottie Lewis taught me the power of expression and encouraged our class to explore different writing styles so that our minds and capabilities developed together. She pushed us to be creative writers and to not be afraid to take a chance.

ADAM AGRON

Thank you for sticking up for me early in my career. You had nothing to gain from it, but I never forgot the gesture. Adam also introduced me to his friend who is a New York Times best-selling author. This author met with me and sent my manuscript to his agent in New York City. I learned a lot from both men, and my book is better because of it.

SUANNE LAQUEUR

Thank you to my Project Manager with Canoe Tree Press for walking me through the final stages of bringing this book to life. I appreciate your patience and candor with me as I navigated this unfamiliar territory for the first time. I consider you my writing coach and hope to work with you again in the future.

AMY BACHELDER JEYNES

Thank you to my editor for polishing the material, ensuring the information flows properly, and making sure the storylines are clear whether the reader is a dear friend or someone's uncle who receives the book as a gift. You made it look easy and helped me become a better writer in the process. I am forever grateful for your time, effort, and expertise.

Nena Tatum

Thank you for editing the manuscript and pushing me to improve my vocabulary. You might be a retired English teacher, but no doubt, you still have what it takes! I hope neither one of us needs a big bat for many years.

Sports for a Cause

I need to thank the following people who played an instrumental role in this wild idea of mine, to create a nonprofit to help children in New Orleans. This group helped from day one and volunteered their time as the Board of Directors: Beth Tosti, Eric Vinton, Kieran Cain, Mike Duvarney, and Jeff Manson. Thanks to the current Board of Directors: Kaitlyn Anderson, Pat Wall, Tom Miller, and Jeff Dowdle. Both groups believed in the cause and allowed me to make mistakes and grow from them. I also want to thank Megan Martinez, Temi Dada, Tami Brown, Andrew Elliott, Jeff Plush, and Horacio Ruiz for their encouragement and support.

New Orleans Friends

This group of people shared their business contacts, houses, cars, and, most importantly, their hearts with a stranger from Denver, Colorado, who had a big idea and enough energy to back it up. They went through hell and still found a way to smile and demonstrate a positive attitude for years as they worked tirelessly to rebuild their city.

Jay Cicero, A.C., Brett Forshag, Tony Biagas, Denise Thornton, Bob Bourg, Allen Woods, Pastor Nick, Ron Maestri, Walter Tillman, Charlie Bosworth, Ward "Mack" McClendon, Letitia "Tish" Youngblood, Andrew Miragliotta, Josephine Duchane, Horacio Ruiz, and Smitty. We are not related, but I consider them my NOLA family and would run through a brick wall for each one of them.

Randy and Julie West

To two of the funniest and kindest neighbors in the world, thank you for letting me sit on your porch night after night to discuss the latest updates about the book. You believed in this project from day one, and I appreciate the feedback on the manuscript. I hope Randy's offer to be my security guard if I ever go on a book tour remains valid.

To Beth, Kaden, and Emily

Thank you for being the shining stars in my world and for supporting me as I spent *many* hours and months organizing and editing this book. I love you more than chocolate chip cookies, and those are my favorite! Kaden and Emily, I hope someday you will look at the book as a special gift long after I am gone. If you ever need advice, I know in my heart that anyone mentioned in this book will gladly help you as you blaze your trail in life. Whatever career path you choose, remember to dream big and chase it with everything you can!